NATIONAL GEOGRAPHIC
KiDS

A European common frog makes a splash diving into clear water.

ALMANAC 2015

NATIONAL GEOGRAPHIC
WASHINGTON, D.C.

National Geographic Kids Books
gratefully acknowledges the following people for their help with the
National Geographic Kids Almanac 2015.

Curtis Malarkey, Julie Segal, and Cheryl Zook of the National Geographic Explorers program; Truly Herbert, National Geographic Communications; and Chuck Errig of Random House

Amazing Animals

Suzanne Braden, Director, Pandas International

Dr. Rodolfo Coria, Paleontologist, Plaza Huincul, Argentina

Dr. Sylvia Earle,
National Geographic Explorer-in-Residence

Dr. Thomas R. Holtz, Jr., Senior Lecturer, Vertebrate Paleontology, Department of Geology, University of Maryland

Dr. Luke Hunter, Executive Director, Panthera

Dereck and Beverly Joubert,
National Geographic Explorers-in-Residence

"Dino" Don Lessem, President, Exhibits Rex

Kathy B. Maher, Research Editor,
NATIONAL GEOGRAPHIC magazine

Kathleen Martin, Canadian Sea Turtle Network

Barbara Nielsen, Polar Bears International

Andy Prince, Austin Zoo

Christopher Sloan

Julia Thorson, translator, Zurich, Switzerland

Dennis vanEngelsdorp, Senior Extension Associate, Pennsylvania Department of Agriculture

Going Green

Eric J. Bohn, Math Teacher, Santa Rosa High School

Stephen David Harris, Professional Engineer, Industry Consulting

Catherine C. Milbourn, Senior Press Officer, EPA

Brad Scriber, Senior Researcher,
NATIONAL GEOGRAPHIC magazine

Paola Segura and Cid Simões,
National Geographic Emerging Explorers

Dr. Wes Tunnell, Harte Research Institute for Gulf of Mexico Studies, Texas A&M University—Corpus Christi

Super Science

Tim Appenzeller, Chief Magazine Editor, NATURE

Dr. Rick Fienberg, American Astronomical Society, Press Officer and Director of Communications

Dr. José de Ondarza, Associate Professor, Department of Biological Sciences, State University of New York, College at Plattsburgh

Lesley B. Rogers, Managing Editor (former), NATIONAL GEOGRAPHIC magazine

Dr. Enric Sala, National Geographic Visiting Fellow

Abigail A. Tipton, Director of Research (former), NATIONAL GEOGRAPHIC magazine

Erin Vintinner, Biodiversity Specialist, Center for Biodiversity and Conservation at the American Museum of Natural History

Barbara L. Wyckoff, Research Editor (former), NATIONAL GEOGRAPHIC magazine

Culture Connection

Dr. Wade Davis,
National Geographic Explorer-in-Residence

Deirdre Mullervy, Managing Editor, Gallaudet University Press

Wonders of Nature

Anatta, NOAA Public Affairs Officer

Dr. Robert Ballard,
National Geographic Explorer-in-Residence

Douglas H. Chadwick, wildlife biologist and contributor to NATIONAL GEOGRAPHIC magazine

Drew Hardesty, Forecaster, Utah Avalanche Center

History Happens

Dr. Sylvie Beaudreau, Associate Professor, Department of History, State University of New York

Elspeth Deir, Assistant Professor, Faculty of Education, Queens University, Kingston, Ontario, Canada

Dr. Gregory Geddes, Lecturer, Department of Global Studies, State University of New York—Orange, Middletown-Newburgh, New York

Dr. Fredrik Hiebert, National Geographic Visiting Fellow

Micheline Joanisse, Media Relations Officer, Natural Resources Canada

Dr. Robert D. Johnston,
Associate Professor and Director of the Teaching of History Program, University of Illinois at Chicago

Dickson Mansfield, Geography Instructor (retired), Faculty of Education, Queens University, Kingston, Ontario, Canada

Tina Norris, U.S. Census Bureau

Parliamentary Information and Research Service, Library of Parliament, Ottawa, Canada

Karyn Pugliese, Acting Director, Communications, Assembly of First Nations

Geography Rocks

Glynnis Breen, National Geographic Special Projects

Carl Haub, Senior Demographer, Conrad Taeuber Chair of Public Information, Population Reference Bureau

Dr. Mary Kent, Demographer,
Population Reference Bureau

Dr. Walt Meier, National Snow and Ice Data Center

Dr. Richard W. Reynolds,
NOAA's National Climatic Data Center

United States Census Bureau, Public Help Desk

Dr. Spencer Wells,
National Geographic Explorer-in-Residence

Contents

Awesome Adventure

100

Super Science

118

Fun and Games

154

Culture Connection

174

Wonders of Nature

200

History Happens

222

Geography Rocks

254

Dai women in Yunnan, China, have buckets of fun at the Water Splashing Festival. The Buddhist celebration takes place every spring.

Animal Discoveries

From "WALKING" SHARKS to FLYING FROGS, here are some species recently found in the wild.

Epaulette Shark

Forget swimming: One of the newly discovered species of epaulette shark can also "walk" on its fins along the ocean floor. Discovered off the coast of Indonesia, *Hemiscyllium halmahera* feeds on bottom-dwelling invertebrates in tide pools and coral reefs. Another cool fact? It can survive for about an hour in the low-oxygen conditions of tide pools by increasing blood flow to its brain and shutting down less essential body functions.

Cambodian Tailorbird

Discovered outside Cambodia's bustling capital of Phnom Penh, this orange-topped warbler was first spotted at a construction site. It gets its name for the intricate way it "tailors" its nest by weaving leaves together.

Helen's Flying Frog

This amphibian, discovered close to Ho Chi Minh City in Vietnam, uses its huge webbed feet and hands to parachute across the lowland ever-green forest canopy. But one of these large, white-bellied frogs was simply sitting on a log when it caught the eye of researcher Jodi Rowley, who later named the species "Helen" after her mom.

Olinguito

This may be the cutest new species discovery yet! The olinguito—found in a forest in Colombia, South America—is described as a "cross between a teddy bear and a house cat." And with its big, wide eyes, round ears, and fuzzy, orange-brown coat, it's easy to see why this carnivore can be mistaken for a furry friend. But this animal isn't so cuddly: The canopy dweller has sharp, curved claws, along with textured foot pads, to allow it to grip branches and climb trees high in the Andes Mountains.

The 100th Anniversary
Sinking of the *Lusitania*

THE *LUSITANIA*

The captain of the R.M.S. *Lusitania* had been warned. The year was 1915, World War I raged across Europe, and the German government declared that all Allied ships would be in danger of attack in British waters. Still, the British ocean liner set out on its planned course from New York City, New York, U.S.A., to Liverpool, England, with 1,900 passengers and crew members on board.

The *Lusitania* never made it. On May 7, 1915, as the ship cruised along the southern coast of Ireland, a German submarine, also known as a U-boat, torpedoed and sank the ship. It took less than 20 minutes for the giant ship to plunge to the murky depths of the Atlantic Ocean, taking more than 1,100 people along with it.

The event sparked outrage around the world from those who believed the Germans' act was unlawful. In the United States—home to nearly 130 of the *Lusitania* victims—public opinion on Germany swiftly shifted from a neutral standpoint to a strong desire to declare war on the country. Two years later, the U.S. officially entered World War I, joining the Allied powers to defeat Germany in 1918.

Now 100 years later, the sinking of the *Lusitania* remains a key turning point in World War I's time line. This year, people around the world will mark the anniversary with memorial services to honor those who lost their lives on the *Lusitania* and commemorate this monumental event that helped shape our world's history.

SURVIVORS FROM THE *LUSITANIA*

LUSITANIA MAY 7 1915

ELEPHANT SIGN LANGUAGE

HEADS UP!

While elephants don't sit around chatting with each other like you and your friends do, they do express emotions through gestures similar to sign language. After studying a family of African elephants in the wild for decades, biologist Joyce Poole noticed that subtle movements and gestures were actually ways in which the pachyderms communicate.

"I noticed that when I was narrating the elephants' behavior to others, I was able to predict what they would do next perhaps 90 percent of the time," Poole says.

What are some of the ways elephants express themselves? If one feels threatened, it may spread its ears out wide to appear bigger (top right) or stand up on a log or an anthill to look taller. A mama elephant may show her little one love by wrapping her trunk around her calf's leg or belly, or by touching its mouth. And an elephant who wants to initiate a game might wiggle its head from side to side or lie down on the ground, hoping others may clamber on top.

They display a sense of humor, too: After repeatedly observing elephants appearing to trip and fall in front of her car, Poole figured out that the animals were just messing around. "It is one of the behaviors that led me to say that elephants have a sense of self and a sense of humor," says Poole. "They *know* that they are funny."

I WANT TO GO THIS WAY. LET'S GO TOGETHER.

I'M FEELING UNEASY OR AMBIVALENT.

SPACE BALLOONS

Just how high can balloons travel? How about all the way to Saturn? That's just what a team of scientists in the United States is working on. The hot-air balloon is being designed to orbit Saturn's biggest moon, Titan. It will also transport equipment on unmanned missions and possibly send photos back to Earth.

But getting a balloon to withstand Titan's extreme environment is no easy feat. Temperatures hover around 300 degrees below zero Fahrenheit (-184°C) on Titan. Researchers developing the balloon hope that a specially created material made of polyester fibers will do the trick.

While the balloon is still being tested, scientists plan to get it off the ground soon. And once it takes off? There's hope that this type of balloon mission can continue in the future to shed more light on some of the greatest mysteries of our solar system—and beyond.

NATIONAL GEOGRAPHIC KIDS
SCANNER

SCAN THIS PAGE!
GET BONUS MOBILE CONTENT! Download the free NG Kids scanner app. Directions on inside front cover.

One-Way Ticket TO MARS

AN ARTIST'S DEPICTION OF MARS ONE'S

Forget a dream vacation to Tahiti or Disney World. How about a trip to Mars? The only catch is that you may never come back. At least that's what Dutch-based company Mars One is proposing through a project they say will send four people on a one-way mission to Mars in 2023. But this trip's not just about exploring: Mars One wants to colonize the red planet, too. So, after eight years of full-time training, the select crew will travel to Mars in 2023 and live there for the rest of their lives. Sound scary? Not to everyone: More than 200,000 have already applied!

REAL-LIFE
Lightsabers?

Darth Vader, watch out! Physicists at Harvard University and the Massachusetts Institute of Technology (MIT) in Massachusetts, U.S.A., created a real-life system that behaves like a lightsaber in the Star Wars movies. By binding together photons—massless particles of light—in a special optical material, laser beams of light can be pushed and pulled, just like the beam of a lightsaber. So while you may not be able to fight the Dark Side with your saber just yet, you may be able to do so one day without having to travel to a galaxy far, far away.

SPONGEBOB SQUAREPANTS 2

KUNG FU PANDA 3

HOTEL TRANSYLVANIA 2

HOT MOVIES
in 2015*

- SpongeBob SquarePants 2
- The Penguins of Madagascar
- Jurassic World
- Hotel Transylvania 2
- Kung Fu Panda 3
- Alvin and the Chipmunks 4
- The Smurfs 3
- Star Wars: Episode VII

*Release dates and titles are subject to change.

KING RICHARD III FOUND IN PARKING LOT!

You just never know what—or who—may be buried beneath your feet. Case in point: Researchers recently discovered the skeleton of King Richard III, who died in battle in 1485, under a parking lot in England. The remains, unearthed during an archaeological dig by the team from the University of Leicester in the United Kingdom, matched the DNA of a living relative of Richard, giving researchers proof that the skeleton in fact belonged to the famed leader. This discovery solved the decades-long mystery surrounding the whereabouts of his body.

Can Dogs Sense Emotions?

Your pooch may know you better than you think. A recent study shows that dogs yawn more in response to their owners' yawns than they do to strangers' yawns. To test the pets, researchers had the dogs watch both their owners and strangers yawn or pretend to yawn. The result? The dogs in the study yawned more in response to their owners' yawns and yawned less when they saw fake yawns. This, researchers say, suggests that pups can actually sense their owners' emotions. No wonder your pup is considered man's best friend!

Cool Events in 2015

Songkran Festival

Thailand gets wet and wild in this countrywide water fight!

April 13–15

World Turtle Day

Come out of your shell and celebrate turtles big and small!

May 23

FIFA Women's Soccer World Cup Canada

Watch the best soccer players in the world kick it in Canada. Score!

June 6–July 5

International Left-Handers Day

Give a high five to your favorite southpaw today!

August 13

International Chocolate Day

Treat yourself to an extra cupcake today. Sweet!

September 13

Rugby World Cup

The world's best rugby players are set to scrum in matches all around England.

September 18–October 31

International Music Day

Turn up the tunes as you celebrate all things music. Did someone say dance party?

October 1

150th Anniversary of Alice in Wonderland

Lewis Carroll's famous character is 150 years old. And she still doesn't look a day over 7.

November 26

SAND SCULPTING CHAMPIONSHIPS

Each February, some of the world's best artists head down under for the annual Australian Sand Sculpting Championships in Surfers Paradise along the continent's Gold Coast. But this competition isn't just about building simple castles: Artists use more than 198 tons (180 MT) of sand to mold and carve elaborate designs, like amazingly real-looking animals, mythical creatures, fierce pirates, and crazy faces. Hoping to see the sculptures for yourself but don't live down under? There are similar competitions around the world in places like Fort Myers Beach, Florida, U.S.A.; San Diego, California, U.S.A.; Jesolo, Italy; and Fiesa, Portugal.

sports funnies uh-oh!

Pro soccer players are superfierce, but they can be superfunny, too! As we gear up for the FIFA Women's World Cup Canada 2015, here are some players caught in some silly positions!

Christie Rampone of the U.S.A. makes a kick during the finals match against Japan in the 2011 FIFA World Cup in Frankfurt, Germany.

Brazil's Aline Pellegrino chases the ball during a 2012 soccer match against the U.S.A. in Chiba, Japan.

17

Amazing Animals

Emperor penguins leap and glide at floe's edge on the Ross Sea's Cape Washington in Antarctica.

WHAT IS
Taxonomy?

Since there are billions and billions of living things, called organisms, on the planet, people need a way of classifying them. Scientists created a system called **taxonomy**, which helps to classify all living things into ordered groups. By putting organisms into categories we are better able to understand how they are the same and how they are different. There are seven levels of taxonomic classification, beginning with the broadest group, called a domain, down to the most specific group, called a species.

Biologists divide life based on evolutionary history, and they place organisms in three domains depending on their genetic structure: Archaea, Bacteria, and Eukarya. (See p. 131 for "The Three Domains of Life.")

SAMPLE CLASSIFICATION
LLAMA

Domain:	Eukarya
Phylum:	Chordata
Class:	Mammalia
Order:	Artiodactyla
Family:	Camelidae
Genus:	*Lama*
Species:	*glama*

Where do animals come in?

Animals are a part of the Eukarya domain, which means they are organisms made of cells with nuclei. More than one million species of animals have been named, including humans. Like all living things, animals can be divided into smaller groups, called phyla. Most scientists believe there are more than 30 phyla into which animals can be grouped based on certain scientific criteria, such as body type or whether or not the animal has a backbone. It can be pretty complicated, so there is another, less complicated system that groups animals into two categories: vertebrates and invertebrates.

Chinese stripe-necked turtle

TIP
Here's a sentence to help you remember the classification order:
Dear **P**hillip **C**ame **O**ver **F**or **G**ood **S**oup.

BY THE NUMBERS

There are 11,092 vulnerable or endangered animal species in the world. The list includes:

- **1,140 mammals**, such as the snow leopard, the polar bear, and the fishing cat.

- **1,313 birds**, including the Steller's sea eagle and the Madagascar plover.

- **2,110 fish**, such as the Mekong giant catfish.

- **847 reptiles**, including the American crocodile.

- **835 insects**, including the Macedonian grayling.

- **1,948 amphibians**, such as the Round Island day gecko.

- **And more**, including 21 arachnids, 723 crustaceans, 236 sea anemones and corals, 164 bivalves, and 1,707 snails and slugs.

Vertebrates Animals WITH Backbones

Fish are cold-blooded and live in water. They breathe with gills, lay eggs, and usually have scales.

Amphibians are cold-blooded. Their young live in water and breathe with gills. Adults live on land and breathe with lungs.

Reptiles are cold-blooded and breathe with lungs. They live both on land and in water.

Birds are warm-blooded and have feathers and wings. They lay eggs, breathe with lungs, and usually are able to fly. Some birds live on land, some in water, and some on both.

Mammals are warm-blooded and feed on their mothers' milk. They also have skin that is usually covered with hair. Mammals live both on land and in water.

Bird: Bald eagle

Fish: Clown anemonefish

Invertebrates Animals WITHOUT Backbones

Sponges are a very basic form of animal life. They live in water and do not move on their own.

Echinoderms have external skeletons and live in seawater.

Mollusks have soft bodies and can live either in or out of shells, on land or in water.

Arthropods are the largest group of animals. They have external skeletons, called exoskeletons, and segmented bodies with appendages. Arthropods live in water and on land.

Worms are soft-bodied animals with no true legs. Worms live in soil.

Cnidaria live in water and have mouths surrounded by tentacles.

Worm: Earthworms

Cnidaria: West Coast sea nettle

Arthropod: Red-kneed tarantula

Cold-blooded versus Warm-blooded

Cold-blooded animals, also called ectotherms, get their heat from outside their bodies.

Warm-blooded animals, also called endotherms, keep their body temperature level regardless of the temperature of their environments.

Incredible Animal Friends

IS IT TIME FOR MY HOPPING LESSON?

GORILLA GOES APE FOR RABBIT
ERIE, PENNSYLVANIA, U.S.A.

Samantha the western lowland gorilla seemed to like her new roommate, Panda the Dutch rabbit. But her keepers at the Erie Zoo grew worried one day when the rabbit hopped over to Samantha's favorite stuffed animal. They knew the ape was crazy about her toy and feared the 200-pound (91-kg) Samantha might get upset if the rabbit got too close. But the gorilla didn't sweat it. She just moved the toy so Panda could pass by. That's when keepers realized the roomies were best buds.

Too shy to live with other apes, Samantha was paired with the rabbit to keep from getting lonely. Keepers introduced them slowly, first letting the duo see each other through a mesh screen. Eventually, Panda moved into the ape's exhibit. "Almost immediately, they were sitting side by side," zoo CEO Scott Mitchell says.

The pair was practically inseparable. They liked watching visitors walk by their exhibit together, and Samantha often let the rabbit nibble on her hay. Keepers even saw the gorilla stroke Panda under his chin. Says Mitchell, "Their friendship was one of a kind."

THANKS, I THINK I SMELL GREAT TOO!

PUP BABYSITS PIGLETS
ORANIENBURG, GERMANY

The litter of boar piglets living at the Lehnitz animal sanctuary loved trying to get piggyback rides from their best bud, Baby the French bulldog. "Sometimes, one of the boars will try to scramble onto Baby's back," says Norbert Damm, who works at the sanctuary. "She'll just playfully shake the piglet off."

The football-size boars arrived at the sanctuary where the dog lives after they were found alone and freezing in a nearby forest. "Baby cuddled with them, just as their mom would've done," Damm says. The pup stuck close to the pigs afterward. The fuzzy crew enjoyed dashing around the garden together and snuggling up for naps until the boars were big enough to move to a nature reserve. Guess you could say these guys were hog wild about each other!

I KNEW PIGGING OUT WOULD MAKE THEM SLEEPY!

BABOON BEFRIENDS BUSH BABY
NAIROBI, KENYA

It's easy to see that Dina the yellow baboon and Bushy the bush baby are best friends. They're always giving each other bear hugs—even when they're on the move. Bushy wraps her arms around the baboon's tummy and holds on upside down as Dina crawls around their enclosure at the Nairobi Animal Orphanage.

The critters bonded after arriving at the reserve as infants. Now, the baboon protects her pal from other animals and makes sure Bushy eats enough. Bushy, who's naturally nocturnal, even changed her sleeping schedule so she's awake at the same time as Dina. "The friendship is rare," primate expert Barbara Smuts says. "But the animals are great for each other."

I'M NOT SAYING WHO, BUT ONE OF US NEEDS A BATH.

Bet you didn't know

6 phenomenal facts about families

1 European **shrew** families often **travel** with each member **holding** on to **another's** tail.

2 Born on land, **poison dart** frog **tadpoles wriggle** onto a parent's back for a ride to water.

3 Cassowaries— **large flightless** birds—are raised by **their dads.**

4 Up to **700** black widow **spiders** can hatch from **one** grape-size egg sac.

5 **Mother** elephants use their **trunks** to lift **newborns** to their feet.

6 **Meerkats** can have up to **12 babies a year.**

APE BRUSHES TEETH

WHERE'D I PUT THE MOUTH-WASH?

Central Kalimantan, Borneo

Siswi the orangutan would make a dentist proud. The 34-year-old ape has been spotted scrubbing her teeth with a toothbrush! So, does Siswi scrub her chompers to prevent cavities? Not exactly. She's likely copying people she's seen brushing their teeth at a nearby river (not to mention she may enjoy the minty taste of toothpaste). Yet another reason might explain why the animal cleans her teeth—she's getting ready to mug for the camera. "Siswi's much more likely to start brushing if someone's about to take a picture," orangutan expert Biruté Mary Galdikas says. "She's a bit of a diva."

CAT HAS TWO FACES

TALK ABOUT MEOW MIX!

South Florida, U.S.A.

This is one two-faced cat. Venus's unique mug is divided down the middle—one side is jet black, while the other is light orange.

Why does Venus have such a dramatic look? Every animal's body contains sets of genes passed down from parents. These microscopic molecules determine how the animal will look, including the color of its skin, hair, or fur. "It's possible that the genes that decide fur color came together in an unusual way in Venus," cat researcher Leslie Lyons says. "This may have led to her odd coloring." Who wouldn't want face time with this cool cat?

DO ANIMALS LOVE EACH OTHER?

It's a boy! Romani the Asian elephant has just given birth. After nursing, the baby falls asleep and his mom positions herself directly over him. All is quiet in the barn, and the elephant keeper dims the lights. Then this first-time mom does something remarkable: Like a human mother tucking her child into bed, she gently covers her baby with hay.

Is it love? Scientists used to say that love belonged only to humans. Now they aren't so sure. Jaak Panksepp, a neuroscientist at Washington State University, believes that feelings such as love are hardwired into animals' brains and control their behavior.

The most important sensation is the need to feel good. Like people, many animals feel good when they have something to look forward to—and somebody they care about. Keep reading for more stories of animal love.

CARE BEAR

One day, Else Poulsen, a zookeeper at the Detroit Zoo, puts extra branches in Triton the polar bear's enclosure. Why? Poulsen is playing matchmaker. She's bringing a second bear, a female named Bärle, to live with Triton. One look at Bärle turns Triton to mush. It takes a while, but he eventually wins her over with gifts of sugar maple branches.

Later, their cub is born. In the wild, Triton would be long gone. Male polar bears don't stick around once mating season is over, and they do not help raise their young. But Triton continues to bring Bärle gifts, including a plastic toy that Poulsen fills with small treats such as raisins. "They have a strong bond," Poulsen says.

HOW COME YOU ALWAYS GET TO SIT UP FRONT?

SISTER ACT

Glitter and Golden are the oldest twin chimpanzees known to survive in the wild. And they're very close. How close? Their bond is so strong that they even share food—a rare sight in the wild.

Take, for instance, when Golden and their mother are pigging out on freshly hunted monkey meat, a special treat for chimps in the forests of Tanzania. But no fair—Glitter doesn't have any! A frustrated Glitter holds out her hand and begs. While the mom ignores her pleas, Golden hands over some of her meat. She has no reason for doing that, unless, of course, she truly loves her twin.

DEVOTED DAD

In India's Ranthambore National Park, two orphaned Bengal tiger cubs are missing. Their mother died, and the cubs' den is empty. Has the ruling male tiger killed the defenseless babies?

Forest rangers set up camera traps and catch a photo of a male tiger named Zalim. But one of the missing cubs is also in the picture! Zalim isn't preying on them; he's traveling with them. It turns out he's taken over the role of the mother. For example, when the cubs kill a goat, Zalim lets them eat it instead of taking it for himself as most males would do. And when another tiger threatens one of his "kids," Zalim makes the bully back off. This is one big cat that's really earning his stripes.

I'M STARVING! DID DAD TELL YOU WHAT'S FOR DINNER?

UM, YEAH. YOU DEFINITELY HAVE FISH BREATH.

SPECIAL DELIVERY

It's lunchtime at the Philadelphia Zoo. A keeper brings a bucket of catfish to the otter exhibit, and an otter mom and her five hungry pups come running. But not Banjo, the pups' dad. At 19, Banjo is one of the world's oldest otters.

The otters start chowing down, except Banjo. He never worries about getting fed, because his pups always take care of him. One of them races over and drops a fish at Banjo's feet. The pup scampers off and Dad eats.

Does Banjo's caring family contribute to his long life? "Absolutely," says carnivore curator Tammy Schmidt. "That's part of his secret."

1 The freshwater-loving **AMAZON RIVER DOLPHIN** can be found in the Amazon and Orinoco Rivers in South America. Following a flood, they can swim through parts of forests.

2 DON'T LET THE NICKNAME FOOL YOU: **"KILLER WHALES" ARE ACTUALLY DOLPHINS.**

3 SOME WILD DOLPHINS PLAY CATCH WITH **COCONUTS.**

4 The **SMALLEST DOLPHIN,** Hector's dolphin, is only four feet long (1.2 m). It's one of the rarest types, and it is shorter than an orca's dorsal fin.

15 COOL THINGS ABOUT

5 RISSO'S DOLPHINS CAN HOLD THEIR BREATH FOR **30 MINUTES.**

6 Every dolphin has a **SIGNATURE WHISTLE** it uses to identify itself.

7 A dolphin **"SLEEPS"** for about eight hours a day, although it is never fully unconscious. Only half its brain is asleep at a time!

8 NEWBORN DOLPHINS HAVE A TINY **PATCH OF HAIR** ON THEIR SNOUTS.

9

THE IPAD is the latest high-tech tool researchers are using to help enhance communication between humans and dolphins.

10

Dolphins have a special superpower that makes finding their way underwater easier. They use a type of sonar called echolocation to hunt and navigate.

11

JUST LIKE HUMANS, DOLPHINS GET ONE SET OF TEETH TO LAST A LIFETIME.

DOLPHINS

12

IF A **DOLPHIN BECOMES SICK,** OTHER DOLPHINS WILL TAKE TURNS

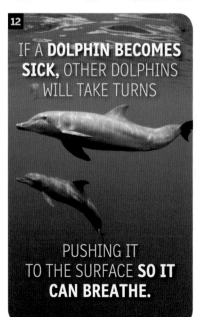

PUSHING IT TO THE SURFACE **SO IT CAN BREATHE.**

13

A DOLPHIN'S BEAKLIKE SNOUT IS CALLED A ROSTRUM.

14

A DOLPHIN BREATHES AIR THROUGH A **BLOWHOLE** LOCATED AT THE **TOP OF ITS HEAD.**

15

A PINK BOTTLENOSE DOLPHIN WAS DISCOVERED IN A LOUISIANA, U.S.A., LAKE.

OCEAN SUPERSTARS

The fascinating lives of 6 sea turtle species

Think all sea turtles are the same? Think again! Each of these species stands out in its own way.

1 GREEN SEA TURTLE: THE NEAT FREAK

In Hawaii, U.S.A., green sea turtles choose a "cleaning station"—a location where groups of cleaner fish groom the turtles by eating ocean gunk, like algae and parasites, off their skin and shells. In Australia, the turtles rub against a favorite sponge or rock to scrub themselves. Neat!

2 KEMP'S RIDLEY: THE LITTLE ONE

They may be the smallest sea turtles, but they're not so tiny: Adults weigh as much as many ten-year-old kids, and their shell is about the size of a car tire. They're speedy, too: It takes them less than an hour to dig a nest, then lay and bury their eggs.

3 OLIVE RIDLEY: THE ULTRA-MOM

Every year, hundreds of thousands of female olive ridley sea turtles take over beaches to lay their eggs and then bury them before disappearing back into the sea. Call it safety in numbers: With thousands of turtles swarming the shoreline, they're sure to overwhelm any predator.

4 LEATHERBACK: THE MEGA-TURTLE

These giants among reptiles have shells about as big as a door and weigh as much as six professional football players! Their size doesn't slow them down, though. A leatherback can swim as fast as a bottlenose dolphin.

5 HAWKSBILL: THE HEARTY EATER

What's the hawksbill's favorite snack? Sponges! These turtles gobble about 1,200 pounds (544 kg) of sponges a year. The turtles can safely eat this sea life, which is toxic to other animals. That means there are plenty of sponges to snack on!

6 LOGGERHEAD: THE TOUGH GUY

The loggerhead sea turtle's powerful jaws can easily crack open the shells of lobsters, conchs, and snails to get at the meat inside. Some loggerheads swim a third of the way around the world to find food.

Meet the
PENGUINS

Check out 10 of the world's coolest penguin species.

Rockhopper

Both northern and southern rock-hopper penguins are expert climbers. They use their sharp claws to hop and scramble up steep cliffs to nest. The two species live in the subarctic. Only northern rock-hoppers are endangered.

Little

More than a half million tourists a year watch the nightly parade of these blue-gray, football-size penguins from New Zealand and Australia returning to their burrows after foraging at sea.

Adélie

Adélie penguins must win a deadly game of freeze tag while crossing thin ice in Antarctica. Leopard seals lurk below, watching for movement. If an Adélie sees a predator, it "freezes" until the danger passes.

Emperor

Emperor penguins are the largest species—as tall as a seven-year-old kid. They can dive 1,853 feet (565 m) straight down and hold their breath underwater for up to 22 minutes.

Galápagos

Instead of fighting frost-bite, these penguins battle sunburn. That's because they live on the Galápagos Islands at the Equator. They shade their feet with their flippers to avoid sunburn.

Gentoo

When a gentoo parent returns from hunting subantarctic seas, it races away from its chicks. But hungry chicks will follow. Once a chick is fed and full, it won't bother chasing its parent anymore.

Royal

Royal penguins spend about four months each year eating and sleeping at sea—somewhere between Australia and Antarctica.

Macaroni

Every October, about 18 million macaroni penguins nest on the hill-sides and cliffs of Antarctic and sub-Atlantic shorelines. Macaronis have the largest population of all penguins.

African

The only species that breeds on the coast of Africa, the African penguin faces land predators such as leopards, rats, snakes, and mongooses. It is known for its mating call, which sounds like a braying donkey.

Yellow-eyed

Unlike penguins that nest together in crowded colonies, yellow-eyed penguins hide in coastal forests and shrubland far from any other penguin's nest.

5 COOL THINGS ABOUT KOALAS

A koala doesn't look like the kind of creature that keeps campers awake at night or dines on food that would give you a serious stomachache. There's a lot more to these living "teddy bears" than cotton-ball ears and a laid-back lifestyle. Check out five amazing things about these wild, loud, and lovable creatures from Australia.

1. Loudmouths
Imagine a burp so loud it brings you to your knees, followed by a snore that rattles the rafters. Combine them and you have the typical bellow of a koala. Why so noisy? Male koalas grunt with gusto to broadcast their whereabouts to distant females or to scare rivals.

2. Toxic Diet
Koalas eat one to two pounds (450 to 900 g) of eucalyptus leaves each day. The leaves are not only poisonous—they're also tough to digest and provide little nutrition. But koalas have a specially adapted digestive system that extracts every drop of energy from the leaves while neutralizing their toxins.

3. Mistaken Identity
The Europeans who first settled in Australia mistook these tree dwellers for a type of bear, and the name "koala bear" stuck. However, a koala is actually a marsupial—a type of mammal that protects and nurtures its tiny newborns in a pouch.

4. Feisty Guys
A koala may look like a stuffed animal, but you'd be sorry if you tried to cuddle a wild one. Their long, sharp claws—supremely adapted for climbing trees—are used as daggers when two male koalas argue over territory or a mate.

5. Awesome Moms
Born blind, hairless, and no bigger than a jelly bean, a baby koala spends six months sleeping and drinking milk in its mother's pouch. Eventually, it will poke its head out to eat pap—a poopy soup from its mother that builds resistance to eucalyptus poison. When the joey leaves the pouch, the mama koala carries it on her back or belly as she climbs trees and teaches the tiny koala by example.

Snowy Owls

How these birds of prey
keep on the move
to survive
in cold
climates

A young male owl began life in the Arctic about five months ago. This winter he flew hundreds of miles south to Logan International Airport near Boston, Massachusetts, U.S.A. His white feathers are tipped with brown stripes, but they'll soon be almost all white. Suddenly, the owl launches, gliding silently toward the water's edge. He stretches out his talons and snatches an unsuspecting duck. Dinner is served.

Raptors on the Move

Snowy owls migrate to and from their Arctic breeding grounds each spring and fall in a quest for food. Logan Airport is a popular winter

WHO'S WHO?
ADULT MALES ARE
ALL WHITE; FEMALES
HAVE STYLISH BROWN-
AND-WHITE FEATHERS.

destination for them in the northeastern United States since the habitat looks like a tundra and there's plenty to eat there, too. But not all snowy owls migrate so far south. Some stay in the Arctic, hunt there, and endure the harsh winter in constant darkness. Though temperatures can plummet to minus 40°F (-40°C) the owls are kept warm by their layers of feathers. Researchers used to think snowy owls always flew south in the winter, but after tracking the birds with electronic transmitters, they've realized that some stay in the north by the coast, feasting on seabirds.

Tundra Life

In the spring, a female owl migrates to find a good nesting site. She lands on the tundra near Barrow, Alaska, where there's a good supply of small rodents called lemmings to feast on.

WHERE'S DINNER? CHICKS
HUDDLE IN THEIR NEST.

By May, the female sits atop a nest of eight eggs, which hatch in mid-June. They snuggle under their mother's wings and against the featherless brood patch on her belly to keep warm. Their father provides food for the whole family. The chicks grow quickly, each eating about two lemmings a day.

When the owlets are about two months old, they learn to fly. By October, the chicks are ready to strike out on their own. Silently, they glide into the darkness to their winter destinations.

35

FREAKY frogs!

Nearly 6,000 species of frogs hop, burrow, climb, swim, and even soar in exotic ecosystems around the world—and your own neighborhood. Their sometimes startling adaptations make them remarkable survivalists. Here are some frogs whose freakish good looks and bizarre lifestyles will make you become a frog fan.

WARNING LABEL

From the top, the Oriental fire-bellied toad from Korea, China, and southeastern Russia appears to be a mild-mannered frog. If threatened, though, it flashes its brightly colored belly to warn predators, "Look but don't touch." Not only is it toxic, it's also covered with sharp warts.

An amphibian is a **frog, toad**, newt, **salamander**, or caecilian.

CLEARLY SEE-THROUGH

From Central and South America, glass frogs are translucent (kind of see-through, like fogged glass). This type of camouflage makes them appear nearly invisible or like a bump on a leaf. Some even have green bones to blend in and trick predators. If you flip over a glass frog, you can see its heart beating through its skin.

FROG-ZILLA!

At 7 pounds (3.2 kg) and with a sitting length of 12.5 inches (31.8 cm), the Goliath frog from Cameroon and Equatorial Guinea is bigger than a Chihuahua. The world's largest frog, it can leap ten times its body length, or about 10 feet (3 m) each hop. Its body and legs can stretch 29.5 inches (75 cm) long, a little longer than a tennis racket.

FLYING FROG

Why hop when you can fly?
These amphibians, which live high
up in the rain forest canopy in Indonesia,
Malaysia, and Thailand, glide from tree to tree to
escape predators or search for food. With its webbed
feet and side skin flaps, this four-inch (10-cm)-long frog can
glide up to 50 feet (15 m). That's like flying from the pitcher's
mound to home plate on a Little League field.

Frogs live on **every** continent **except** Antarctica.

BIG GULP

Go ahead and yell, "Hey, big mouth!" The
Amazon horned frog won't be offended. That's
because its mouth is 1.6 times wider than its
entire body length. It eats anything it can fit
inside that mega-mouth, including rodents,
snakes, lizards, and even other frogs. And it
swallows the prey whole. Sometimes its eyes
are bigger than its stomach. Some Amazon
horned frogs have attempted to eat prey that
was larger than themselves.

KISS ME AND CROAK

A golden poison frog has enough poison on its skin to kill several
men. This tiny toxic frog from Colombia doesn't make its own
poison. It absorbs toxins from the insects that it eats. Unlike most
frogs, it boldly rests out in the open for everyone to see. Its color
warns enemies to leave it alone. Being armed with enough poison
to drop half a football team means there's no need to hide.

BURPING UP BABY

The male Darwin's frog of Argentina and Chile gives
"birth," but in his own weird way. After the female lays
eggs, the male guards them for about 20 days. Then he
swallows them, and the tadpoles grow and morph into
frogs inside his throat pouch. After 50 to 60 days, daddy
belches up more than a dozen baby frogs. Yum!

THE BIGGEST SMALLEST DISCOVERY

In 2009, on the rain forest floor in Papua
New Guinea, scientists discovered the planet's
smallest frog species, known only by its
scientific name, *Paedophryne amauensis*.
How small is it? A couple of them could sit
on a dime and still have room!

Meerkat CITY

Meerkats always have something to do. These mongoose relatives live in busy communities, with no time to sit around being bored. In their family groups of up to 40 members, everyone pitches in to get all the jobs done.

A SENTINEL KEEPS WATCH.

Guards

Meerkats are very territorial. Guards, called sentinels, are always on the lookout for rival meerkats that try to move in on their territory. If a sentinel (left) spots any intruding meerkats, it sends out an alarm call. The whole group gathers together and stands tall to try to scare away the rivals. If that doesn't work, meerkats quickly decide whether to fight or retreat.

Predators such as eagles or jackals rate a different warning call. When the sentinel spots a predator, it lets out an alarm call that sends all the meerkats scurrying into the nearest bolt hole—an underground safety den where the eagle can't follow.

Babysitters

Within a meerkat group, the alpha, or leader, female and the alpha male are usually the only ones that have babies. When their babies are too young to follow along while they search for food, meerkat parents have to go without them. So they leave their pups with babysitters—other adult meerkats in the group. The pups stay inside their family's underground burrow for the first three weeks of life, protected and cared for by the babysitters.

Diggers

Picture yourself looking for a tasty bug to eat (below) when suddenly you hear the alarm call for "eagle." You dash left, you dash right, and you finally find a bolt hole.

Bolt holes provide fast getaways for meerkats in danger. Members of the group cooperate to make sure bolt holes are properly dug out, that nothing is blocking the entry, and that there are enough bolt holes in every area.

Meerkats are built to be superdiggers. All four of their paws have long, sturdy claws that they use like rakes. They dig to find food, such as lizards and other small reptiles, insects and their larvae, and scorpions.

HOME SWEET BURROW

DIGGING FOR FOOD

WILD DOGS OF AFRICA

The puppy-dog eyes and pleading squeals of a five-month-old African wild dog named Cici can mean only one thing: dinnertime. An older sister in Cici's pack responds, dragging over a meaty impala bone. In African wild dog society, puppies have all the power. "It's up to the older siblings to take care of the puppies," says Micaela Gunther, a scientist who studies wild dogs, including Cici's family. "The doting grown-ups even deliver toys, such as a strip of impala skin perfect for puppy tug-of-war." Imagine your big brother or sister working hard to hand you snacks and games while you eat, play, and rest all day.

DOG DAYS

Like wolves, wild dogs live in a pack of up to 15 dogs. Pups stay in the pack for about two years. Then some may break off to start packs of their own, while others stay with their mom and dad.

When the pups are newborn, every member of the pack works together to provide for them. At first the puppies stay near the den, often under the watch of a babysitter while the pack hunts. Returning pack members throw up meat for the pups. Sound gross? Puppies love these leftovers.

PACK ATTACK

By the time the pups are six months old, they join the pack on hunting expeditions. First they learn how to stalk prey, and eventually they participate in the kill. Single 60-pound (27-kg) dogs rarely catch larger prey on their own, but a pack of 20 proves that there really is strength in numbers. Together they can take down a zebra or wildebeest weighing up to 1,000 pounds (454 kg).

Hunting wild dogs often pursue herds of gazelle for miles, fresh dogs trading places with tired ones. Eventually the weakest of the chased animals tires. The dogs surround it and attack from every direction. This teamwork is bred from the pack's intense social bonding, such as the daily greeting ceremonies and puppy play sessions. Team-building is the reason wild dogs spoil the pups, who grow up united and ready to contribute to the strength of the pack.

SUPER SNAKES

Snakes are masters of disguise, skilled hunters, and champion eaters. More than 2,500 species of snakes slither around the world. Check out these surprising facts about snakes.

AMAZON TREE BOA

SNAKES SMELL WITH THEIR TONGUES.

Smell that mouse? A snake uses its tongue to help it smell. It flicks its long, forked tongue to pick up chemical molecules from the air, ground, or water. The tongue carries the smelly molecules back to two small openings—called the Jacobson's organ—in the roof of the snake's mouth. Cells in the Jacobson's organ analyze the scent. *Mmm,* lunch!

SNAKES CHANGE THEIR SKIN.

Snakes literally grow out of their skin. Every few months, most start rubbing against the ground or tree branches. Starting at the mouth, a snake slithers out of its too-tight skin. Like a sock, the skin comes off inside out. *Voilà*—the snake has a fresh, shiny look. Nice makeover.

EMERALD TREE BOA

CONSTRICTORS GIVE WICKED HUGS.

Boas, anacondas, pythons, and other snakes called constrictors are amazing squeezers. This kind of snake wraps its muscular body around a victim and squeezes until the animal suffocates. The twisted talent comes from muscles attached to 200 or more vertebrae in a snake's backbone. (Humans are born with only 33 vertebrae.)

DIONE RAT SNAKE

SOME SNAKES CAN DISAPPEAR.

Snakes are great hunters, but often they're the prey. Birds, raccoons, foxes, and other animals have a taste for snakes. One way to hide: camouflage. Many snakes sport colors and patterns that allow them to blend in with their surroundings. For instance, a green tree python looks like a vine when it coils itself around a branch. A yellow eyelash viper blends in with flowers. And a rainbow boa disappears on gnarled tree stumps.

BRAZILIAN RAINBOW BOA

PUFF ADDER

SNAKE VENOM CAN KILL.

By sinking two hollow, pointy fangs into their prey, many snakes inject venom to paralyze or kill victims before devouring them. Africa's black mamba is thought to be one of the world's deadliest snakes. Up to 14 feet (4.3 m) long and as skinny as a pool cue, the black mamba strikes fast. Two drops of its venom can kill a human. It's a snake to be respected—from a distance.

SNAKES DON'T CHEW.

A snake's lower jawbone is hinged very loosely in back, so the snake can open superwide. The snake's backward-curved teeth are designed to grab prey and move it down its throat. Loosely attached ribs and elastic skin expand as the food moves on down. Boas and other huge snakes can even eat goats and deer. After a big meal, snakes can go weeks without food.

GREEN TREE PYTHON

SEDGE VIPER

SNAKES "SEE" HEAT.

Some snakes—such as pythons, rattlesnakes, and copperheads— can't see well and use other senses to find prey. These creatures have openings called pit holes in front of their eyes. These pits sense the heat given off by warm-blooded prey. The snakes' heat vision allows the vipers to track prey day or night.

5 COOL THINGS ABOUT HARP SEALS

With their irresistible faces and fluffy fur, harp seals are some of the cutest animals around. But their snow-white pelts and icy habitat make harp seals especially vulnerable to hunters, global warming, and other environmental threats. Here's more about harp seals—and why it's extra-important to protect these adorable animals.

1 6,000-MILE JOURNEY

Each year, harp seals migrate more than 6,000 miles (9,600 km), spending summers feeding in northern Arctic coastal waters and heading back south in the fall to breed. They migrate in small groups of up to 20 individuals. By late February, harp seals gather in large herds. As many as one million form an enormous herd found on the floating mass of pack ice in the Gulf of St. Lawrence in Canada. Once breeding season is over, the seals travel back north for the summer.

2 SEE-THROUGH COAT

When a harp seal pup is born, its coat has a yellow tint. But it turns completely white within a couple of days. The fine, silky fur is almost transparent. This allows the pup's skin to absorb the sun's rays, which helps it stay warm. The whitecoats, as they are called, look like this only for about two weeks. Then they molt, or shed, their white fur. Their new coats are gray.

3 HEART TRICK

When a young harp seal sees a polar bear, instinct takes over. The pup can't escape the predator by running away, so it hides—in plain sight. The ball of white fur plays possum. The seal lies motionless with its head tucked into its chubby neck, looking like a heap of snow (below). The pup's heart rate slows from about 80 to 90 beats a minute to only 20 to 30 beats. If the trick works, the bear doesn't see the harp seal and moves on. Then the seal can stretch out and relax. Whew!

4 DEEP DIVERS

It's not unusual for a harp seal to hold its breath for 5 minutes. But when it needs to, the seal can stay underwater for as long as 20 minutes and dive more than 800 feet (244 m) down. That's six times deeper than a scuba diver can go safely. Harp seals can get places fast, too—100 feet (30 m) down in 15 seconds. As the seals zip through the water hunting for fish, they also stay alert for orcas and sharks that might eat *them*.

5 QUICK-CHANGE ARTISTS

By the time a harp seal is 14 months old, it has changed coats—and nicknames—five times. A whitecoat at first, it then becomes a graycoat, a ragged jacket, a beater, and finally a bedlamer. At four years old a harp seal has a silvery gray coat with a few spots—and it's called a spotted harp. Some females look like that the rest of their lives. Males, as well as many females, develop a distinctive black pattern that is shaped like a harp, which explains the name of the species.

DID YOU KNOW?
Harp seals are known as "earless" seals because they don't have external earflaps.

MONKEY TROUBLE

A YOUNG BABOON TAKES A DANGEROUS SWIM.

It's a chilly winter morning in Botswana's Okavango Delta in Africa. A troop of chacma baboons wades across a narrow stream. But an eight-month-old infant named Chobe is left behind. She frantically paces the shore and calls out. The others ignore her as they move through the cold water without her.

Because the baboons' territory is flooded for half of the year, they must cross water all day. They move from island to island to find food and to escape predators such as lions and leopards.

1

DANGEROUS CROSSING

To cross the stream, bigger kid baboons hitch a ride with one of their parents, climbing onto the adult's back. Chobe usually gets a lift across the water with her dad, but today he's gone on ahead. So she has to figure out a way to get across the water and keep up with her troop. A young baboon cannot survive alone in the wild.

2

CAUGHT IN THE CURRENT

Chobe begins to wade into the cold stream. The water quickly becomes too deep for her, so she starts to swim clumsily. Midway, the strong current drags her downstream, farther from the shore. Her screams turn to gurgles as she starts to swallow water.

4

COMFORT AFTER A CLOSE CALL

Chobe's tiring fast, but just then, her feet find a shallow bank in the stream and she races out of the water. She sits on the shore, shivering. Her mother soon arrives, holds her close, and grooms her. Grooming is a great form of comfort for baboons. In no time, Chobe is running around with the other young baboons.

3

STAYING SAFE WITH DAD

Baboons have to learn to survive on their own, and sometimes that involves dangerous lessons. Chobe got a taste of what it's like to be an independent member of the troop. She decides she isn't quite ready to be a grown-up yet ...so she makes sure to find her father and hop onto his back at the next water crossing.

Animal Rescues

KOALA
QUEENSLAND, AUSTRALIA

RESCUE FROM TREE

Dogs viciously attack a young male koala, biting and shaking him. Somehow the koala escapes and struggles up a tree to seek shelter. Without medical care, he'll die of his wounds.

Home owners finally notice the injured animal and call Moreton Bay Koala Rescue. The rescuers gently place the wounded animal in a large cage and drive him to the Australia Zoo Wildlife Hospital. During the trip, they decide to name the koala Lewis.

GROWING STRONGER
The staff changes Lewis's bandages and cleans his wounds every day. It takes more than three months for the koala's arms and legs to heal. After eight months, Lewis is scaling trees over 60 feet (18 m) tall and gathering his own leaves. He's ready to return to the wild.

BACK TO THE BUSH
Lewis is driven back to the area where he was rescued, and then carried in a cage deep into the bush—far from private property and dogs. After a half-hour hike, the release team opens the cage. At first, Lewis is a bit hesitant. But then he quickly climbs up the tree, without looking back.

DOLPHIN TURKISH COAST

For months two male dolphins, named Tom and Misha, have been attractions in a moneymaking scheme near the coast of Turkey. Tourists pay to swim with the 9-foot (2.7-cm)-long dolphins in a small, 13-foot (4-m)-deep swimming pool.

The business owner neglects them. No one cleans the pool. A thick pile of dolphin waste and uneaten, rotting fish builds up on the bottom, creating a terrible stench. The contaminated water makes the dolphins sick, and the pair rapidly lose weight. The stressed, cooped-up dolphins fight each other. They're only weeks from dying.

RESCUE FROM POOL

HELP ARRIVES
A local organization called the Dolphin Angels hears about the desperate situation and begins a protest campaign. Soon the Born Free Foundation, an animal rights group in England, joins the cause. Once they win custody of Tom and Misha, the rescuers put their plan into action to release the dolphins back to the wild.

AROUND THE WORLD

ELEPHANT

ZAMBIA, AFRICA

In the Kapani Lagoon in Zambia, Africa, a baby elephant playfully rolls around in the sticky mud to chill out. But when it stands up, one of its feet sinks deep into the mud and gets stuck. The terrified baby squeals to its mother. She ignores the muddy danger and tries to yank her calf out with her strong trunk. The mud traps the heavy mother too, swallowing her legs like thick cement. Without help, the two elephants will slowly dehydrate and die in the heat—if the lions and hyenas don't find them first.

HELP ON THE WAY

An employee at a nearby safari lodge hears the animals' cries and sees their dangerous situation. The staff of the lodge alerts the government wildlife department, and help is on the way in the form of heavy rope, lots of manpower, and a tractor!

HELP ARRIVES

BACK TO THE HERD

After many tries the rescuers are able to pull the baby elephant out of the mud using rope and having a good old-fashioned tug-of-war. On the other hand, extracting the mother elephant from the mud pit requires a lot more effort—the rope, the manpower, and the tractor. Free at last, mother and child are happily together again and eager to rejoin the herd.

A team of wildlife experts carries the two dolphins out of the pool on stretchers and loads them into a van. To fight the infections and parasites, a veterinarian gives them strong doses of antibiotics. The rescuers haul the dolphins out to a large floating pen enclosed with deep nets in the Mediterranean Sea.

BACK TO THE WILD

After 20 months of rehabilitation the dolphins are ready. Scuba divers remove part of the sea pen's netting, opening the door to freedom. Tom cautiously swims through the opening. Misha follows, and then— *see ya!* They take off and never look back.

ROCK-A-BYE
MONKEY

Gleefully vaulting from branch to branch, Intan, a six-week-old monkey, is so daring—and so uncoordinated. She slips, then screams for help while dangling from 60 feet (18 m) up a tree. Mom and other females in the troop rush to her rescue.

Ebony langurs, a kind of monkey, spend most of their lives high in the forest canopy. There they effortlessly leap from tree to tree. But today is Intan's first day in a real tree in a real forest. The troop was just released from captivity into the forest of Bromo Tengger Semeru National Park on the island of Java in Indonesia.

Monkey Business

Illegally captured from the wild and sold as pets, the monkeys in this troop are survivors. The Indonesian Conservation Department rescued them, bringing them to a center where caregivers prepare them for release back into the wild. Little Intan is born while the troop is at the center.

When the monkeys are released, biologists and photographers hide on an observation platform high in a tree to watch them settle in. But the monkeys easily find the observers.

Nice Trip. See You Next Fall!

Intan's mother becomes exasperated as she rescues her baby from climbing predicaments. After a few falls, she carries Intan to the not-so-secret blind, and puts her in photographer Djuna Ivereigh's lap.

Before Ivereigh can move the baby from her lap, Intan leaps up to play with a stick. Chasing it across the platform, Intan accidentally topples over the edge. The humans watch in horror as the baby tumbles 25 feet (8 m) to the ground!

Shrieking langurs rush toward the motionless monkey. Scooping up Intan, Mom gently rocks her baby. Very soon, Intan peeks out, unharmed. She bounds away for more monkey mischief.

The dirty looks the others give Ivereigh suggest their opinion of her babysitting skills. The near-disastrous result may achieve one goal, though: No troop member will ever trust a human with one of its own again.

INTAN ENJOYS ACROBATICS.

INTAN CUDDLES WITH HER MOM WHEN SHE'S READY TO REST.

According to an ancient Indian legend, the Raven turned one out of every ten bears white to remind people of a time when Earth was covered by snow and ice.

Secrets of the Spirit Bear

A rare animal creates a mysterious sight in the forest.

On a cold, rainy October night in the rain forest, a hulking white form with a ghostly glow appears in the distance. No, it's not the ghost of a black bear. It's a spirit bear, also called a Kermode bear, which are black bears with white hair. They live almost exclusively in one place: the Great Bear Rainforest along the coast of British Columbia, Canada. Researchers want to figure out why the bears with white coats have survived here. Fewer than 200 spirit bears call this area home.

WHITE COAT CLUES

For many animals, unusual white coloration can make it hard to survive since they may have

trouble hiding from predators. But the Kermode bears' coloring may actually help them survive and give them an edge while catching salmon.

"A white bear blends into the background during the day and is more successful catching fish," explains biologist Thomas Reimchen. "There is an advantage to one bear in some conditions and the other in different conditions."

TALE OF TWO ISLANDS

Canada's Gribbell Island has the highest concentration of Kermode bears, followed by neighboring Princess Royal Island. These isolated islands may be another key to the bears' survival since there's no competition from grizzly bears, and wolves are the only natural threat. The islands' trees provide shelters, and rivers are filled with salmon.

Even though spirit bears have flourished on these islands, new threats such as logging worry scientists and the members of the Native American Gitga'at First Nation, who have lived with and protected spirit bears for centuries. That's why researchers are working hard to understand the biology of the spirit bear. As they do, they can find the best ways to ensure its survival.

BIG CATS

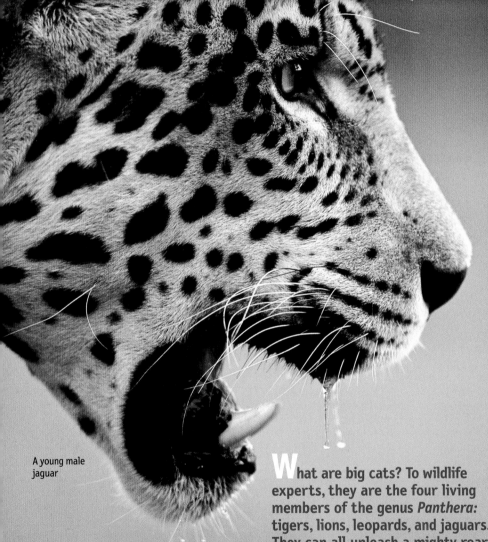

A young male
jaguar

Learn more about animals in peril and ways
you can help with National Geographic
Kids Mission: Animal Rescue series.
Visit kids.nationalgeographic.com/
mission-animal-rescue.

What are big cats? To wildlife
experts, they are the four living
members of the genus *Panthera*:
tigers, lions, leopards, and jaguars.
They can all unleash a mighty roar
and, as carnivores, they survive
solely on the flesh of other animals.
Thanks to powerful jaws; long, sharp
claws; and daggerlike teeth, big cats
are excellent hunters.

WHO'S WHO?

FUR

Most tigers are orange-colored with vertical black stripes on their bodies. This coloring helps the cats blend in with tall grasses as they sneak up on prey. These markings are like fingerprints: No two stripe patterns are alike.

BIG CATS MAY HAVE a lot of features in common, but if you know what to look for, you'll be able to tell who's who in no time.

TIGERS

JAGUARS

A jaguar's coat pattern looks similar to that of a leopard, as both have dark spots called rosettes. The difference? The rosettes on a jaguar's torso have irregularly shaped borders and at least one black dot in the center.

LIONS

Lions have a light brown, or tawny, coat and a tuft of black hair at the end of their tails. When they reach their prime, most male lions have shaggy manes that help them look larger and more intimidating.

LEOPARDS

A leopard's yellowy coat has dark spots called rosettes on its back and sides. In leopards, the rosettes' edges are smooth and circular. This color combo helps leopards blend into their surroundings.

JAGUAR
100 to 250 pounds
(45 TO 113 KG)
5 to 6 feet long
(1.5 TO 1.8 M)

LEOPARD
66 to 176 pounds
(30 TO 80 KG)
4.25 to 6.25 feet long
(1.3 TO 1.9 M)

BENGAL TIGER
240 to 500 pounds
(109 TO 227 KG)
5 to 6 feet long
(1.5 TO 1.8 M)

AFRICAN LION
265 to 420 pounds
(120 TO 191 KG)
4.5 to 6.5 feet long
(1.4 TO 2 M)

CHEETAHS: Built for SPEED

This wild cat's body makes it an incredible predator.

Breathing deeply, the cheetah prepares her body for the chase. Head low, eyes focused on an impala, she slowly inches forward. In three seconds this streamlined, superfast cat is sprinting at 60 miles an hour (96 km/h), eyes locked, laserlike, on the fleeing impala.

Long, muscular tail for balance in tight turns

The legendary Jamaican runner Usain Bolt is the world's fastest human. Bolt ran 200 meters in 19.19 seconds, about 23 miles an hour (37 km/h), but that's slow compared with the cheetah. Cheetahs can run about three times faster than Bolt. At top speed a sprinting cheetah can reach 70 miles an hour (113 km/h). Next time you're in a car on the highway, imagine a cheetah racing alongside you. That will give you an idea of how fast this speedy cat can run.

Several adaptations help cheetahs run so fast. A cheetah has longer legs than other cats. It also has a

Small, short face with enlarged nostrils to take in lots of air

long, extremely flexible spine. These features work together so a running cheetah can cover up to 23 feet (7 m) in one stride—about the length of five ten-year-olds lying head to feet in a row.

Most other cats can retract their claws when they're not using them. Cheetahs' claws stick out all the time, like dogs' claws. Cheetahs use these strong, blunt claws like an athlete uses cleats on track shoes—to help push off and quickly build up speed. The large center pad on the cheetah's foot is covered with long ridges that act like the treads on a car tire. A sprinting cheetah needs to be able to stop fast, too. It is able to spread its toes wide, and its toe pads are hard and pointed. This helps a cheetah turn quickly

Strong, blunt claws and ridged footpads to grip the ground

and brake suddenly. It can stop in a single stride from a speed of more than 20 miles an hour (32 km/h).

All these body adaptations add up to extraordinary hunting abilities. A cheetah stalks up close to a herd of impalas, then streaks forward with lightning speed. As the herd bolts, the cat singles out one individual and follows its twists and turns precisely. As it closes in on its prey the cheetah strikes out with a forepaw, knocks the animal off its feet, and clamps its jaws over the prey's throat.

Snow Leopard SECRETS

High-tech tools help scientists understand how to save these big cats.

On a cool summer night, a snow leopard curiously sniffs an overhanging boulder for a strong scent sprayed by other cats. He rubs his cheeks on the boulder, scrapes the ground with his hind paws, and then urinates.

This act—called scraping—is how snow leopards communicate with one another. A scrape tells other snow leopards what they're doing and may reveal whether a snow leopard is male or female, has cubs, or is looking for a mate.

Recently, researchers studying the 4,000 to 7,000 snow leopards in the wild have set up motion-activated cameras at scraping sites in an effort to gather more information on these elusive cats and expose new details about how many snow leopards there are, how long they live, and how we can protect them.

Even though snow leopards live in some of the most rugged mountain terrain on Earth, people pose the biggest threat to their survival. Poachers can sell a snow leopard's hide and bones for thousands of dollars. Herders often kill any snow leopard that attacks their livestock. Hunters target ibex, wild sheep, and other animals for food and trophies—removing important snow leopard prey.

Like a snow leopard reality show, the cameras expose everything that happens. The images also help researchers count the number of snow leopards in an area and reveal whether prey animals, livestock, or poachers are nearby.

Other researchers will gently trap the wild cats and put satellite radio collars on them to track where the cats roam and to learn new things about how and where they live. Technology like this is essential to help researchers protect snow leopards in the wild and preserve their habitat.

Despite their name, snow leopards are not snow-colored. Their spotted gray or beige fur actually stands out against a snowy background—but blends in with rocks.

MARKING TERRITORY

TWO CUBS

CHASING DOWN PREY

TIGERS in the Snow

These wild cats survive the cold of eastern Russia.

Many Amur tigers have beachfront property—they live in Russian forests on the edge of the Sea of Japan.

Silently moving through the trees, a tigress stalks her prey. Deep snow covers the ground, and with each step the big cat sinks to her belly. She knows the snow will muffle any sounds, so she can sneak up on a wild boar that is rooting around for pine nuts. A few yards away, the tiger pauses, crouches, and then launches her 280-pound (127-kg) body toward her prey. Snow sprays up with each leap as she prepares to pounce on the boar with her plate-size paws. A powdery cloud fills the air. Then the snow settles, revealing the three-foot (0.9-m)-long tail and orange, black, and white body. Now stained red, the tigress grasps the boar in her mouth.

She carries her catch behind some larch trees, and her two cubs join her from a nearby hill. Camouflaged in the trees, they were watching their mother hunt. Soon, they'll start hunting for themselves. But for now, they are content with the meal their mother has provided, followed by a nap.

These Siberian, or Amur, tigers live in the eastern reaches of Russia—farther north than any other tiger subspecies. Thick coats of fur insulate their bodies from the freezing winter temps. In the summer, their coats blend in with the forest, making them nearly impossible to see.

HUNGER GAMES

The tiger trio is among the some 400 Amur tigers that researchers think are left in the wild. As recently as 50 years ago, there were plenty of deer and wild boar, the staples of a tiger's diet. Today, those prey animals are harder to find. People hunt

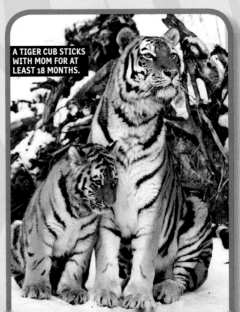

A TIGER CUB STICKS WITH MOM FOR AT LEAST 18 MONTHS.

them, and logging companies and fires destroy the forest where they live. Some tiger habitat is protected, but the cats wander beyond these safe zones in search of prey. Half of all tiger cubs die young because they are sick, killed by hunters, or orphaned. Cubs that survive leave Mom at about 18 months old, relying on the hunting skills they learned growing up. Sometimes a young male must travel far to find unclaimed land that has enough food. But the odds are that his journey will take him through areas where people live.

TROUBLESHOOTING

It is late winter when the male tiger leaves his mother's care. When he scratches against a tree, he catches his paw on something. He's walked into a wire snare, and the more he moves, the tighter it gets. A little while later, he hears voices. People. They stay behind the trees, and one of them raises a gun. The tiger roars at the sharp pain in his backside, then lies down and falls asleep. He's been shot by a researcher's tranquilizer gun, not a hunter. Unable to find enough food in the snowy forest, this tiger started taking livestock and dogs in a nearby town. Dale Miquelle and his team are called in to fix the problem. "Relocating them gives them a second chance," Miquelle says. Otherwise, the farmer would track down the tiger and shoot him.

The researchers quickly weigh and measure the tranquilized tiger. Then they fit a collar with a radio transmitter around his neck. This will let Miquelle's team keep track of the tiger's whereabouts for at least three years.

NEW TERRITORY

Two hours later, the tiger wakes up in the back of a truck about 150 miles (241 km) from the town. The cage gate opens, and the wild cat leaps out. Unfamiliar with the territory, he searches for signs of other tigers. He comes across a birch tree with a strong odor. Another male sprayed the tree and left scrape marks and urine on the ground to tell others, "Occupied. Keep moving."

The young tiger walks on. Miquelle's team monitors his movements using signals from the radio collar. They hope he can find food, avoid other males, find his own territory, and eventually mate with a local female. The tiger spots a deer ahead. Melting snow drips from the trees, masking his footsteps as he ambushes his prey. His odds just got a little better.

THIS TIGER'S SCRATCHES ON TREES ARE MESSAGES FOR OTHER TIGERS.

In the 1930s, only about 30 Amur tigers were left in the wild.

ICE-COLD WATER QUENCHES THIS TIGER'S THIRST.

53

Family Pride

Lion cubs grow up strong with help from moms, aunts, and big sisters.

Hidden among tall grass and bushes in Africa, a mother cub rests while her two lion cubs bury their faces in her belly to nurse. At five weeks old, they've eaten only mother's milk since birth. In a couple of weeks they'll start to eat meat, but first they must meet the pride, or family group.

Family First

After their nap, the mother takes the cubs to the woods near a river, where they're greeted by six young cats, the cubs' cousins. More lions lounge nearby. They are familiar with the new-comers because their mom has been wearing their scent when she has returned to the pride for group hunts.

A shaggy mane surrounding a mas-sive male lion's head appears from behind the rock. The pride ruler. The mother lion waits to see if he recognizes her cubs as his offspring. If not, he will kill them on the spot. He pads over to the cubs and sniffs their heads. They bat his nose with tiny paws. He bats back, growling. He finally decides the cubs are his and plops down to rest.

Pride Power

It's time for the lions to eat. Hunting is an organized family affair: It will take several lions to overpower something like a one-ton (907-kg) buffalo bull. While the females fan out and surround a small group of buffalo, the younger cubs quietly watch from a distance.

A lioness sprints toward a bull, and the other lions jump on, digging in their teeth as they pull the bull down. Then the whole pride runs over to claim some meat. The pride's large male chases away the females and eats his fill. When he moves away, the rest of the pride fights over any leftovers. The two cubs gnaw small pieces with their new teeth.

The distracted pride doesn't notice a new male lion approaching. He wants to take over the pride and its territory, so he challenges the pride leader, who is older and weaker. Eventually, the injured old ruler limps away, abandoning the pride. The new male moves to his next victims: the cubs. He wants his own offspring, so these cubs must go. But the older females fight him off, and the twins' mother escapes with her cubs.

Again on the move, the twins stay close to their mother. She and two of her sisters have split from the pride to save their offspring. Even a small group is better protected than a lone lion with cubs, so they're hoping it will be enough to survive.

A MALE LION ACCEPTS HIS OWN CUB AS IT APPROACHES TO PLAY.

YOUNG LIONS PRACTICE HUNTING SKILLS AS THEY PLAY.

HUNTING IS A GROUP EFFORT, ESPECIALLY WHEN PREY IS AS BIG AS THESE BUFFALO.

NATIONAL GEOGRAPHIC KiDS
SCANNER

SCAN THIS PAGE!
GET BONUS MOBILE CONTENT! Download the free NG Kids scanner app. Directions on inside front cover.

BIZARRE Insects

Check out some of the strangest bugs on Earth!

The bright-colored head of the puss moth caterpillar warns predators to stay away. This species, one of the most toxic caterpillars in North America, can spray acid from its head when it is attacked.

puss moth caterpillar

walking leaf

giraffe-necked weevil

No surprise, this bug gets its name from its extra-long neck. The males have longer necks than females do, which they use to fight other males for mating rights.

This flat, green insect is a master of disguise: It's common to mistake this bug for an actual leaf, thanks to its large, feathery wings. This clever camouflage provides protection from potential predators.

thorn bugs

spiny katydid

One tiny thorn bug may not be a match for a bigger predator, but when grouped together on a branch, these spiky bugs create a prickly pack no bird wants a bite of!

This katydid is covered in sharper-than-knive spikes. If a predator attacks, this species springs into action, defending itself by jabbing an enemy with its spiny legs and arms.

cockshafer beetle

The wild, feathery antennae on the male cockshafer may be cool to look at, but they're also helpful tools. They enable the bug to sniff for food and feel out its surrounding environment.

acorn weevil

The acorn weevil's hollow nose is longer than its body, and perfect for drilling through the shells of acorns. A female will feast on the nut by sucking up its rich, fatty liquid, and then lay her eggs in the acorn.

pink grasshopper

Though most grasshoppers are green or brown, some—like this pink nymph—are much brighter. Pink grasshoppers are rare, most likely because they are easy for predators to spot.

man-faced stinkbug

There are more than 4,500 species of stinkbugs worldwide, including this brilliant yellow species, whose shield-shaped body displays a unique pattern resembling a tribal mask. Like all stinkbugs, this species secretes a foul-smelling liquid from scent glands between its legs when it feels threatened.

rhinoceros beetle

Ounce for ounce, this insect, which gets its name from the horn-like structure on the male's head, is considered one of the world's strongest creatures. It is capable of carrying up to 850 times its own body weight.

5 SILLY Pet Tricks

1 GOAT SKATEBOARDS

Jumping on her skateboard, Happie the goat zips down driveways and cruises along sidewalks. The animal first showed her zeal for wheels when she tried to leap on a bicycle that owner Melody Cooke was riding. Cooke decided to get Happie her very own skateboard and train her to ride. After a lot of practice and goodies, the goat learned some sweet boarding moves: Happie can coast for more than 100 feet (30 m) without stopping. Talk about being on a roll.

2 HORSE PLAYS B-BALL

Before he makes a slam dunk, Amos the miniature horse looks around to see if people are watching. "Amos definitely likes an audience," owner Shelly Mizrahi says. To teach him to "play" basketball, Mizrahi gave Amos carrot slices each time he touched his nose to a hoop set on a short stand. Later Amos learned to pick up a small ball with his teeth and place it in the hoop. Scoring baskets has become the horse's all-time favorite activity. The hoofed athlete once dunked the ball a hundred times in a row. "Amos can also paint and play a xylophone with a mallet," Mizrahi says. "But if I place a paintbrush, a musical instrument, and a basketball in front of him, he always goes for the basketball."

4 PIG JAMS ON HORNS

Why won't you see Jax the cat's paw prints on the floor? Because the kitty can move around on a large, rolling ball! "Jax has always loved perching on narrow surfaces," owner Samantha Martin says. "I thought she'd like even cooler balancing acts." To prepare for the trick, Jax practiced standing on a smaller ball set in a bowl so it couldn't move. Then Martin placed her on a bigger ball at one end of a short track. On the other end were yummy cat treats. The clever kitty quickly figured out that if she inched backward on the ball, she could move it down the track—and get her delicious reward.

CAT WALKS ON BALL 3

Mudslinger the pig could be a real hog when it came to music. He enjoyed creating tunes with horns, and once he got started, he sometimes didn't want to stop. Trainer John Vincent introduced the pig to the horns by tooting some in front of him. After watching his owner, the curious pig tried squeezing the instruments with his mouth to make noise. Whenever he continued, Vincent fed him juicy grapes to keep him motivated. The curly-tailed rock star created new sound patterns whenever he played.

5 MACAW TAKES UP SKIING

Luna the hyacinth macaw loves to fly—down a ski slope! Owner Mark Steiger knew the eight-year-old bird would be a natural skier. "Hyacinth macaws like Luna have strong legs," he says. First, Luna practiced walking while clutching handles on tiny skis with her claws. Then Steiger taught her to slide down a custom-made four-foot (1.2-m)-tall slope on the skis, rewarding the bird with treats at the bottom. The macaw even learned to take a "ski lift" up her slope. With her hardy beak, she grasps onto a metal ring that her owner uses to pull her up the slide. Just before Luna whooshes back down, she leans forward like a competitive skier. "She picked that up all on her own," Steiger says. "Luna's a total pro."

Lifestyles of the

Celebs and royalty aren't the only ones lapping up luxury. With decked-out doghouses, private jets, and cat crowns, the lifestyles of some pets are totally drool-worthy. In 2013, U.S. pet owners spent about $55 billion on their furry companions. "Pets are an important part of the family," says Bob Vetere, associate president of the American Pet Products Association. "Some owners like to shower their animals with nice things."

Loving your pet doesn't have to cost an arm and a paw. Hugs, kisses, snacks, and attention are all your furry friend needs to feel like royalty.

COCO'S LOOKIN' GOOD WITH HER FLASHY LOCKS.

KITTY GLITTER ▲

Like many pampered pets, Coco the cat has all the must-have fashion accessories. When this kitty wants to show off her rock-star style, she slips on a hot-pink wig. For a more elegant look, the feline fashionista dons a faux fur coat and tiara. This kitty is sitting pretty!

THIS DOG FEELS RIGHT AT HOME IN HIS POOCH PALACE.

◄ CANINE CASTLES

Coco Puff the Yorkshire terrier and Rio the Doberman pinscher love to kick back in their two-bedroom doghouse. Many people are buying custom-made homes like this one for their pets. "Owners want an area where their dogs feel relaxed," says Michelle Pollak of La Petite Maison, which builds luxury pet homes. Fancy doggie digs can have wood floors, bay windows, and balconies. Some are big enough to hold six people!

RICH and FURRY

BASED ON A WORK BY THOMAS GAINSBOROUGH CALLED "THE BLUE BOY," THIS PAINTING FEATURES A SERIOUSLY DAPPER-LOOKING KITTY!

▶ JOIN THE CLUB

Frank the bulldog's favorite hangout isn't a dog park—it's a country club! The Club Beverly Hills is an ultra-fancy resort that caters to canines. "Dogs are so excited when they arrive here, they leap out of the car," owner Marjorie Lewis says. Members start their visits by running around a specially made fitness course. To relax, posh pets can soak in a hot tub, get massages, or do yoga with a human instructor.

CATS ON CANVAS ▲

Tiger the tabby's owners wanted more than just photographs of their beloved feline. So they asked an artist to paint a portrait. "Pet paintings are a tribute to the bond people share with their animals," says Rebecca Collins of Art Paw portrait studio. Collins and her team create pet paintings (starting at $135) based on snapshots. They'll even re-create famous works of art and add your pet to the scene.

DOG DOES YOGA!

RICOCHET THE GOLDEN RETRIEVER LIVES THE HIGH LIFE WITH A GOURMET MEAL ON A PLANE.

◀ JET-SET PETS

Beijit the golden retriever travels in style. When she flies on private jets with her owners, they hire a pet flight attendant to care for her. "Our animal customers get majorly pampered," says Carol Martin, owner of Sit 'n Stay Global. The company's pet flight attendants serve fresh-cooked entrées on fine china and give thirsty critters chilled spring water in crystal bowls. After the plane lands, pet flight attendants become pet nannies, caring for their animal clients while the owners go sightseeing. *Bone* voyage!

BEIJIT ENJOYS THE VIEW.

REAL ANIMAL HEROES!

THESE ANIMALS SHOW AMAZING BRAVERY.

DOG SAVES KID FROM TRUCK

Geo the German shepherd mix follows ten-year-old Charlie Riley everywhere. Naturally the pup goes along on family walks.

One day Charlie, his mom, and two younger brothers are standing at a street corner. Geo is sitting at Charlie's side. Suddenly ...

"We hear a roar," Charlie's mother says. An out-of-control pickup jumps the curb. It's heading straight for Charlie!

But Geo makes a flying leap. "He hits me so hard I fall over," Charlie says. The speeding truck slams into Geo instead. They rush an injured Geo to the animal hospital for emergency surgery.

"My dog could have died," Charlie says. And my son could have too, thinks his mother. But he didn't—thanks to Geo.

CAT RESCUES COUPLE

Three years after adopting a stray cat named Tiger, Michelle and Rod Ramsey are in bed with blinding headaches. Suddenly Tiger bursts into their room and howls. When Tiger won't stop, Michelle stumbles down the hall and lets him outside. That's when she sees her older cat staggering and calls the vet. "You have carbon monoxide poisoning," the veterinary assistant says when she hears Michelle slurring. Carbon monoxide is a deadly gas. Invisible and odorless, it's leaking out of the Ramseys' heating system.

Paramedics arrive. An emergency helicopter airlifts the Ramseys to the hospital. They both survive. All thanks to a cat no one else wanted.

BLIND FELINE DEFEATS ROBBER

Homer the blind cat weighs only four pounds. Gwen Cooper adopted the little stray in Miami, Florida, U.S.A., when he was three weeks old. Because of an eye infection that left him blind, he would have been euthanized if she hadn't taken him in.

Homer never lets blindness stop him. "He's a bold little adventurer," Cooper says. "He's fearless." The cat proves this one night when his growling wakes up Cooper. He's never growled before. Surprised, Cooper opens her eyes. A burglar is standing at the foot of her bed! Cooper reaches for her phone to call 911.

"Don't do that!" the intruder says. The sound of his voice pinpoints his exact location, and blind Homer leaps. No match for a snarling cat with extended claws, the would-be robber flees.

PAW ENFORCEMENT

DOGS ON DUTY SNIFF OUT SMUGGLERS.

NON-POISONOUS GOPHER SNAKES **ARE USED FOR TRAINING.**

Walking his beat at the Honolulu International Airport in Hawaii, Taylor stops to observe two women waiting for a flight to the U.S. mainland. Taylor's partner, Inspector Edna Tanaid, has no reason to believe the women might be smugglers, but Taylor smells trouble. He's a skilled, no-nonsense detective that works for the federal government. There's only one thing Taylor likes more than busting smugglers—the mouthwatering flavor of meaty dog treats. Taylor is a beagle mix. And you're in trouble if he sits down next to you and wags his tail so hard it looks ready to fly off.

BUSTED BY A DOG

"Where are your fruits?" Tanaid asks.

"We aren't carrying any," the women reply. Taylor excitedly wags, pants, and aims his sensitive nose back and forth at the women's jacket pockets. Sure enough, they have mangoes in their pockets. Tanaid seizes the contraband, or illegal goods, and gives Taylor some extra petting along with his meaty reward.

Sniffing around may sound like fun—and for Taylor, it is—but it's important work. Mangoes could contain the larvae of the Mediterranean fruit fly, a variety that lives in Hawaii but not in the continental United States. If these fruit flies reach the mainland, they could devastate American crops, costing billions of dollars.

Taylor was born with his great nose, but before putting it to work, he and his canine colleagues get about three months of training at the National Detector Dog Training Center in Georgia. There the new recruits learn the basic scent of contraband and how to find it in bags, boxes, and pockets—an advanced game of hide-and-seek.

CANINES AT WORK

In addition to sniffing around travelers and baggage, dog teams also examine U.S. and international mail, which is a huge job. Janelle Michalesko checks out arriving cargo and mail with her canine partner, Khaz, at JFK Airport in New York City. Khaz is equal parts Chesapeake Bay and Labrador retriever, a big energetic mix that makes him perfect for patrolling long warehouses and inspecting big boxes.

GOOD JOB

Along with the fruits and vegetables they discover, Khaz and Michalesko regularly find mailed meat products that could carry diseases. The handler guesses that it would take her a full day to search a warehouse that Khaz can clear in 15 minutes. Other breeds do different jobs. Tiny, fearless Jack Russell terriers, for instance, are perfect for finding brown tree snakes in cargo leaving Guam, a U.S. island in the Pacific Ocean. If stowaway snakes spread to Hawaii, it could doom the state's rare birds.

SMART PUPS

For sniffing baggage and passengers at airports, beagles are the ideal breed. "They're very friendly and people usually aren't intimidated by them," says Andrew Bateman, a Customs and Border Protection (CBP) handler who, with pup partner Cayenne, guards the Hartsfield-Jackson Atlanta International Airport. Detector dogs don't just smell well; they're trained to smell the difference between contraband and safe snacks.

Someone might assume a dog as valuable as Cayenne was raised in a special kennel and trained from birth. "She was actually found on the side of the road on a highway," Bateman says. All detector dogs that deal with agricultural items were adopted. Many, like Cayenne, are found at animal shelters, while others are donated by owners or breeders.

"I couldn't for the life of me figure out why somebody would give away a dog that's so handsome," says handler Jonathan Saito about his stocky beagle partner, Bruno, a former pound dog. "He's just an incredible dog to work with. We say 'work,' but actually, it's a game for the dogs."

Tanaid agrees. "Taking in one of these dogs and giving it a second chance at doing an important public service is great. And the dogs love what they do."

DOGS SEARCH CARS AND LUGGAGE.

Protecting American Agriculture

IN ONLY TWO DAYS, TAYLOR FOUND ALL THIS.

15 Cutest Animals of 2015

From arctic foxes to zebras, baby animals easily qualify as some of the cutest creatures on Earth. Here's NG Kids' roundup of cuddly critters that are sure to make you say *awww*.

1

OUT AND ABOUT

A young Emperor penguin stays fluffy to fight the chill in Antarctica. A chick stays snug in its mother's brood pouch for two months. As it grows older, adults leave chicks in groups called crèches while they go off to fish.

2

BEAR-Y CUTE

Talk about *panda*-monium: A collection of giant panda cubs rests in a crib at a research center in China where they're being bred to help boost the endangered animal's numbers in the wild.

3 REAL TROOPERS

A family—or troop—of ring-tailed lemurs get close and cuddly in a zoo enclosure. In the wild, lemurs live in groups of up to 30 animals. They travel as a pack foraging for food during the day and spend their nights huddled together as they snooze.

4 SUMMER STYLE

Hi, there! This adorable arctic fox pops out of his burrow in Alaska. This animal's thick fur changes color with the seasons, going from grayish brown in the summer to white in the winter.

5 STUCK ON YOU

This itsy-bitsy amphibian may look harmless, but watch out! The Amazon milk frog gets its name from the milky-colored fluid it secretes when threatened. Native to South America, milk frogs spend most of their lives high in the rain forest canopy and hardly ever touch the ground.

6

MUG SHOT

Why so glum? "Grumpy Cat" Tardar Sauce became an Internet sensation after her owner's brother posted a video on YouTube. But this kitty's not really mad: Her frowny face is likely a result of feline dwarfism.

7

FUR BABY

A harp seal pup soaks up the sun on ice off the coast of the Gulf of St. Lawrence in Canada. Born with very little body fat, the pups have thick, white fur that traps heat from the sunlight to keep them warm and snug.

8

PUPPY LOVE

Abandoned by the side of the road as a puppy, Tuna the chiweenie (that's part Chihuahua, part dachshund) was so traumatized, he'd squirm on his belly instead of walking. Now? The puppy is thriving in an adopted home, and pics of his adventures—and his funny outfits—have earned him fans around the world. How's that for a happy ending?

9

SHOW-OFF

Just call him four eyes: A bespectacled dolphin steals the show at a water park in Phuket, Thailand. Considered one of the smartest mammals on the planet, dolphins can recognize themselves in a mirror and can hear sounds underwater that are 15 miles (24 km) away.

10

HOW *DEER*

Gimme a kiss! A roe deer plants one on her friend in Olympic National Park, Washington, U.S.A., as they graze in a spring meadow. In the wild, fawns stay protected from predators like red foxes and bears by hiding in long grass until they're ready to join the rest of the herd—usually at six weeks old.

11

HOOFIN' IT

Catch me if you can! A young zebra flocks in a field of flowers in Namibia, Africa. Speedy zebras, which can walk just 20 minutes after they're born, tend to run in a zigzag pattern to confuse predators.

12

MONKEYING AROUND

A golden snub-nosed monkey perches atop a branch high in the mountains of China. These elusive monkeys travel in groups of up to 400 monkeys. That smushed-in nose isn't just there to look cute: It may also be an adaptation to protect the primates from extremely cold temps.

13

PLAYTIME

Hey mom, wake up! Two polar bear cubs climb on their resting mom in Wapusk National Park in Manitoba, Canada. In the wild, playful polar bear cubs tend to stick by their mama's side for about two years. During that time, she will protect them and teach them how to hunt.

14

STANDOUT

Chameleons usually do a pretty good job of blending into their backgrounds. Not this guy. With its bright blue skin and helmet-shaped head, the panther chameleon definitely stands out. The lizards, which can grow to be as long as a cat, are native to the tropical forests of Madagascar, and are also very popular pets.

15

HEAD COUNT

It's a raccoon totem pole! Three baby raccoons—or kits—create a too-cute tower as they poke their heads out of a tree. After building a den in the hollow of a tree or a burrow, raccoon mamas give birth to litters of about two to five kits. Babies stay with their mom until they are over one year old.

Prehistoric TIME LINE

HUMANS HAVE WALKED on Earth for some 200,000 years, a mere blip in Earth's 4.5-billion-year history. A lot has happened during that time. Earth formed, and oxygen levels rose in the millions of years of the Precambrian time. The productive Paleozoic era gave rise to hard-shelled organisms, vertebrates, amphibians, and reptiles.

Dinosaurs ruled the Earth in the mighty Mesozoic. And 64 million years after dinosaurs became extinct, modern humans emerged in the Cenozoic era. From the first tiny mollusks to the dinosaur giants of the Jurassic and beyond, Earth has seen a lot of transformation.

THE PRECAMBRIAN TIME

4.5 billion to 542 million years ago

- The Earth (and other planets) formed from gas and dust left over from a giant cloud that collapsed to form the sun. The giant cloud's collapse was triggered when nearby stars exploded.
- Low levels of oxygen made Earth a suffocating place.
- Early life-forms appeared.

THE PALEOZOIC ERA

542 million to 251 million years ago

- The first insects and other animals appeared on land.
- 450 million years ago (m.y.a.), the ancestors of sharks began to swim in the oceans.
- 430 m.y.a., plants began to take root on land.
- More than 360 m.y.a., amphibians emerged from the water.
- Slowly the major landmasses began to come together, creating Pangaea, a single supercontinent.
- By 300 m.y.a., reptiles had begun to dominate the land.

What Killed the Dinosaurs?

WAS IT AN ASTEROID, A VOLCANO, OR BOTH? Scientists seeking to explain the disappearance of dinosaurs 65 million years ago believe that a huge impact, such as from an asteroid or comet, a massive bout of volcanic activity, or the combination of the two events might have choked the sky with debris that starved Earth of the sun's energy. The resulting greenhouse gases may have caused the temperature to soar, causing half of the world's species—including the dinosaurs—to die in a mass extinction.

DINO TIMES

THE MESOZOIC ERA

251 million to 65 million years ago

The Mesozoic era, or the age of the reptiles, consisted of three consecutive time periods (shown below). This is when the first dinosaurs began to appear. They would reign supreme for more than 150 million years.

TRIASSIC PERIOD

251 million to 199 million years ago

- Appearance of the first mammals. They were rodent-size.
- The first dinosaur appeared.
- Ferns were the dominant plants on land.
- The giant supercontinent of Pangaea began breaking up toward the end of the Triassic.

JURASSIC PERIOD

199 million to 145 million years ago

- Giant dinosaurs dominated the land.
- Pangaea continued its breakup, and oceans formed in the spaces between the drifting landmasses, allowing sea life, including sharks and marine crocodiles, to thrive.
- Conifer trees spread across the land.

CRETACEOUS PERIOD

145 million to 65 million years ago

- The modern continents developed.
- The largest dinosaurs developed.
- Flowering plants spread across the landscape.
- Mammals flourished, and giant pterosaurs ruled the skies over the small birds.
- Temperatures grew more extreme. Dinosaurs lived in deserts, swamps, and forests from the Antarctic to the Arctic.

THE CENOZOIC ERA—TERTIARY PERIOD

65 million to 2.6 million years ago

- Following the dinosaur extinction, mammals rose as the dominant species.
- Birds continued to flourish.
- Volcanic activity was widespread.
- Temperatures began to cool, eventually ending in an ice age.
- The period ended with land bridges forming, which allowed plants and animals to spread to new areas.

DINO Classification

Classifying dinosaurs and all other living things can be a complicated matter, so scientists have devised a system to help with the process. Dinosaurs are put into groups based on a very large range of characteristics.

Scientists put dinosaurs into two major groups: the bird-hipped ornithischians and the reptile-hipped saurischians.

Ornithischian

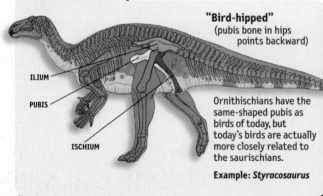

ILIUM

PUBIS

ISCHIUM

"Bird-hipped"
(pubis bone in hips points backward)

Ornithischians have the same-shaped pubis as birds of today, but today's birds are actually more closely related to the saurischians.

Example: *Styracosaurus*

Saurischian

ILIUM

PUBIS

ISCHIUM

"Reptile-hipped"
(pubis bone in hips points forward)

Saurischians are further divided into two groups: the meat-eating Theropoda and the plant-eating Sauropodomorpha.

**Example:
*Tyrannosaurus rex***

Within these two main divisions, dinosaurs are then separated into orders and then families, such as Stegosauria. Like other members of the Stegosauria, *Stegosaurus* had spines and plates along the back, neck, and tail.

SOME DINOSAURS HAD 1,000 TEETH.

ALL DINOSAURS WALKED ON THEIR TOES.

LIKE BABY HUMANS, *PSITTACOSAURUS* CRAWLED BEFORE IT WALKED.

MOST DINOSAURS COULD SWIM.

4 NEWLY DISCOVERED DINOS

Humans have been searching for—and discovering—dinosaur remains for hundreds of years. In that time, at least 1,000 species of dinos have been found all over the world, and thousands more may still be out there waiting to be unearthed. Recent discoveries include the dog-size, 230-million-year-old *Eodromaeus*, found in Argentina and believed to be one of the world's earliest predators. For more exciting dino discoveries, read on.

4 *Xenoceratops foremostensis*
(Ornithischian)
Alien horn-faced
Length: 20 feet (6 m)
Time Range: Late Cretaceous
Where: Alberta, Canada

1 *Nasutoceratops titusi*
(Ornithischian)
Big nose horned face
Length: 15 feet (5 m)
Time Range: Late Cretaceous
Where: Utah, U.S.A.

3 *Nyasasaurus parringtoni*
(Saurischian)
Lake Nyasa lizard
Length: 6.5–10 feet (2–3 m)
Time Range: Early Triassic
Where: Tanzania, Africa

2 *Pegomastax africanus*
(Ornithischian)
Thick jaw from Africa
Length: Less than 2 feet (0.6 m)
Time Range: Early Jurassic
Where: South Africa

OLDEST DINO EVER?

Just when you thought dinos couldn't get any older, the oldest dinosaur (*Nyasasaurus parringtoni*) has been found in Africa. The fossils push back the dawn of the dinosaurs to around 240 million years ago—about 10 to 15 million years earlier than previously thought. But there's not enough information yet to say whether the creature was a true dinosaur or whether it was the dinosaur's closest cousin.

Dynamite DINO AWARDS

Spiky body armor. Razor-sharp teeth. Unimaginable strength. No doubt, all dinos are cool. But whether they were the biggest, the fiercest, or the biggest-brained of the bunch, some stand out more than others. Here are seven of the most amazing dinos ever discovered.

Supersize Appetite

Big Brain

Cool Camo

Scientists think that **Tyrannosaurus rex** could gulp down 500 pounds (227 kg) of meat at a time—that's like eating 2,000 hamburger patties in one bite!

Troodon, a meat-eater the size of a man, had a brain as big as an avocado pit—relatively large for a dinosaur of its small stature. Because of its big brain, scientists think **Troodon** may have been the smartest dino and as intelligent as modern birds.

The birdlike **Sinornithosaurus** had feathers similar to those of modern birds. It may have also had reddish brown, yellow, and black coloring that kept this turkey-size raptor camouflaged as it hunted in the forest.

Heavy-weight

The heaviest of all dinosaurs, *Argentinosaurus* is believed to have weighed 220,000 pounds (99,790 kg)—more than 15 elephants.

Built for Speed

Ornithomimids, a group of dinosaurs that resembled ostriches, would have given the world's fastest man a run for his money. Some of these long-limbed, toothless meat-eaters are thought to have clocked speeds of 50 miles an hour (80 km/h).

Pint-Size Predator

Microraptor zhaoianus, the smallest meat-eating dinosaur, measured just 16 inches (40 cm) tall. With long toe tips for grasping branches, it's thought to be closely related to today's birds.

Super Spines

Known as the "spine lizard," *Spinosaurus* had huge spines sticking out of its back, some taller than a fourth grader! Weighing up to 22 tons (20,000 kg), it may have been the biggest meat-eating dinosaur.

DINOSAUR MYTHS

BUSTED!

CHECK OUT THESE PREHISTORIC PUZZLES.

Some ideas about dinosaurs are just plain wrong, but they still can be hard to get rid of. (Have you heard the one about *Stegosaurus* having a brain in its rump? It didn't.) Here's another myth about *Stegosaurus*, along with more news about other dinos you may know.

THE MYTH *STEGOSAURUS'* BRAIN WAS ONLY THE SIZE OF A WALNUT.

WHERE IT PROBABLY CAME FROM

In 1877, a paleontologist named O.C. Marsh studied the first *Stegosaurus* found. He measured plaster casts of the inside of the tiny braincase and announced it had "the smallest brain of any known land vertebrate." Newspapers began trumpeting the tiny brain. Publishers found they could sell books if they included the not-very-smart *Stegosaurus*, saying it had "a brain no larger than a walnut."

WHAT WE KNOW NOW

More than a century later, Ashley Morhardt of Ohio University's WitmerLab wondered if the walnut story was true. Using computers, she produced a digital cast of *Stegosaurus'* brain cavity. She modeled the brain's odd shapes in a software program and figured out each shape's volume. Then she added them up. The brain was really the size of *two* walnuts! "*Stegosaurus* was still probably pretty dumb, though," Morhardt says.

THE MYTH

DINOSAURS FOUND IN THE "DEATH POSE" DIED IN AGONY.

WHERE IT PROBABLY CAME FROM

Head pulled back upside down over the hips, tail stretched forward. The death pose is common among theropods, which were two-legged, mostly meat-eating dinosaurs. Paleontologists long wondered why. One thought the dinos had died while sleeping. Others believed that they'd been poisoned, suffocated, or died in agony. Or that dead dinos might have become fossilized pretzels as they dried out.

WHAT WE KNOW NOW

What if the dead dinosaurs ended up in a lake or a stream? wondered Alicia Cutler and Brooks Britt of Brigham Young University. To test this idea, they placed dead chickens in buckets of water. The heads swung back almost instantly! In water, the head and neck float. That allows ligaments between the backbones to shorten, pulling the neck into a tight arch. A chicken placed on dry sand didn't take the death pose, even months after drying out.

THE MYTH

ONLY LITTLE DINOSAURS HAD FEATHERS.

WHERE IT PROBABLY CAME FROM

Paleontologists have been finding extremely well-preserved skeletons of small, nonflying feathered dinosaurs in China's Liaoning Province. Scientists think the feathers might have kept them warm or helped attract mates. It seemed only little dinosaurs had feathers. The biggest was *Beipiaosaurus*, which was seven feet (2.1 m) long. Other feathered dinos were pip-squeaks, like *Sinosauropteryx*. But a feathered *Tyrannosaurus rex*? No way!

WHAT WE KNOW NOW

Recently, Chinese and Canadian scientists reported a huge new dinosaur with long feathers covering most of its body. *Yutyrannus* was 30 feet (9.2 m) long and 40 times heavier than *Beipiaosaurus*. And it was a tyrannosaur, three-quarters the length of its ginormous later relative, *T. rex*. So maybe the terrifying Tyrant King was really soft and fluffy.

STUMP YOUR PARENTS

AMAZING ANIMALS QUIZ

Do your parents know all about animals? Find out by testing their smarts on all sorts of species. (All questions are based on information in this chapter.)

ANSWERS BELOW

1 **True or false?** Glass frogs have black bones.

2 **Which dino is believed to have been the smartest?**
a. *T. rex*
b. *Troodon*
c. *Apatosaurus*
d. Barney

3 **Where do a majority of Amur tigers in the wild live?**
a. Russia
b. China
c. Hawaii
d. Antarctica

4 **A snake can smell with its _____.**
a. tongue
b. nose
c. teeth
d. feet

5 **What is an extended lion family called?**
a. a team
b. a clan
c. a pride
d. a litter

Not **STUMPED** yet?
Check out the *National Geographic Kids Quiz Whiz* collection for more crazy **ANIMAL** questions!

ANSWERS: 1. False. They have green bones to help them blend in with leaves; 2. b; 3. a; 4. a; 5. c

HOMEWORK HELP

Wildly Good Animal Reports

beluga whale

Your teacher wants a written report on the beluga whale. Not to worry. Use these organizational tools so you can stay afloat while writing a report.

STEPS TO SUCCESS: Your report will follow the format of a descriptive or expository essay (see p. 117 for "How to Write a Perfect Essay") and should consist of a main idea, followed by supporting details and a conclusion. Use this basic structure for each paragraph as well as the whole report, and you'll be on the right track.

1. Introduction
State your **main idea**.
The beluga whale is a common and important species of whale.

2. Body
Provide **supporting points** for your main idea.
The beluga whale is one of the smallest whale species.
It is also known as the "white whale" because of its distinctive coloring.
These whales are common in the Arctic Ocean's coastal waters.

Then **expand** on those points with further description, explanation, or discussion.
The beluga whale is one of the smallest whale species.
Belugas range in size from 13 to 20 feet (4 to 6.1 m) in length.
It is also known as the "white whale" because of its distinctive coloring.
Belugas are born gray or brown. They fade to white at around five years old.
These whales are common in the Arctic Ocean's coastal waters.
Some Arctic belugas migrate south in large herds when sea ice freezes over.

3. Conclusion
Wrap it up with a **summary** of your whole paper.
Because of its unique coloring and unusual features, belugas are among the most familiar and easily distinguishable of all the whales.

KEY INFORMATION

Here are some things you should consider including in your report:

> What does your animal look like?
> To what other species is it related?
> How does it move?
> Where does it live?
> What does it eat?
> What are its predators?
> How long does it live?
> Is it endangered?
> Why do you find it interesting?

SEPARATE FACT FROM FICTION: Your animal may have been featured in a movie or in myths and legends. Compare and contrast how the animal has been portrayed with how it behaves in reality. For example, penguins can't dance the way they do in *Happy Feet*.

PROOFREAD AND REVISE: As with any great essay, when you're finished, check for misspellings, grammatical mistakes, and punctuation errors. It often helps to have someone else proofread your work, too, as he or she may catch things you have missed. Also, look for ways to make your sentences and paragraphs even better. Add more descriptive language, choosing just the right verbs, adverbs, and adjectives to make your writing come alive.

BE CREATIVE: Use visual aids to make your report come to life. Include an animal photo file with interesting images found in magazines or printed from websites. Or draw your own! You can also build a miniature animal habitat diorama. Use creativity to help communicate your passion for the subject.

THE FINAL RESULT: Put it all together in one final, polished draft. Make it neat and clean, and remember to cite your references.

Going Green

An old elevated train line in New York City, New York, U.S.A., has been transformed into a park called the High Line.

1 Putting on a
WARM SWEATER
instead of
TURNING UP THE HEAT
can keep 1,000 pounds (454 kg) of carbon dioxide out of the atmosphere every year.

2 In the U.S. and Great Britain, a **FRUIT OR VEGETABLE TRAVELS** an average of 1,200 miles (1,931 km) from farm to table!

3 EARTH-FRIENDLY
BAMBOO
grows quickly and can be used to make everything from **FLOORS AND CLOTHES TO RADIOS AND EVEN AN IPAD STYLUS (PEN)**.

15 COOL THINGS ABOUT

4 **REDUCE** the number of **VAMPIRE APPLIANCES** in your home. A TV and its remote use more energy while they are off during the day than they do when you watch TV for four hours.

5

EARTH HOUR occurs every March, when people turn off their lights for an hour to raise awareness about climate change. In 2013, people in 153 countries and territories took part.

6 A DESIGNER HAS CREATED **"LIVING" SHOES** —ONCE YOU HAVE WORN THEM OUT YOU CAN PLANT THEM AND THEY WILL SPROUT FLOWERS.

7 WORLDWIDE, PEOPLE RECYCLE ABOUT ONE-THIRD OF ALL ALUMINUM PRODUCTS. THAT'S **19.8** **MILLION TONS** (18 MILLION MT).

8 A year's worth of the **AVERAGE AMERICAN KID'S LAUNDRY** would weigh 500 pounds (227 kg). That's heavier than a gorilla!

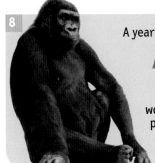

9 A designer has created a cell phone with a casing **MADE OUT OF GRASS.** After the life of the phone is over, it decomposes and the keys and screen **CAN BE RECYCLED.**

10 # GO PORTABLE
TO REDUCE YOUR CARBON FOOTPRINT.
Laptop computers use **50 TO 90 PERCENT LESS ENERGY** than desktop computers.

11 Carbon dioxide, the gas that makes your soda fizzy, is **ALSO LINKED TO CLIMATE CHANGE.**

GOING GREEN

12 **INSTEAD OF GAS-GUZZLING LAWN MOWERS, THE INTERNET COMPANY GOOGLE USES GOATS TO** ## TRIM ITS LAWN.

13

14 ELECTRIC CARS COST **TEN CENTS LESS PER MILE** (1.6 km) to drive than a car that runs on gas. A trip between San Francisco and Los Angeles, California, U.S.A., costs $34 less in an **ELECTRIC CAR.**

15 ## ONE MILLION PLASTIC BAGS **ARE USED EVERY MINUTE.**

AS MUCH AS # 90% of the energy used by standard lightbulbs escapes as heat and is not converted into **USABLE LIGHT.**

Habitat

WHERE HAVE THE ANIMALS GONE?

All around the world, countless animals are being driven out of their habitats as a result of deforestation, or trees being cut down for lumber or logs or to clear land. Here, you can check out two endangered animals and their fight for survival.

SPIDER MONKEY WITH BABY

TWO ADULT SPIDER MONKEYS

BROWN SPIDER MONKEY

A farmer living in South America and deep in one of Colombia's rain forests has spotted a rare species of spider monkey thought to be extinct in the region.

Spider monkeys spend most of their lives high in tree branches. They travel in social groups called troops. A spider monkey swings from branch to branch as easily as you walk from your living room to the kitchen. Its tail has a grip strong enough to support the animal's entire weight, leaving the other four long limbs free to pick tasty nuts, fruits, and leaves.

Hunting and habitat loss have threatened all species of spider monkeys. Some are critically endangered, although those living in national parks are safe from hunters and habitat loss.

Suddenly, you hear whoops and wails. You spot a few dark shapes swinging from the highest branches—brown spider monkeys! "This is the only population found within a national protected area," says Nestor Roncancio, a Wildlife Conservation Society researcher. "It's one of the largest fragments of forest left with good habitat for the species."

Destruction

IBERIAN LYNX

CAPTIVE-BRED LYNX RECEIVES BOTTLE FEEDING

"You need patience, luck, and a guide who knows where to look to see an Iberian lynx in the wild," says Miguel Rodrigues, your local lynx expert. Today you have all three. "There, behind that bush," he says. You grab the binoculars, focus, and spot the hornlike tufts of black fur poking above the leaves. You've caught a glimpse of the world's most endangered cat!

Unfortunately, these cats have nearly vanished from Earth. With less than 300 Iberian lynx left in the wild, they live in just a few pockets of protected forests in Spain and possibly Portugal. Their habitat has been chopped down to make way for farms, tree plantations, cities, dams, and highways.

Scientists took emergency action. They began breeding captive lynx and releasing them in protected areas. The captive-bred lynx have since raised cubs.

You wonder if the lynx you've spotted behind the bush is one of these success stories. With so few of these cats left in the world, you feel lucky to have seen one. "The lynx is a relatively small feline that doesn't need much space," says conservationist Dan Ward. So you hope that humans and these wild cats can be good neighbors.

GLOBAL WARMING

Polar bear
on a piece of
melting iceberg

Climate Change, Explained

Fact: The world is getting warmer. The summer of 2013 is tied with 2009 as the world's fifth-warmest summer since records began in 1880. Summer 2013 temperatures were 1.12°F (.62°C) higher than the average summer temperature in the 20th century. This is the direct effect of climate change, which refers not only to the increase in the Earth's average temperature (known as global warming), but also to the long-term effects on winds, rain, and ocean currents. Global warming is the reason glaciers and polar ice sheets are melting—resulting in rising sea levels and shrinking habitats. This makes survival for some animals a big challenge. Warming also means more flooding along the coasts and drought for inland areas.

Why are temperatures climbing?

Some of the recent climate changes can be tied to natural causes—such as changes in the sun's intensity, the unusually warm ocean currents of El Niño, and volcanic activity—but human activities are a major factor as well.

Everyday activities that require burning fossil fuels, such as driving gasoline-powered cars, contribute to global warming. These activities produce greenhouse gases, which enter the atmosphere and trap heat. At the current rate, Earth's global average temperature is projected to rise from 2 to 11.5°F (1 to 6.4°C) by the year 2100, and it will get even warmer after that. And as the climate continues to warm, it will unfortunately continue to affect the environment and our society in many ways.

Greenland's Giant Canyon

Think the Grand Canyon in Arizona, U.S.A., is huge? Well, imagine a canyon nearly twice as long! That's just what sits under Greenland's Ice Sheet, a thick layer of frozen water that covers an area about a quarter of the size of the continental United States.

The recently discovered canyon, which runs as deep as a half a mile (800 m) and as long as 466 miles (750 km), was likely part of a massive river system before an ice sheet covered it millions of years ago. Scientists think that water once flowed in the canyon from the interior of Greenland coast and may one day play a major role in transporting meltwater below the ice into the Arctic Ocean.

Rising sea levels

Global warming is taking a toll on Greenland. In 2009, record-high temperatures caused changes in the ice sheet, like the 150-foot (46-m)-deep Birthday Canyon, carved by meltwater. And although the chances of Greenland's entire ice sheet melting are remote, there is enough frozen fresh water there to raise sea levels by about 20 feet (6 m), which would impact coastlines around the world. It's very important for scientists to have a better understanding of what lies beneath the ice so they can predict how water will flow if—or when—things start to melt.

A massive canyon rests below Greenland's ice sheet.

Scientists are concerned that Greenland's ice sheet has begun to melt in summer. Birthday Canyon, shown here, was carved by meltwater.

Pollution
Cleaning Up Our Act

So what's the big deal about a little dirt on the planet? Pollution can affect animals, plants, and people. In fact, some studies show that more people die every year from diseases linked to air pollution than from car accidents. And right now nearly one billion of the world's people don't have access to clean drinking water.

A LITTLE POLLUTION = BIG PROBLEMS

You can probably clean your room in a couple of hours. (At least we hope you can!) But you can't shove air and water pollution under your bed or cram them into the closet. Once released into the environment, pollution—whether it's oil leaking from a boat or chemicals spewing from a factory's smokestack—can have a lasting environmental impact.

KEEP IT CLEAN

It's easy to blame things like big factories for pollution problems. But some of the mess comes from everyday activities. Exhaust fumes from cars and garbage in landfills can seriously trash the Earth's health. We all need to pitch in and do some house-cleaning. It may mean bicycling more and riding in cars less. Or not dumping water-polluting oil or household cleaners down the drain. Look at it this way: Just as with your room, it's always better not to let Earth get messed up in the first place.

SCAN THIS PAGE!
GET BONUS MOBILE CONTENT! Download the free NG Kids scanner app. Directions on inside front cover.

Bottled Up!

Sure, water is good for you. But before you sip, think about how often you use plastic water bottles—and what you're doing with them when you're done. For every six water bottles we use, only one will wind up in a recycling bin. The rest end up in landfills or as litter on land or in rivers, lakes, and oceans, taking many hundreds of years to disintegrate. So, what can you do? Fill up from the tap and drink out of a refillable steel container. And if you do use a plastic bottle, make sure to recycle it.

Declining Biodiversity
Saving All Creatures Great and Small

Earth is home to a huge mix of plants and animals—perhaps 100 million species—and scientists have officially identified and named only about 1.9 million so far! Scientists call this healthy mix biodiversity.

THE BALANCING ACT

The bad news is that half of the planet's plant and animal species may be on the path to extinction, mainly because of human activity. People cut down trees, build roads and houses, pollute rivers, overfish, and overhunt. The good news is that many people care. Scientists and volunteers race against the clock every day, working to save wildlife before time runs out. By building birdhouses, planting trees, and following the rules for hunting and fishing, you can be a positive force for preserving biodiversity, too. Every time you do something to help a species survive, you help our planet to thrive.

WILDLIFE BIODIVERSITY

Insects, Centipedes, and Millipedes

Other Animals

Mammals

Florida manatee

Habitats Threatened
Living on the Edge

Even though tropical rain forests cover only about 7 percent of the planet's total land surface, they are home to half of all known species of plants and animals. Because people cut down so many trees for lumber and firewood and clear so much land for farms, hundreds of thousands of acres of rain forest disappear every year.

SHARING THE LAND

Wetlands are also important feeding and breeding grounds. People have drained many wetlands, turning them into farm fields or sites for industries. More than half the world's wetlands have disappeared within the past century, squeezing wildlife out. Balancing the needs of humans and animals is the key to lessening habitat destruction.

Toucan

91

Bet you didn't **know**

6 FUN FACTS about **GOING GREEN**

1 You can **create electricity** out of both **cow manure** and **elephant dung.**

2 Some **cars** can run on **used french-fry oil.**

3 A **newly invented lightbulb** has to be **changed only once** every 20 years!

4 A **cyclist** invented a **bike helmet** made from **recycled newspapers.**

5 It can take up to **200 years** for an **aluminum** can to **decompose.**

6 A **wind farm** in Texas, U.S.A., with more than **600 turbines** provides power to **265,000 homes.**

GREEN inventions

BACK VIEW ▶

ELECTRIC TRICYCLE

Imagine if your bicycle had all the features of a car, right down to a windshield wiper, a trunk for stashing your stuff, and even a motor. The Emcycle encloses the rider in a rain-shielding shell complete with locking doors and three wheels so it won't topple over at stop signs. As with a bicycle, you pedal the Emcycle and steer with handlebars. But pedaling also charges an electric motor that boosts your speed to 40 miles an hour (64 km/h). "That makes you feel like Superman—it amplifies your pedal power two to three times," inventor Michael Scholey says. A dashboard on the handlebars features battery and speed displays, plus controls for the turn signals, heater, and headlights. You can even add a radio and cup holder. Talk about riding in style.

MUSICAL SHOWER

You love singing in the shower, but your family doesn't seem to appreciate your, um, talent. Here's a way to quiet the unappreciative booing—and help protect the planet. The H2O Shower Powered Radio, which runs on energy created by the flow of water, drowns out your shower voice. To set it up, attach the radio to the base of the showerhead. When you turn on the shower, water runs through the radio, rotates a tiny turbine (similar to a waterwheel), and creates energy to power the radio. The device can even store enough juice to keep playing for up to an hour, post-shower. Rock on.

WET RADIO ▼

H₂O Power

POWER ON/OFF   SEEK+   SEEK−   VOL+   VOL−

8 FUN WAYS to Get Outside

Staying inside all day? Snooze! It's time to step outside and explore the world around you. Here's a roundup of eight activities that will get you outdoors and keep you energized.

1 TAKE A HIKE!

Immerse yourself in the great outdoors by hiking. Organize your family and friends for a walk in your local park, or hit some mountain trails for a challenging and scenic route. Don't forget to pack snacks and water to stay fueled while you walk.

2 PICK IT UP

Grab some gloves and a trash bag, then hit your local park creek to pick up trash. You'll get some fresh air and exercise—and help the environment, too.

3 DESIGN YOUR OWN HEADLAMP

Color-coordinate your camping gear by going online and designing your own headlamp. Princeton Tec Spectrum lets you choose your own look for everything from the headlamp's body to the battery door.

Check out the *Get Outside Guide* for more ideas!

4 STARGAZING!

On a clear night you can really see, well, forever! Take an evening stroll in your neighborhood to explore the starry skies. Enhance your view with a smartphone app offering a 3-D map of the stars, constellations, and galaxies.

5 THE AMAZING RACE

Get into the competitive spirit by organizing an obstacle race with your neighborhood pals. Set up a series of silly—but safe—stunts (Think: jumping rope, crossing the monkey bars, and hula-hooping), then see who can get through it the fastest. Ready? Go!

6 LIGHT UP THE SOCCER FIELD

Have an electrifying game of soccer—literally! By kicking the SOCCKET ball you can create enough energy to light an LED lamp for several hours.

7 INDOOR PICNIC

Bring the outdoors inside with the PicNYC Table. Its aluminum tabletop frame forms a deep area for growing a lush lawn where you can picnic. You can even sprout an herb garden instead of grass!

Rainy Day Fun

8 GET GROWING

You don't need a huge patch of land to grow a garden. Select a small square of backyard or even a flowerpot on your balcony, plant some seeds, water them daily, then watch your blooms blossom!

World Energy & Minerals

Almost everything people do—from cooking to powering the International Space Station—requires energy. But energy comes in different forms. Traditional energy sources, still used by many people in the developing world, include burning dried animal dung and wood. Industrialized countries and urban centers around the world rely on coal, oil, and natural gas—called fossil fuels because they formed from decayed plant and animal material accumulated from long ago. Fossil fuel deposits, either in the ground or under the ocean floor, are unevenly distributed on Earth, and only some countries can afford to buy them. Fossil fuels are also not renewable, meaning they will run out one day. And unless we find other ways to create energy, we'll be stuck. Without energy we won't be able to drive cars, use lights, or send emails to friends.

TAKING A TOLL

Environmentally speaking, burning fossil fuels isn't necessarily the best choice, either: Carbon dioxide from the burning of fossil fuels, as well as other emissions, are contributing to global warming. Concerned scientists are looking at new ways to harness renewable, alternative sources of energy, such as water, wind, and sun.

DIGGING FOR FOSSIL FUELS

This illustration shows some of the different kinds of onshore and offshore drilling equipment. The type of drilling equipment used depends on whether the oil or natural gas is in the ground or under the ocean.

The mining of coal made the industrial revolution possible, and coal still provides a major energy source. Work that people once did using picks and shovels is now done with mechanized equipment. This diagram shows some kinds of coal mines currently in use.

CHINA'S POLLUTION PROBLEM

On any given day, a dense cloud of smog hovers over Beijing and other parts of China, an obvious sign of the country's environmental crisis. Now, the Chinese government is trying to curb the pollution by taking steps to limit the use of coal, including a ban on the construction of coal-fired power plants in certain regions. Experts hope this move will encourage the use of natural gas and nuclear power and eventually improve the country's air quality. Whether China will ever be smog free is unknown, but this is a positive step toward solving the country's pollution problem, one plant at a time.

Alternative Power

WIND
Strong winds blowing through the mountains in California (U.S.A.) spin windmill blades on an energy farm, powering giant turbines that generate electricity for the state.

HYDROELECTRIC
Hydroelectric plants, such as this one at Santiago del Estero in Argentina, use dams to harness running water to generate clean, renewable energy.

GEOTHERMAL
Geothermal power, from ground-water heated by molten rock, provides energy for this power plant in Iceland. Swimmers enjoy the warm waters of a lake created by the power plant.

SOLAR
Solar panels on Samso Island in Denmark capture and store energy from the sun, an environmentally friendly alternative to fossil fuels.

BIODIESEL
This Aero L-29 Delfin, nicknamed BioJet 1, was the first jet aircraft powered by 100 percent biodiesel fuel. Biodiesel—which can be made from vegetable oil, animal fats, or french-fry grease—is cleaner and emits fewer pollutants than fossil fuels do into the air.

STUMP YOUR PARENTS

GOING GREEN QUIZ

How much do your parents know about protecting the planet? Find out with this quiz.

ANSWERS BELOW

① About how many Iberian lynx are left in the wild?
- a. 3
- b. 30
- c. 300
- d. 300,000

② True or false? You can create electricity out of both cow manure and elephant dung.

③ Where have scientists recently discovered a giant canyon?
- a. under Greenland's ice sheet
- b. on the moon
- c. in the Atlantic Ocean
- d. in Antarctica

④ How can you promote biodiversity?
- a. follow hunting and fishing rules
- b. build a birdhouse
- c. plant a tree
- d. all of the above

⑤ What's the biggest threat to the future of brown spider monkeys living in South America?
- a. drought
- b. cold temperatures
- c. lack of bananas
- d. hunting and habitat loss

Not **STUMPED** yet?
Check out the *National Geographic Kids Quiz Whiz* collection for more crazy **ENVIRONMENT** questions!

ANSWERS:
1. c; 2. True; 3. a; 4. d; 5. d

HOMEWORK HELP

Write a Letter That Gets Results

Knowing how to write a good letter is a useful skill. It will come in handy anytime you want to persuade someone to understand your point of view. Whether you're emailing your congressperson or writing a letter for a school project or to your grandma, a great letter will help you get your message across. Most important, a well-written letter leaves a good impression.

Check out the example below for the elements of a good letter.

Your address

Date

Salutation
Always use "Dear" followed by the person's name; use Mr., Mrs., Ms., or Dr. as appropriate.

Introductory paragraph
Give the reason you're writing the letter.

Body
The longest part of the letter, which provides evidence that supports your position. Be persuasive!

Closing paragraph
Sum up your argument.

Complimentary closing
Sign off with "Sincerely" or "Thank you."

Your signature

Abby Jones
1204 Green Street
Los Angeles, CA 90045

March 31, 2015

Dear Mr. School Superintendent,

I am writing to you about how much excess energy our school uses and to offer a solution.

Every day, we leave the computers on in the classroom, the TVs are plugged in all the time, and the lights are on all day. All of this adds up to a lot of wasted energy, which is not only harmful for the Earth, as it increases the amount of harmful greenhouse gas emissions into the environment, but is also costly to the school. In fact, I read that schools spend more on energy bills than on computers and textbooks combined!

I am suggesting that we start an Energy Patrol to monitor the use of lighting, air-conditioning, heating, and other energy systems within our school. My idea is to have a group of students dedicated to figuring out ways we can cut back on our energy use in the school. We can do room checks, provide reminders to students and teachers to turn off lights and computers, replace old lightbulbs with energy-efficient products, and even reward the classrooms that do the most to save energy.

Above all, I think our school could help the environment tremendously by cutting back on how much energy we use. Let's see an Energy Patrol at our school soon. Thank you.

Sincerely,

Abby Jones

Abby Jones

COMPLIMENTARY CLOSINGS

Sincerely, Sincerely yours, Thank you, Regards, Best wishes, Respectfully,

With the Matterhorn looming in the background, an Alpine climber scales the cold, icy north face of Obergabelhorn above Zermatt, Switzerland.

Awesome Adventure

DARE to EXPLORE

KAKANI KATIJA
Biological Oceanographer

WANT TO BE A BIOLOGICAL OCEANOGRAPHER?
STUDY: Mathematics, physics, and marine biology
WATCH: *NOVA* and *Nature* on PBS
READ: *Twenty Thousand Leagues Under the Sea* by Jules Verne

"Never stop learning. Learn as much as you can and never close yourself off to any opportunity."

SEA NETTLE JELLYFISH

"My team and I plunged into the water. We couldn't turn on any bright lights until we reached our destination nearly a hundred feet (30 m) down, or the jellies would be scared off. So we dived through the sea in darkness. Finally we made it to our site. I switched on an underwater lamp and panned it around me. Jellyfish were everywhere! It was incredible.

"My job is to watch how marine animals move through the water—many glide along with amazing efficiency. Then I think about how to design underwater vehicles that move in the same way. This may help us invent submarines that whisk you to the deepest parts of the ocean. Our oceans are so important and we've explored only a sliver of them. There's much more to see."

A GROUP OF JELLYFISH IS CALLED A SMACK.

BRADY BARR
Herpetologist

WANT TO BE A HERPETOLOGIST?
STUDY: Biology, anatomy, and ecology
WATCH: *Dangerous Encounters With Brady Barr* on Nat Geo WILD
READ: *Crocodile Encounters!* by Brady Barr

"Learn everything you can about the animals you're interested in, have a passion, and stay true to your hopes and dreams."

A herpetologist is a scientist who studies reptiles and amphibians.

"If you want to catch a one-ton (907-kg) crocodile, sometimes you just have to jump on its back and ride it out. I don't always do things the normal way—I've caught a croc with a ball of string, tracked great white sharks with remote-controlled helicopters, and even dressed up as a hippo, a crocodile, and a baboon to get closer to animals.

"Once I climbed down a croc burrow in Costa Rica thinking the sides of the burrow were just mud walls. But then I realized they weren't walls at all. They were actually crocs covered in mud, and I realized this when they suddenly opened their eyes!

"I'm scared every single day, but being afraid keeps me safe. You make one mistake and you could lose a part of your body. But don't ever let anyone tell you that you can't do something."

REAL-LIFE CROC

A CROCODILE CAN'T STICK OUT ITS TONGUE.

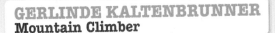

GERLINDE KALTENBRUNNER
Mountain Climber

WANT TO BE A MOUNTAIN CLIMBER?
STUDY: Geography, geology, and meteorology
WATCH: Nat Geo Adventure's *First Ascent*
READ: *Climbing Everest: Tales of Triumph and Tragedy on the World's Highest Mountain* by Audrey Salkeld

"Your passion doesn't have to be mountaineering—it could be art or playing an instrument—but it's important to always feel your passion from the inside."

KALTENBRUNNER ON K2

NATIONAL GEOGRAPHIC KIDS SCANNER

SCAN THIS PAGE!
GET BONUS MOBILE CONTENT! Download the free NG Kids scanner app. Directions on inside front cover.

"Early one morning while climbing Dhaulagiri I, a mountain in Nepal, my tent was swept down by an avalanche when I was still inside it. I tumbled about 130 feet (40 m) downhill. I couldn't tell what was happening and when it stopped, I was buried in the snow and wasn't even able to tell if I was up or down. Thankfully, after an hour of digging and climbing, I was able to reach the surface and climb out of the snow.

"There are many challenges in mountain climbing. But climbing is not all about the danger. When I reach the top of a mountain, it's always a very calm, quiet moment for me, when I can say 'thank you' to the universe for allowing me to have the experience."

MOUNT EVEREST WAS ONCE KNOWN AS "PEAK 15."

BARRINGTON IRVING
Pilot

WANT TO BE A PILOT?

STUDY: Algebra, chemistry, biology, and geography

WATCH: *Flight Simulator* or *X-Plane*

READ: *Popular Science* and *Popular Mechanics* to keep up with technology

THE PILOT FUELS HIS AIRPLANE.

IRVING IN THE COCKPIT

"You have to have confidence. **If you don't believe, no one else will.** Confidence will always keep you going."

"❝I was flying from Saudi Arabia to Egypt when a wall of sand suddenly rose up in front of the plane. As I flew into the sandstorm, grains began seeping into the cockpit through vents. All I could do was hope that none of it got into the engine turbochargers, which would have been disastrous. Luckily I made it through the storm unharmed.

"My trip around the world took 97 days and included 145 hours of flying. Sometimes I flew more than 12 hours in a row before making a stop. And there were times after landing when I had to crawl from the plane on my elbows because I lost my leg strength during the long flight.

"But being a pilot is totally worth it. You have the opportunity to explore the world from amazing heights."

THE FIRST AIRPLANE FLIGHT LASTED 12 SECONDS.

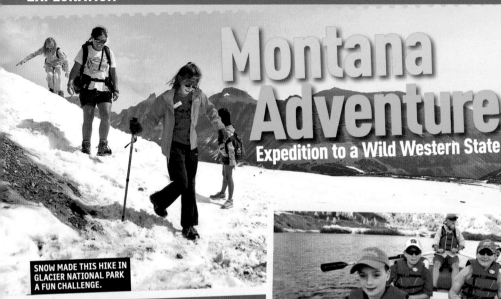

Montana Adventure

Expedition to a Wild Western State

SNOW MADE THIS HIKE IN GLACIER NATIONAL PARK A FUN CHALLENGE.

PADDLING DOWN THE MISSOURI RIVER

Spotting a grizzly bear, uncovering dinosaur fossils, hiking, and floating down the Missouri River are just a few of the wild adventures that 15 young explorers experienced in Montana, U.S.A., after winning the Hands-On Explorer Challenge (HOEC), an essay and photo competition.

While exploring northwestern Montana, the winners walked in the footsteps of Lewis and Clark's historic expedition along the Missouri River, played in snow (yes, in July!), saw mountain goats and bighorn sheep, and dug for dinosaur bones and other prehistoric fossils, all while taking photographs of their adventures. They even watched a huge grizzly bear on the shore of St. Mary Lake. "We were on a boat, so we were able to do it safely," says Ben Zino, 11, of Salisbury, North Carolina. "It was awesome!"

Glacier National Park

MONTANA

UNITED STATES

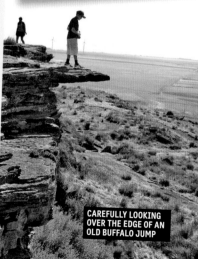

A GRIZZLY BEAR SIGHTING FROM THE SAFETY OF A BOAT

On a visit to an Indian Reservation, team members played traditional Blackfeet games, learned a few words in the Blackfoot language, and peered over a 50-foot (15-m)-cliff that was used long ago as a buffalo jump. "Blackfeet and other Native Americans used to hunt buffalo by herding them off a cliff," says Jackson Jacobs, 9, of Hillsboro, Tennessee. "They used every part of the buffalo they killed for things such as clothes, cooking pots, food, and shelter."

HOEC team members were on the move all day, every day. "We did so many cool things on this expedition that I can't pick a favorite," says Emily Marshall, 10, of Ashburn, Virginia. "I loved it all!"

CAREFULLY LOOKING OVER THE EDGE OF AN OLD BUFFALO JUMP

MYSTERY IN THE SKIES

What happened to Amelia Earhart?

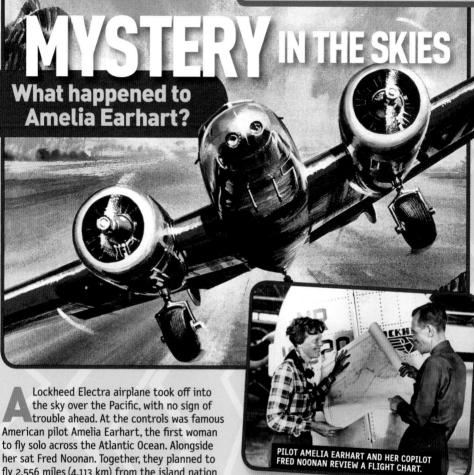

PILOT AMELIA EARHART AND HER COPILOT FRED NOONAN REVIEW A FLIGHT CHART.

A Lockheed Electra airplane took off into the sky over the Pacific, with no sign of trouble ahead. At the controls was famous American pilot Amelia Earhart, the first woman to fly solo across the Atlantic Ocean. Alongside her sat Fred Noonan. Together, they planned to fly 2,556 miles (4,113 km) from the island nation of Papua New Guinea to Howland Island in the South Pacific Ocean, the third-to-last leg in a trip around the world. The date was July 2, 1937. That was the last time anyone ever saw them.

Earhart's disappearance remains a mystery. Now, more than 75 years later, new research is shedding light on what may have happened during that fateful flight.

SPLASH AND SINK

The most widely accepted explanation for what happened to Earhart is that her plane crashed into the ocean. According to a U.S. Coast Guard boat keeping radio communication with the Electra during the flight, Earhart said she was searching for the island but could not find it— and that she was running low on fuel. No under-water wreckage has been found, but searches continue. A recent expedition used a deep-sea sonar system to scan a wide area around which the Electra likely went down, but it did not find any sign of a plane.

CRASH LANDING

Others think the Electra landed on the remote Pacific atoll Nikumaroro and that Earhart and Noonan lived as castaways. Newly discovered evidence found on Nikumaroro—such as fragments of glass made in the U.S. and a cosmetics jar—have caused speculation that Earhart lived there for an unknown amount of time before she died. But despite multiple expeditions to the island, no plane or other conclusive evidence has been found.

LEGACY

Other less likely theories—including one claiming that Earhart acted as a spy during World War II and then changed her identity— are still floating around, offering extra ideas for what happened. As the search for answers continues, one thing remains certain: Amelia Earhart will always be one of the most celebrated aviators in history.

SECRETS OF THE

DARING SCIENTISTS SEARCH FOR

A bizarre world lies under the sparkling Atlantic Ocean off the islands of the Bahamas, a world few have seen. Here, a system of super-deep underwater caves called blue holes contain odd-looking creatures, six-story-high rock formations, and even ancient human remains. Scuba-diving scientists must dodge whirl-pools and squeeze through narrow tunnels to study blue holes—but their risky expedi-tions uncover amazing secrets.

CREATURE FEATURE

FANGED CRUSTACEAN

WEIRD WATER

NEON PINK CAVE WATER!

Dive about 30 feet (9 m) into some blue holes, and the water turns pink. It looks nice—but it's poison-ous. Because of a weak current here, rainwater and salt water mix in a way that traps a layer of toxic gas where pink bacteria thrive. To avoid getting ill, divers do not linger here.

In other blue holes, ocean tides can whip up whirlpools that look like giant bathtub drains. Scientists must circle carefully, or else risk being sucked in.

Farther down, the caves become dark and twisty. Anthropologist and National Geographic explorer Kenny Broad and his team have found many odd species here, including a tiny, transparent crustacean that is venomous (above).

Blue holes also contain fossils of animals— even birds. During the last ice age, these areas were dry and made perfect perches for the fliers. In one watery cave, a 12,000-year-old owl's nest was found surrounded by lizard bones—leftovers from the owl's meals.

BLUE HOLES

CLUES ABOUT UNDERWATER CAVES.

HOW BLUE HOLES FORMED

During past ice ages—the most recent about 18,000 years ago—water levels dropped and new land was exposed. Rain ate away at the land, forming holes that became deep caves. The caves filled with water after sea levels rose again. The deepest known blue hole is about 660 feet (200 m) deep.

BONE-CHILLING DISCOVERY

The most amazing find in the blue holes? Human skeletons. Scientists were able to trace the remains back 1,400 years to the time of the Lucayans—the first people believed to live in the Bahamas. No one is sure how the bones ended up in the submerged caves. But the team thinks the Lucayans might have used these areas as burial sites for their dead. With more investigation, the mystery of the skeletons may soon be solved. But scientists believe that other secrets are waiting to be uncovered in blue holes. "There are hundreds left that no human has seen," Broad says. "It's a whole other world for exploration."

A BLUE HOLE OFF BELIZE

109

1 YOU CAN START A FIRE WITH THE BATTERY OF A CELL PHONE, STEEL WOOL, AND DRY STICKS.

2 Wireless operators aboard the *Titanic* called for help using SOS in 1912.

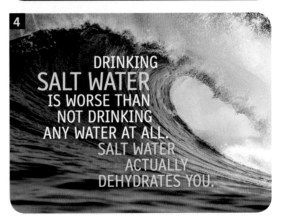
TITANIC
19— —12
LONDON

3 Some people say TWINKIES are the best food for a survival kit because they never seem to spoil, but their shelf life is only 45 days.

4 DRINKING SALT WATER IS WORSE THAN NOT DRINKING ANY WATER AT ALL. SALT WATER ACTUALLY DEHYDRATES YOU.

15 COOL THINGS ABOUT

5 EATING INSECTS has helped people survive in the wilderness. Insects are a good source of protein and fat.

6
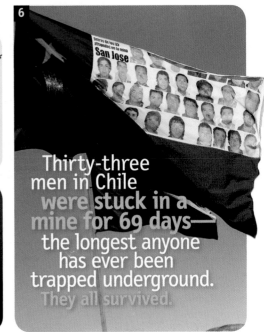
San Jose

Thirty-three men in Chile were stuck in a mine for 69 days— the longest anyone has ever been trapped underground. They all survived.

7

SOS
● ● ●   ▬ ▬ ▬   ● ● ●
THE SIGNAL FOR SOS, WHICH CAN BE USED AS A VISUAL OR AUDIO CALL FOR HELP, IS THREE SHORT, THREE LONG, AND THEN THREE SHORT SIGNALS.

8 YOU LOSE **10** PERCENT OF YOUR BODY HEAT THROUGH YOUR HEAD.

9 The best way to **SURVIVE A TORNADO** if you're outside and nowhere near a shelter is to flatten yourself on the ground like a pancake.

10

A New York, U.S.A., man was stuck in an elevator for 41 hours.

11 PEOPLE HAVE BEEN POISONED BY SNAKE VENOM EVEN AFTER THE SNAKE IS DEAD.

SURVIVAL 6

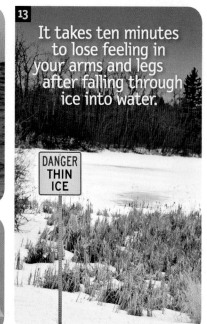

12 PUNCHING OR KICKING A SHARK IN ITS MOST SENSITIVE AREAS—NOSE, EYES, AND GILLS—CAN SEND IT SWIMMING THE OTHER DIRECTION IN THE MIDDLE OF AN ATTACK.

13 It takes ten minutes to lose feeling in your arms and legs after falling through ice into water.

DANGER THIN ICE

14 Some lizards' tails are constructed to break off easily so they can escape in an attack. **Usually a new tail is regenerated in a few months.**

15 THE INTERNATIONAL **SIGN OF DISTRESS** WHEN USING FIRE IS TO BUILD THREE FIRES IN A TRIANGLE.

SURVIVAL STORY

ORANGUTAN
TO THE RESCUE

After getting lost in the rain forest, National Geographic explorer Agustín Fuentes receives some very unlikely help. Read on to find out how Fuentes found his way home.

All Agustín Fuentes wanted to do was find the rare maroon leaf monkey. He'd been spending some time at Camp Leakey, an orangutan research camp on Borneo, a large, mountainous island in southeast Asia, and he got the urge to take a day trip into the dense rain forest to seek one out. So he packed up his compass, headlamp, and small backpack, and off he went.

After four hours of following marked trails, Fuentes thought he caught a glimpse of a maroon leaf monkey. But then it scampered away into the rain forest. He had a decision to make: Should he stay on the trails and hope he sees the monkey again? Or should he follow it?

"I took a risk and went off trail," Fuentes says.

Bad move. Forty-five minutes later, Fuentes found himself deep in the rain forest, with no maroon leaf monkey in sight. He used his compass to make a guess as to which direction he was heading and kept walking.

"Another 30 minutes passed, and I began to get a little nervous," says Fuentes. "Darkness was coming on quickly."

Fuentes tried to find comfort in the fact that he was in a place where another human had likely never been. As he looked around the rain forest, there was so much to admire.

"At one point, I spotted a shimmering metallic blue pool in an opening. I moved closer, and the blue image vibrated. Suddenly, hundreds of blue butterflies took flight before me," he says. "They had been feasting on wild pig droppings on the ground a few feet away."

Pulling out his compass, Fuentes headed south, thinking he'd eventually hit the river, if not a trail first. It paid off. After about 20 minutes, he saw an unmarked trail. Seconds later, he heard a rustling. He shone his headlight toward the sound. It was an orangutan! And not just any orangutan: Fuentes recognized right away that she was one of the tribe being rehabilitated at camp.

"We looked at each other, and she held out her hand to me." he says. "Then she led me, hand-in-hand, to camp. Just like me, she was heading back for the evening."

HOW TO
SURVIVE A
KILLER BEE ATTACK!

1 Buzz Off
Killer bees—or Africanized honey bees—only attack when their hive is being threatened. If you see several bees buzzing near you, a hive is probably close by. Heed their "back off" attitude and slowly walk away.

2 Don't Join the Swat Team
Your first instinct might be to start swatting and slapping the bees. But that just makes the buzzers angry. Loud noises have the same effect, so don't start screaming, either. Just get away.

3 Don't Play Hide-and-Seek
Hives are often near water, but don't even think about outlasting the bees underwater. They'll hover and attack when you come up for air, even if you try to swim for it.

4 Make Like Speedy Gonzalez
Killer bees will chase you, but they'll give up when you're far enough away from the hive (usually about 200 yards [183 m]). Take off running and don't stop until the buzzing does.

5 Create a Cover-Up
Killer bees often go for the face and throat, which are the most dangerous places to be stung. While you're on the run, protect your face and neck with your hands, or pull your shirt over your head.

HOW TO SURVIVE A
BEE STING!

1. De-Sting Yourself
First, get inside or to a cool place. Then, remove the stinger by scraping a fingernail over the area, like you would to get a splinter out. Do not squeeze the stinger or use tweezers unless you absolutely can't get it out any other way.

2. Put It on Ice
Wash the area with soap and water and apply a cool compress to reduce swelling. Continue icing the spot for 20 minutes every hour. Place a washcloth or towel between the ice and your skin.

3. Treat It Right
With a parent's permission, take an antihistamine and gently rub a hydrocortisone cream on the sting site.

4. Hands Off
Make sure you don't scratch the sting. You'll just increase the pain and swelling.

5. Recognize Danger
If you experience severe burning and itching, swelling of the throat and/or mouth, difficulty breathing, weakness, or nausea, or if you already know you are allergic to bees, get to an emergency room immediately.

EXTREME
ACTION SPORTS

Forget soccer and softball: Some athletes go above and beyond when it comes to their sport of choice. These activities take a ton of skill—and plenty of guts, too. Here's a roundup of some *extreme*-ly out-there sports!

BASE JUMPING

SPECIAL GEAR
Parachute

WHY IT'S EXTREME
Instead of leaping from an airplane, BASE jumpers parachute from fixed objects, including buildings (B), antennas (A), spans (S), such as bridges, and Earth's formations (E).

EXTREME IRONING

SPECIAL GEAR
Iron, ironing board, and wrinkled clothes

WHY IT'S EXTREME
Thrill-seekers iron their laundry while performing an extreme sport, like riding on a moving car or scuba diving.

SNOWKITING

SPECIAL GEAR
Skis, large kite

WHY IT'S EXTREME
Skiers use large kites to propel themselves across snow and ice—and off mountains.

FLARE SURFING

SPECIAL GEAR
Surfboard, flares

WHY IT'S EXTREME
Surfers create a fiery display while they ride the waves by attaching flares to the backs of their boards.

STILT JUMPING

SPECIAL GEAR
Jumping stilts

WHY IT'S EXTREME
Stride up to nine feet (2.7 m) with these spring-loaded stilts that you can walk, jump, and jog in.

UNDERWATER HOCKEY

SPECIAL GEAR
Hockey puck, stick, swimming pool

WHY IT'S EXTREME
Players hold their breath as they dive to the bottom of the pool to go after the puck and push it to the goal.

STUMP YOUR PARENTS

AWESOME ADVENTURE QUIZ

See if your parents are up to speed by quizzing their knowledge on all things adventure.

ANSWERS BELOW

1 What is a possible theory explaining Amelia Earhart's disappearance?

a. Her plane crashed into the ocean.
b. She landed on a remote island and lived as a castaway.
c. She changed her identity.
d. All of the above.

2 **True or false?** If you're stung by a bee, you should remove the stinger as soon as you can.

3 What does a herpetologist study?

a. insects and spiders
b. plants
c. reptiles and amphibians
d. pets

4 What is a blue hole?

a. a canyon made of blue rocks
b. a superdeep underwater cave
c. the entrance to the Smurfs' underground village
d. a mountain lake

5 What does "BASE" in BASE jumping stand for?

a. Be A Smart Eagle
b. Bravery, Agility, Speed, and Energy
c. Buildings, Antennas, Spans, and Earth's formations
d. It doesn't stand for anything

Not STUMPED yet?
Check out the *National Geographic Kids Quiz Whiz* collection for more crazy ADVENTURE questions!

ANSWERS:
1. d; 2. True; 3. c; 4. b; 5. c

HOMEWORK HELP

How to Write a Perfect Essay

Need to write an essay? Does the assignment feel as big as climbing Mount Everest? Fear not. You're up to the challenge! The following step-by-step tips will help you with this monumental task.

1 **BRAINSTORM.** Sometimes the subject matter of your essay is assigned to you, sometimes it's not. Either way, you have to decide what you want to say. Start by brainstorming some ideas, writing down any thoughts you have about the subject. Then read over everything you've come up with and consider which idea you think is the strongest. Ask yourself what you want to write about the most. Keep in mind the goal of your essay. Can you achieve the goal of the assignment with this topic? If so, you're good to go.

2 **WRITE A TOPIC SENTENCE.** This is the main idea of your essay, a statement of your thoughts on the subject. Again, consider the goal of your essay. Think of the topic sentence as an introduction that tells your reader what the rest of your essay will be about.

3 **OUTLINE YOUR IDEAS.** Once you have a good topic sentence, then you need to support that main idea with more detailed information, facts, thoughts, and examples. These supporting points answer one question about your topic sentence—"Why?" This is where research and perhaps more brainstorming come in. Then organize these points in the way you think makes the most sense, probably in order of importance. Now you have an outline for your essay.

4 **ON YOUR MARK, GET SET, WRITE!** Follow your outline, using each of your supporting points as the topic sentence of its own paragraph. Use descriptive words to get your ideas across to the reader. Go into detail, using specific information to tell your story or make your point. Stay on track, making sure that everything you include is somehow related to the main idea of your essay. Use transitions to make your writing flow.

5 **WRAP IT UP.** Finish your essay with a conclusion that summarizes your entire essay and restates your main idea.

6 **PROOFREAD AND REVISE.** Check for errors in spelling, capitalization, punctuation, and grammar. Look for ways to make your writing clear, understandable, and interesting. Use descriptive verbs, adjectives, or adverbs when possible. It also helps to have someone else read your work to point out things you might have missed. Then make the necessary corrections and changes in a second draft. Repeat this revision process once more to make your final draft as good as you can.

Super Science

Traffic jam? No problem! Scientists at a Dutch corporation have created PAL-V ONE, a flying car with a short takeoff and landing capability so it can take to the air from almost anywhere.

THE UNIVERSE BEGAN WITH A BIG BANG

Clear your mind for a minute and try to imagine this: All the things you see in the universe today—all the stars, galaxies, and planets—are not yet out there. Everything that now exists is concentrated in a single, incredibly hot, dense state that scientists call a singularity. Then, suddenly, the basic elements that make up the universe flash into existence. Scientists say that actually happened about 13.7 billion years ago, in the moment we call the big bang.

For centuries scientists, religious scholars, poets, and philosophers have wondered how the universe came to be. Was it always there? Will it always be the same, or will it change? If it had a beginning, will it someday end, or will it go on forever?

These are huge questions. But today, because of recent observations of space and what it's made of, we think we may have some of the answers. Everything we can see or detect around us in the universe began with the big bang. We know the big bang created not only matter but also space itself. And scientists think that in the very distant future, stars will run out of fuel and burn out. Once again the universe will become dark.

POWERFUL PARTICLE

It's just one tiny particle, but without it the world as we know it would not exist. That's what scientists are saying after the recent discovery of the Higgs boson particle, a subatomic speck related to the Higgs field, which is thought to give mass to everything around us. Without the Higgs boson, all the atoms created in the big bang would have zipped around the cosmos too quickly to collect into stars and planets. So you can think of it as a building block of the universe —and of us!

EARLY LIFE ON EARTH

About 3.5 billion years ago
Earth was covered by one gigantic reddish ocean. The color came from hydrocarbons.

The first life-forms on Earth were Archaea that were able to live without oxygen. They released large amounts of methane gas into an atmosphere that would have been poisonous to us.

About 3 billion years ago
erupting volcanoes linked together to form larger landmasses. And a new form of life appeared—cyanobacteria, the first living things that used energy from the sun.

Some 2 billion years ago
the cyanobacteria algae filled the air with oxygen, killing off the methane-producing Archaea. Colored pools of greenish brown plant life floated on the oceans. The oxygen revolution that would someday make human life possible was now under way.

About 530 million years ago
the Cambrian explosion occurred. It's called an explosion because it's the time when most major animal groups first appeared in our fossil records. Back then, Earth was made up of swamps, seas, a few active volcanoes, and oceans teeming with strange life.

More than 450 million years ago
life began moving from the oceans onto dry land. About 200 million years later dinosaurs began to appear. They would dominate life on Earth for more than 150 million years.

PLANETS

CERES

MARS

EARTH

VENUS

MERCURY

JUPITER

SUN

MERCURY
Average distance from the sun:
   35,980,000 miles (57,900,000 km)
Position from the sun in orbit: first
Equatorial diameter: 3,030 miles (4,878 km)
Length of day: 59 Earth days
Length of year: 88 Earth days
Surface temperatures: -300°F (-184°C)
   to 800°F (427°C)
Known moons: 0
Fun fact: Mercury is home to one of the
   largest craters in the solar system.

VENUS
Average distance from the sun:
   67,230,000 miles (108,200,000 km)
Position from the sun in orbit: second
Equatorial diameter: 7,520 miles (12,100 km)
Length of day: 243 Earth days
Length of year: 225 Earth days
Average surface temperature: 864°F (462°C)
Known moons: 0
Fun fact: It never rains on Venus.

EARTH
Average distance from the sun:
   93,000,000 miles (149,600,000 km)
Position from the sun in orbit: third
Equatorial diameter: 7,900 miles (12,750 km)
Length of day: 24 hours
Length of year: 365 days
Surface temperatures: -126°F (-88°C)
   to 136°F (58°C)
Known moons: 1
Fun fact: Earth traveled more than 5,000
   miles (8,047 km) in the past 5 minutes.

MARS
Average distance from the sun:
   141,633,000 miles (227,936,000 km)
Position from the sun in orbit: fourth
Equatorial diameter: 4,221 miles (6,794 km)
Length of day: 25 Earth hours
Length of year: 1.88 Earth years
Surface temperatures: -270°F (-168°C)
   to 80°F (27°C)
Known moons: 2
Fun fact: Iron-rich soil gives Mars its
   reddish appearance.

This artwork shows the
13 planets and dwarf planets.
The relative sizes and positions
of the planets are shown but
not the relative distances
between them.

SATURN

URANUS

NEPTUNE

PLUTO

HAUMEA

MAKEMAKE

ERIS

JUPITER
Average distance from the sun:
   483,682,000 miles (778,412,000 km)
Position from the sun in orbit: sixth
Equatorial diameter: 88,840 miles (142,980 km)
Length of day: 9.9 Earth hours
Length of year: 11.9 Earth years
Average surface temperature: -235°F (-148°C)
Known moons: 67*
Fun fact: Europa, one of Jupiter's many
   moons, is thought to have an ocean that's
   ten times deeper than any sea on Earth.

SATURN
Average distance from the sun:
   890,800,000 miles (1,433,500,000 km)
Position from the sun in orbit: seventh
Equatorial diameter: 74,900 miles (120,540 km)
Length of day: 10.7 Earth hours
Length of year: 29.46 Earth years
Average surface temperature: -218°F (-139°C)
Known moons: at least 62*
Fun fact: Scientists believe that Saturn's
   rings will eventually disappear.

URANUS
Average distance from the sun:
   1,784,000,000 miles (2,870,970,000 km)
Position from the sun in orbit: eighth
Equatorial diameter: 31,760 miles (51,120 km)
Length of day: 17.2 Earth hours
Length of year: 84 Earth years
Average surface temperature: -323°F (-197°C)
Known moons: 27
Fun fact: Summer on Uranus lasts 42 years.

NEPTUNE
Average distance from the sun:
   2,795,000,000 miles (4,498,250,000 km)
Position from the sun in orbit: ninth
Equatorial diameter: 30,775 miles (49,528 km)
Length of day: 16 Earth hours
Length of year: 164.8 Earth years
Average surface temperature: -353°F (-214°C)
Known moons: 13
Fun fact: Large, dark spots on Neptune's sur-
   face are believed to be enormous storms.

For information about dwarf planets—Ceres,
Pluto, Haumea, Makemake, and Eris—see p. 124.

*Includes provisional moons, which await confirmation
   and naming from the International Astronomical Union.

DWARF PLANETS

Haumea

Eris

Thanks to advanced technology, astronomers have been spotting many never-before-seen celestial bodies with their telescopes. One new discovery? A population of icy objects orbiting the sun beyond Pluto. The largest, like Pluto itself, are classified as dwarf planets. Smaller than the moon but still massive enough to pull themselves into a ball, dwarf planets neverthe-less lack the gravitational "oomph" to clear their neighborhood of other sizable objects. So, while larger, more massive planets pretty much have their orbits to themselves, dwarf planets orbit the sun in swarms that include other dwarf planets as well as smaller chunks of rock or ice.

So far, astronomers have identified five dwarf planets: Ceres (which circles the sun in the asteroid belt between Mars and Jupiter), Pluto, Haumea, Makemake, and Eris. Astronomers are studying hundreds of newly found objects in the frigid outer solar system, trying to figure out just how big they are. As time and technology advance, the family of known dwarf planets will surely continue to grow.

CERES
Position from the sun in orbit: fifth
Length of day: 9.1 Earth hours
Length of year: 4.6 Earth years
Known moons: 0

PLUTO
Position from the sun in orbit: tenth
Length of day: 6.4 Earth days
Length of year: 248 Earth years
Known moons: 5*

HAUMEA
Position from the sun in orbit:
    eleventh
Length of day: 3.9 Earth hours
Length of year: 282 Earth years
Known moons: 2

MAKEMAKE
Position from the sun in orbit: twelfth
Length of day: 22.5 Earth hours
Length of year: 305 Earth years
Known moons: 0

ERIS
Position from the sun in orbit:
    thirteenth
Length of day: 25.9 Earth hours
Length of year: 561 Earth years
Known moons: 1

*Includes provisional moons.

SUPER SUN!

THE SUN IS 99.8 PERCENT OF ALL THE MASS IN OUR SOLAR SYSTEM.

The **SUN'S** surface is **9,932°F!** (5,500°C)

THERE IS real gold in the SUN.

E ven from 93 million miles (150 million km) away, the sun's rays are powerful enough to provide the energy needed for life to flourish on Earth. This 4.6-billion-year-old star is the anchor of our solar system and accounts for 99 percent of the matter in the solar system. What else makes the sun so special? For starters, it's larger than one million Earths and is the biggest object in our solar system. The sun also converts about four million tons (3,628,739 MT) of matter to energy every second, helping to make life possible here on Earth. Now that's *sun*-sational!

Storms on the Sun!

Solar flares are ten million times more powerful than a volcanic eruption on Earth.

Solar storm

With the help of specialized equipment, scientists have observed solar flares—or bursts of magnetic energy that explode from the sun's surface as a result of storms on the sun. Solar storms occur on a cycle of about 11 years, with 2013 being the most recent active year for these types of events. And while most solar storms will not impact the Earth, the fiercer the flare, the more we may potentially feel its effects, as it could disrupt power grids or interfere with GPS navigation systems. Solar storms can also trigger stronger-than-usual auroras, light shows that can be seen on Earth.

Some solar storms travel at speeds of **THREE MILLION MILES AN HOUR** (4.8 million kph).

Sky Calendar
2015

Jupiter

Partial solar eclipse

Leonid meteor shower

January 3–4 Quadrantids Meteor Shower Peak. A nearly full moon will affect visibility this year, but several bright meteors can still be spotted.

February 6 Jupiter at Opposition. The giant planet is at its closest approach to Earth.

February 22 Conjunction of Venus and Mars. Visible in the west just after sunset, these two bright planets will be unusually close together.

April 4 Total Lunar Eclipse. Visible in most of North America, South America, eastern Asia, and Australia.

May 23 Saturn at Opposition. The best time to view the ringed planet. It makes its closest approach to Earth.

August 12–13 Perseids Meteor Shower Peak. One of the best! Up to 60 meteors per hour. Best viewing is in the direction of the constellation Perseus.

September 1 Neptune at Opposition. The blue planet will be at its closest approach to Earth. Because Neptune is so far away, binoculars or a telescope are necessary for viewing. Unless you have a very powerful telescope, Neptune will appear as a small blue dot.

September 28 Total Lunar Eclipse. Visible throughout most of North America, South America, Europe, Africa, and western Asia.

October 21–22 Orionids Meteor Shower Peak. View up to 20 meteors per hour. Look toward the constellation Orion for the best show.

October 28 Conjunction of Venus, Mars, and Jupiter. Visible in the east just before sunrise, these three planets will be unusually close together, forming a triangle.

November 17–18 Leonid Meteor Shower Peak. View up to 15 meteors per hour.

December 7 Conjunction of Moon and Venus. Look east just before sunrise to view Venus unusually close to the crescent moon.

December 13–14 Geminids Meteor Shower Peak. A spectacular show! Up to 120 multi-colored meteors per hour.

Dates may vary slightly depending on your location. Check with a local planetarium for the best viewing time in your area.

DESTINATION SPACE

LAVA PLANET

You open your spacecraft door and step out at the edge of an ocean. Except this is not a normal seashore—it's made of lava. You're on a planet 489 light-years (the distance light travels in one year) from Earth, far outside your solar system. To explore this lava planet, named CoRoT-7b, you wear a heatproof spacesuit. It's 3,990°F (2,199°C) here—hot enough to vaporize a human.

Like Earth, CoRoT-7b is made largely of rock. But since the lava planet is so hot, the rock melts, forming a red-orange lava ocean that covers almost half the planet. The intense heat vaporizes the liquid rock, turning it into rock gas, which rises above the ocean and forms clouds, just as water does on Earth. As you stare into the sky, you see clouds moving toward you.

Suddenly, pebbles start falling from the cloudy sky. The gas rock condensed and now it's raining rocks! You jump inside your spacecraft and speed away from this extreme planet. Clearly it's no place for a vacation!

Destination
The planet CoRoT-7b

Location
The constellation Monoceros

Distance
489 light-years from Earth

Time to reach
13.3 million years

Weather
Sunny and 3,990°F with a chance of rock rain

Half the planet always faces its sun.

Half the planet always faces away from its sun.

Scientists have discovered three other lava planets like CoRoT-7b.

The lava ocean on CoRoT-7b is 28 miles (45 km) deep.

EYE ON THE SKY Watch the night sky for the meteor showers. Sometimes called shooting stars, meteors are space rocks that burn up in Earth's atmosphere.

Viewed from Earth, the brightest objects in the sky are the sun, the moon, and Venus.

5 Freaky Places in Space

THE MOON AND MARS might sound like exciting destinations for an expedition. But some places in space are even more exciting—and weirder—than you've ever imagined. Most of them would squash, freeze, or blow apart a human visitor. But if you could survive the trip, what would these places be like? Blast off to five of the freakiest places in the galaxy to find out.

1 SUNNY SPOT

Your first expedition is to Kepler-16b, a planet 200 light-years from Earth. (One light-year is almost six trillion miles [9.5 trillion km]!) You arrive at dawn as a bright sun spreads light across the planet's surface. Then things get even stranger: A second sun, small and red, joins the first in the sky.

Kepler-16b, discovered in 2011, is the first confirmed planet ever found that orbits two suns. The suns spin around each other as the planet circles them both every 41 days. Kepler-16b is no place for humans. It has a surface made of gas, and temperatures that drop to minus 100°F (-73°C). "It's like a nippy winter in Antarctica," says Laurance Doyle, one of the scientists who discovered the planet.

OCEAN VIEW

Some of the galaxy's strangest places are right here in our own solar system. To travel to Europa, one of Jupiter's moons, you take off in a different kind of spaceship—one that carries a submarine. Europa looks like a gray ball of string. But scientists are quite sure that beneath its crust of about ten-mile (16-km)-thick ice, this moon has a giant ocean. One day they hope to send a spacecraft to Europa that would break through the ice and launch a submarine into the ocean below. The submarine would search for the weird creatures that might live in this wild place.

2

③ ALL NIGHT, ALL DAY

Your visit to a red dwarf planet is filled with extremes because it doesn't rotate like Earth does. It's so close to its sun—a small, red star called a red dwarf—that the sun's gravity holds it locked in place. This means that the planet doesn't have days and nights. Instead, one side is always facing the blazing sun, and the other side is always dark. The planet's locked position creates strange weather. An almost continuous hurricane swirls at the point closest to the red dwarf. Streamers from the storm cascade toward the dark side of the planet.

RED DWARF

SMOOTH STAR

The surface of the neutron star you're looking at is far smoother than glass. Neutron stars are born when a giant star runs out of fuel and its core collapses. The dying star's gravity pulls so tightly that everything—even dust—is flattened. An earthling wouldn't stand a chance of survival, so you observe the star from the safety of your spacecraft.

You watch as a star-quake shakes the ground, creating a mountain—just as earthquakes have done on Earth. But here, the mountain rises and vanishes in an instant, sucked toward the star's center by the extreme gravity. The ground is weirdly smooth once again.

④

⑤ FIREWORKS AND STARDUST

Your last expedition brings you close to a supernova, an exploding star. You watch from your spacecraft as violent nuclear reactions blow apart the star from the inside out. You see an explosion as bright as billions of suns put together. Then, like an immense firework, a colorful wave of gas and dust blasts outward.

The gas and dust hold the ingredients to build everything—from planets to oceans to people. When the universe began, its primary elements were hydrogen and helium. All the rest, from carbon to iron, were created in the interior of stars. The explosion blew these elements far into space, spreading the ingredients for life across the galaxy.

WHAT IS LIFE?

This seems like such an easy question to answer. Everybody knows that singing birds are alive and rocks are not. But when we start studying bacteria and other microscopic creatures, things get more complicated.

SO WHAT EXACTLY IS LIFE?

Most scientists agree that something is alive if it can do the following: reproduce; grow in size to become more complex in structure; take in nutrients to survive; give off waste products; and respond to external stimuli, such as increased sunlight or changes in temperature.

KINDS OF LIFE

Biologists classify living organisms by how they get their energy. Organisms such as algae, green plants, and some bacteria use sunlight as an energy source. Animals (like humans), fungi, and some Archaea use chemicals to provide energy. When we eat food, chemical reactions within our digestive system turn our food into fuel.

Living things inhabit land, sea, and air. In fact, life also thrives deep beneath the oceans, embedded in rocks miles below the Earth's crust, in ice, and in other extreme environments. The life-forms that thrive in these challenging environments are called extremophiles. Some of these draw directly upon the chemicals surrounding them for energy. Since these are very different forms of life than what we're used to, we may not think of them as alive, but they are.

HOW IT ALL WORKS

To try and understand how a living organism works, it helps to look at one example of its simplest form—the single-celled bacterium called *Streptococcus*. There are many kinds of these tiny organisms, and some are responsible for human illnesses. What makes us sick or uncomfortable are the toxins the bacteria give off in our bodies.

A single *Streptococcus* bacterium is so small that at least 500 of them could fit on the dot above the letter *i*. These bacteria are some of the simplest forms of life we know. They have no moving parts, no lungs, no brain, no heart, no liver, and no leaves or fruit. Yet this life-form reproduces. It grows in size by producing long chain structures, takes in nutrients, and gives off waste products. This tiny life-form is alive, just as you are alive.

What makes something alive is a question scientists grapple with when they study viruses, such as the ones that cause the common cold and smallpox. They can grow and reproduce within host cells, such as those that make up your body. Because viruses lack cells and cannot metabolize nutrients for energy or reproduce without a host, scientists ask if they are indeed alive. And don't go looking for them without a strong microscope—viruses are a hundred times smaller than bacteria.

Scientists think life began on Earth some 3.9 to 4.1 billion years ago, but no fossils exist from that time. The earliest fossils ever found are from the primitive life that existed 3.6 billion years ago. Other life-forms, some of which are shown below, soon followed. Scientists continue to study how life evolved on Earth and whether it is possible that life exists on other planets.

MICROSCOPIC ORGANISMS*

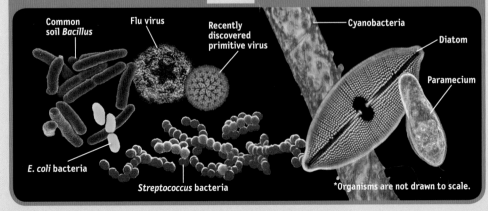

Common soil *Bacillus*

Flu virus

Recently discovered primitive virus

Cyanobacteria

Diatom

Paramecium

E. coli bacteria

Streptococcus bacteria

*Organisms are not drawn to scale.

The Three Domains of Life

Biologists divide all living organisms into three domains: Bacteria, Archaea, and Eukarya. Archaean and Bacterial cells do not have nuclei; they are so different from each other that they belong to different domains. Since human cells have a nucleus, humans belong to the Eukarya domain.

1

BACTERIA

Domain Bacteria: These single-celled microorganisms are found almost everywhere in the world. Bacteria are small and do not have nuclei. They can be shaped like rods, spirals, or spheres. Some of them are helpful to humans, and some are harmful.

2

ARCHAEA

Domain Archaea: These single-celled micro-organisms are often found in extremely hostile environments. Like Bacteria, Archaea do not have nuclei, but they have some genes in common with Eukarya. For this reason, scientists think the Archaea living today most closely resemble the earliest forms of life on Earth.

3

EUKARYA

Domain Eukarya: This diverse group of life-forms is more complicated than Bacteria and Archaea, as Eukarya have one or more cells with nuclei. These are the tiny cells that make up your whole body. Eukarya are divided into four groups: fungi, protists, plants, and animals.

What is a domain? Scientifically speaking, a domain is a major taxonomic division into which natural objects are classified (see p. 20 for "What Is Taxonomy?").

FYI

FUNGI

Kingdom Fungi (about 100,000 species): Mainly multicellular organisms, fungi cannot make their own food. Mushrooms and yeast are fungi.

PROTISTS

Protists (about 250,000 species): Once considered a kingdom, this group is a "grab bag" that includes unicellular and multicellular organisms of great variety.

PLANTS

Kingdom Plantae (about 300,000 species): Plants are multicellular, and many can make their own food using photosynthesis (see p. 216 for "Photosynthesis").

ANIMALS

Kingdom Animalia (about 1,000,000 species): Most animals, which are multicellular, have their own organ systems. Animals do not make their own food.

Your Amazing
eyes

Discover the magic of your body's built-in cameras.

You carry around a pair of cameras in your head so incredible they can work in bright sunshine or at night. Only about an inch (2.5 cm) in diameter, they can bring you the image of a tiny ant or a twinkling star trillions of miles (km) away. They can change focus almost instantly and stay focused even when you're shaking your head or jumping up and down. These cameras are your eyes.

A CRUCIAL PART OF YOUR EYE IS AS FLIMSY AS A WET TISSUE.

A dragonfly darts toward your head! Light bounces off the insect, enters your eye, passes through your pupil (the black circle in the middle of your iris), and goes to the lens. The lens focuses the light onto your retina—a thin lining on the back of your eye that is vital but is as flimsy as a wet tissue. Your retina acts like film in a camera, capturing the picture of this dragonfly. The picture is sent to your brain, which instantly sends you a single command—*duck!*

YOU BLINK MORE THAN 10,000 TIMES A DAY.

Your body has many ways to protect and care for your eyes. Each eye sits on a cushion of fat, almost completely surrounded by protective bone. Your eyebrows help prevent sweat from dripping into your eyes. Your eyelashes help keep dust and other small particles out. Your eyelids act as built-in windshield wipers, spreading tear fluid with every blink to keep your eyes moist and wash away bacteria and other particles. And if anything ever gets too close to your eyes, your eyelids slam shut with incredible speed—in two-fifths of a second—to protect them!

YOUR EYES SEE EVERYTHING UPSIDE DOWN AND BACKWARD!

As amazing as your eyes are, the images they send your brain are a little quirky: They're upside down, backward, and two-dimensional! Your brain automatically flips the images from your retinas right side up and combines the images from each eye into a three-dimensional picture. There is a small area of each retina, called a blind spot, that can't record what you're seeing. Luckily your brain makes adjustments for this, too.

YOUR PUPILS CHANGE SIZE WHENEVER THE LIGHT CHANGES.

Your black pupils may be small, but they have an important job—they grow or shrink to allow just the right amount of light to enter your eyes to let you see.

THE EYEBALL'S TOUGH OUTER LAYERS, THE **CORNEA (1)** AND **SCLERA (2)**, GIVE IT STRENGTH.

THE COLORED **IRIS** ABSORBS BRIGHT LIGHT.

THE **PUPIL** EXPANDS AND CONTRACTS TO LET IN THE AMOUNT OF LIGHT NEEDED TO SEE.

THE **LENS**, WITH THE CORNEA, FOCUSES LIGHT.

COLORLESS, JELLYLIKE **VITREOUS HUMOR** FILLS THE EYEBALL, HELPING IT TO KEEP ITS SHAPE.

A MILLION FIBERS IN THE **OPTIC NERVE** CONNECT THE EYE TO THE BRAIN.

THE **RETINA** CHANGES LIGHT RAYS INTO ELECTRICAL SIGNALS SENT TO THE BRAIN.

Your Amazing heart

YOUR HEART has the power to lift a 3,000-pound (1,360-kg) car, the strength to pump 2,000 gallons (7,570 L) of blood twice around the world in a day, and the stamina to never take a break. And, oh yeah, it keeps you alive, too!

Here are three more heart-pumping facts about this awesome organ.

Your heart beats 100,000 times daily. And each of these little pitter-patters you feel is actually your heart filling with blood, squeezing, then forcing the blood out and throughout your body. This is done with enough power to pump blood to every cell, delivering oxygen and removing carbon dioxide waste.

Thanks to your heart, blood constantly circulates throughout your body to keep you healthy. And every day, your heart pumps more than 2,000 gallons (7,570 L) of blood through 60,000 miles (96,000 km) of blood vessels—a distance greater than two trips around the world.

During its endless journeys to and from your heart, the several quarts of blood in your body travel through three types of vessels: arteries, veins, and capillaries. Most arteries carry oxygen-rich blood away from your heart. Veins deliver oxygen-depleted blood back toward your heart. And tiny capillaries connect arteries and veins, forming a vast network in your tissues and reaching every cell in your body. These fragile vessels are so narrow that the microscopic blood cells have to pass through them single file.

#1 One heartbeat is so powerful that it could shoot water six feet (1.8 m) into the air!

#2 Blood travels 60,000 miles (96,000 km) through your body every day.

#3 You have at least four quarts (3.8 L) of blood in your body.

Heart Parts

- AORTA
- PULMONARY ARTERY
- RIGHT ATRIUM
- LEFT ATRIUM
- RIGHT VENTRICLE
- LEFT VENTRICLE

Your Amazing
brain

Inside your body's supercomputer

You carry around a three-pound (1.4-kg) mass of wrinkly material n your head that controls every single thing you will ver do. From enabling you to think, learn, create, and feel emotions to control- ing every blink, breath, and heartbeat—this fantastic control center is your brain. t is a structure so amazing that a famous scientist once called it the "most complex thing we have yet discovered in our universe."

EMOTION AND PERSONALITY

SPEECH

SMELL

MEMORY AND LEARNING

HEARING

TOUCH

MOVEMENT

SIGHT

BALANCE AND COORDINATION

FRONTAL LOBE
PARIETAL LOBE
OCCIPITAL LOBE
TEMPORAL LOBE

CEREBRUM

CEREBELLUM
BRAIN STEM

BRAIN MAP

THE BIG QUESTION

WHAT TAKES UP TWO-THIRDS OF YOUR BRAIN'S WEIGHT AND ALLOWS YOU TO SWIM, EAT, AND SPEAK?

Answer: The huge hunk of your brain called the cerebrum. It's definitely the biggest part of the brain. The four lobes of the cerebrum house the centers for memory, the senses, movement, and emotion, among other things.

The cerebrum is made up of two hemispheres—the right and the left. Each side controls the muscles of the opposite side of the body.

Bet you didn't know

6 mind-bending facts about the brain

1 **Your brain** generates **enough electricity** to power a **lightbulb.**

2 **Each minute,** about **750** milliliters—or **two soda cans**—of **blood** travel through the **brain.**

3 **Eating chocolate** releases chemicals in the **brain** that make us **happy.**

4 **Exercise can** make **your brain** more **active.**

5 It would take close to **3,000** years to count the **neurons,** or nerve cells, **in your brain.**

6 Pressing your **tongue** to the roof of your mouth **eases** "brain freeze."

That's GROSS!

WHO NEEDS SLOBBERING ZOMBIES AND SLIMY MONSTERS THIS HALLOWEEN? THE BACTERIA LIVING INSIDE YOUR BODY ARE ICKY ENOUGH.

Don't panic, but you're outnumbered by alien life-forms. They look like hairy hot dogs, spiky blobs, and oozing spirals, and they're crawling across—and deep inside—your body right this very minute. They're bacteria!

Your body is built of trillions of itty-bitty living blobs, called cells, that work together to do amazing things, such as hold in your organs or help beat your brother at *Super Mario Kart*. But for every cell you call your own, about ten foreign bacteria are clustering around or near it. You can't see these hitchhikers, but you sure can smell a lot of them. Like any living thing, bacteria eat, reproduce, die, and create waste. A lot of this waste is the source of your body odor, bad breath, and torturous toots. In other words, some bacteria can make your life stink!

If the thought of being a human-shaped planet for microscopic inhabitants makes you queasy, relax. Most of your body's microbes have been harmlessly hanging out in your body for years and are essential for good health. And just like a fingerprint, your bacteria make you who you are, because no two people host the same mix of microorganisms. But that doesn't make things any less disgusting!

Little Monsters

Meet four famous bacteria that call your body "home sweet home..."

1 ACTINOMYCES VISCOSUS
When your dentist breaks out the power tools to jackhammer the brownish coat of slime known as plaque from your teeth, she's really attacking these mouth-dwelling bacteria.

4 BREVIBACTERIUM LINENS

This foul-smelling microbe thrives in the sweat simmering in your sneakers, unleashing an awful stink when you kick off your shoes. It's also used to ferment stinky Limburger cheese.

2 METHANOGENS

About half of all people have these supersimple microbes living in their guts. Methanogens produce methane, a greenhouse gas that animals—including humans—pass into the atmosphere when they, um, toot.

3 ESCHERICHIA COLI

This rod-shaped microbe lives deep in your guts, the body's busiest bacterial neighborhood. Helpful *E. coli* strains produce an important vitamin. Harmful ones make you vomit for days.

More Grossness

Your body's bacterial zoo begins when you're born, as you ingest bacteria from your mom's skin and milk. You also consume lots of harmless and helpful bacteria through food and water every day.

Some bacteria are used by scientists to help produce new vaccines and other medicine.

Your body's bacteria eat everything from salt inside your intestines to chemicals in your sweat.

Belly-button lint—a mix of clothing fibers and dead skin cells—is a hot spot for bacteria. Scientists recently found more than 1,400 species of microbes living in people's navels.

All About YOU

What Your BIRTH ORDER Says About YOU

Whether you're the oldest, the youngest, or an only child, your birth order can shape your personality. "Your position in the family line makes a big impact on the person you are now—and who you'll grow up to be," says psychologist Kevin Leman, author of *The Birth Order Book*. Here's what your sibling status may say about you.

IF THESE PERSONALITY PROFILES DON'T MATCH YOURS, THAT'S OK. THIS IS JUST FOR FUN!

IF YOU'RE THE OLDEST, YOU . . .

are well organized and reliable, excel in school, and have a knack for computers. You're a natural-born leader and like to be in charge of projects, although you don't like big changes. Many firstborns go on to become entertainers.

Celeb matches:
Taylor Swift, Justin Bieber

IF YOU'RE A MULTIPLE . . .

the same birth-order rules apply. If you're a twin or triplet and were born first, your personality is probably like an oldest child's. If you were born last, your personality is probably like a youngest child's. This is usually true even if you have siblings in addition to your twin or triplets.

Celeb matches: Dylan and Cole Sprouse (Dylan's older by 15 minutes.)

IF YOU'RE THE YOUNGEST, YOU . . .

are good at reading people's emotions and understanding how to act accordingly. You aren't scared to say what you think and therefore often get what you want. You love attention and may be the class clown—you could grow up to be a famous comedian.

Celeb matches:
Jack Black, Ariana Grande

IF YOU'RE IN THE MIDDLE, YOU . . .

have a lot of friends and try to resolve fights rather than start them. Always thinking of better ways to do things, you're likely to start a business, such as a lawn-mowing service or lemonade stand. Middle children often become successful business leaders.

Celeb matches:
Donald Trump, Jennifer Lopez

IF YOU'RE AN ONLY CHILD, YOU . . .

rely on your imagination to keep things interesting. An independent person, you're comfortable talking to new people. You're hardworking and goal-oriented, and you like doing things right the first time around. You may become a professional athlete or government leader.

Celeb matches:
Maria Sharapova, Selena Gomez

Awful Afflictions DILEMMA

Would you rather **SUFFER FROM** a **SNEEZING SPREE** that **never ceases,** or **GET A CASE OF** the **HICCUPS** that **lasts forever?**

IF YOU CHOOSE SNEEZING:

You're wise not to stifle a sneeze. It's an important bodily function for blasting boogers and other debris from your air passages. But while a lone sneeze is essential, a long fit can be exhausting. Each ahh-choo involves a mini-workout of the muscles in your face, throat, chest, and abdomen, all working together to expel foreign particles from your nose and mouth at nearly 100 mph (161 kph). Now imagine the ordeal of Donna Griffiths, a 12-year-old English girl who suffered from a sneezing spree that lasted more than 977 days!

IF YOU CHOOSE HICCUPS:

Never-ending hiccups might seem less annoying than ceaseless sneezing, but consider the life-disrupting consequences of well-meaning friends offering a "cure." Iowa, U.S.A., farmer Charles Osborne hiccuped every day for nearly 70 years (doctors think he damaged the hiccup-controlling part of his brain after straining to lift a heavyweight hog). Before he passed away in 1991, Osborne received thousands of letters with homemade remedies. One buddy even fired a double-barreled shotgun just out of sight, hoping to scare away the hiccups.

139

Continents on the Move

1

PANGAEA About 240 million years ago, Earth's landmasses were joined together in one super-continent that extended from Pole to Pole.

2

BREAKUP By 94 million years ago, Pangaea had broken apart into landmasses that would become today's continents. Dinosaurs roamed Earth during a period of warmer climates.

3

EXTINCTION About 65 million years ago, an asteroid smashed into Earth, creating the Gulf of Mexico. This impact may have resulted in the extinction of half the world's species, including the dinosaurs. This was one of several major mass extinctions.

4

ICE AGE By 18,000 years ago, the continents had drifted close to their present positions, but most far northern and far southern lands were buried beneath huge glaciers.

A LOOK INSIDE

The distance from Earth's surface to its center is 3,963 miles (6,378 km) at the Equator. There are four layers: a thin, rigid crust; the rocky mantle; the outer core, which is a layer of molten iron; and finally the inner core, which is believed to be solid iron.

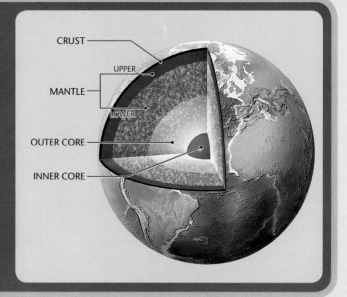

CRUST
UPPER
MANTLE
LOWER
OUTER CORE
INNER CORE

ROCK STARS

The world is full of rocks—some big, some small, some formed deep beneath the Earth, and some formed at the surface. While they may look similar, not all rocks are created equal. Look closely, and you'll see differences between every boulder, stone, and pebble. Here's more about the three top varieties of rocks.

Igneous

Named for the Greek word meaning "from fire," igneous rocks form when hot, molten liquid called magma cools. Pools of magma form deep underground and slowly work their way to the Earth's surface. If they make it all the way, the liquid rock erupts and is called lava. As the layers of lava build up they form a mountain called a volcano. Typical igneous rocks include obsidian, basalt, and pumice, which is so chock-full of gas bubbles that it actually floats in water.

OBSIDIAN   PUMICE

Metamorphic

Metamorphic rocks are the masters of change! These rocks were once igneous or sedimentary, but thanks to intense heat and pressure deep within the Earth, they have undergone a total transformation from their original form. These rocks never truly melt; instead, the heat twists and bends them until their shapes substantially change. Metamorphic rocks include slate as well as marble, which is used for buildings, monuments, and sculptures.

MARBLE   SLATE

Sedimentary

When wind, water, and ice constantly wear away and weather rocks, smaller pieces called sediment are left behind. These are sedimentary rocks, also known as gravel, sand, silt, and clay. As water flows downhill it carries the sedimentary grains into lakes and oceans, where they get deposited. As the loose sediment piles up, the grains eventually get compacted or cemented back together again. The result is new sedimentary rock. Sandstone, limestone, and shale are sedimentary rocks that have formed this way.

SANDSTONE

SCAN THIS PAGE!
GET BONUS MOBILE
CONTENT! Download
the free NG Kids
scanner app. Directions
on inside front cover.

1 The Chol Indians of Mexico believe **crystals** have magical powers.

2 Legend says that the mineral aquamarine was found in the treasure chests of mermaids. Sailors wore it for **good luck.**

4 Egypt's PYRAMIDS AT GIZA AND THE SPHINX are made of limestone, a rock that consists mostly of calcite. That's a mineral formed by the remains of tiny sea creatures.

3 INVENTED IN 1839, THE FIRST SUCCESSFUL **cameras used silver** TO HELP PROCESS PHOTOGRAPHS.

15 COOL THINGS ABOUT

5 **Salt** was once considered so valuable that ancient Roman soldiers were paid partly in the mineral **instead of money.**

6 THE HOPE DIAMOND IS VALUED AT MORE THAN $200 MILLION. ITS FORMER OWNER DONATED THE **45.5-carat gemstone** TO THE SMITHSONIAN INSTITUTION IN 1958— AND SENT IT BY REGULAR MAIL.

7 Natural ice formations, such as **ICEBERGS AND ICICLES,** are considered minerals.

8
The brightly colored rock called **opal** is Australia's national gemstone.

9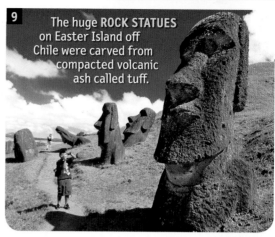
The huge **ROCK STATUES** on Easter Island off Chile were carved from compacted volcanic ash called tuff.

10
FLUORITE CAN GLOW UNDER ULTRA-VIOLET LIGHT.

11
SAPPHIRES AND **RUBIES** ARE THE SAME MINERAL: CORUNDUM.

ROCKS AND MINERALS

12
The gold burial mask of **KING TUT** is decorated with blue rocks called lapis lazuli and the minerals turquoise, carnelian, and quartz.

12

13
THE **HOBA METEORITE** WEIGHS ABOUT 66 TONS (60 MT). THE OUTER SPACE ROCK CONTAINS MINERALS RARELY FOUND ON EARTH'S SURFACE

14
Ancient humans chipped away at **flint** to make **arrowheads** and other **sharp weapons** and **tools**.

15
THERE ARE MORE THAN **4,000** KNOWN MINERALS.

Kaboom!

How demolition experts bring down buildings

1 BEFORE

TEXAS STADIUM

2 EXPLODING!

3 AFTER

Deafening explosions and fiery flashes raced in waves around Texas Stadium. Concrete supports fell like trees, and the steel beams across the top of the building crashed to the ground. Soon a large dust cloud hovered over the rubble. The football arena was gone.

For nearly 40 years, the Dallas Cowboys played home football games at Texas Stadium in Irving. But after the team moved to the new Cowboys Stadium in 2009, the old stadium was no longer needed. So city officials planned to demolish it.

When a structure isn't useful anymore, sometimes the best way to bring it down is also dramatic to watch. Teams of experts can use carefully timed explosions to make a building, bridge, or other structure collapse in a matter of seconds. Let's take a look behind the scenes of the stadium's spectacular demolition.

CONTROLLED DESTRUCTION

The first step to figuring out the most efficient way to demolish Texas Stadium was to study its original plans. Demolition experts take advantage of gravity as much as possible, using the weight of the building to help it collapse. An initial team took out parts of the structure such as walls and ramps so that the whole building perched only on its basic supports, particularly at the lower level of the structure.

EXPLOSIVE SITUATION

Texas Stadium had 12 concrete support structures, called abutments, which circled the outside of the building and held up the roof's six steel beams, called trusses. The team planning the explosion did test blasts to figure out how much dynamite was needed to bring these supports down in the safest way possible. The demolition crew then drilled 3,300 holes into the concrete supports where they placed sticks of dynamite. Special explosives called linear-shaped charges, equipped with a fast-burning, fuse-like cord, cut through the steel in the roof trusses. The charges were linked together so that the concrete supports holding up each of the six trusses exploded at exactly the same time. If they didn't, the roof trusses might not fall to the ground.

SO LONG, STADIUM

After six months of planning, it was time for the explosion. Police and firefighters stopped traffic on highways surrounding Texas Stadium. People gathered at a safe distance to watch. After a countdown, the press of a button set off the series of explosions that, in 60 seconds, left nothing but a massive pile of rubble.

DEMOLITION IN CHINA

1 BEFORE

A BRIDGE IN CHINA WAS DEMOLISHED IN MUCH THE SAME WAY AS TEXAS STADIUM.

2 EXPLODING!

3 AFTER

CRASH AND BURN

PREP TIME FOR TEXAS STADIUM DEMOLITION	NUMBER OF HOLES FOR EXPLOSIVES	TIME TO LOAD EXPLOSIVES	POUNDS OF EXPLOSIVES	TIME TO BRING DOWN TEXAS STADIUM	COST OF DEMOLITION
6 months	3,300	5 days	more than 2,000 (907 kg)	60 seconds	$6 million

COOL inventions

WAY UP!

WALL WALKER

It took a radioactive arachnid's bite to turn Peter Parker into Spider-Man, but engineering students at Utah State University have devised an easier way to gain wall-climbing superpowers. Their Personnel Vacuum Assisted Climber enables its wearer to crawl up walls, even on the roughest surfaces. The climber straps on a backpack equipped with powerful vacuum motors. The motors connect to two handheld suction units that stick to the wall when the motors are engaged. Fast climbers could scramble to the Empire State Building's observation deck in about half an hour. They'll want to take the elevator back down, though—the prototype's battery lasts only 30 minutes!

VACUUM POWER

PUSH FOR PIZZA

Your belly's grumbling but the refrigerator is bare. Don't panic! Just push the button inside the box-shaped magnet on your fridge and—*mamma mia!*—a piping-hot pizza arrives at your door in 30 minutes. It might seem magical, but the V.I.P. Fridge Magnet actually contains a transmitter that enables your cell phone to place an order with the local pizzeria. Right now, this amazing magnet is available only to customers of Red Tomato Pizza in the United Arab Emirates, but its inventors predict it will catch on elsewhere. Pizza party, anyone?

ORDER BUTTON

Push for hunger

THIS IS ONE VACUUM I'M NOT SCARED OF.

SUPER SCOOPER

Scooping up after your dog is a dirty job. Leave it to a kid to help invent a device that takes out the grossest part of this chore. Together with his father, nine-year-old Connor Reynolds created the Pooch Power Shovel, a rechargeable vacuum that picks up piles left by dogs. The unit's powerful motor whisks pieces straight into a biodegradable bag, saving you from any close encounters. When the bag's full, just toss it out and replace it. You'll spend less time fetching Fido's "presents" and more time playing fetch!

BIKE RADIO

As much as you might like to rock out while you ride, wearing headphones on a bicycle is just too risky. Soundmatters' handlebar-mounted speakers make your music collection good to go. Just link these rechargeable wireless speakers to a portable music player (such as an iPod touch, iPhone, or Android phone), then enjoy loud-and-clear playback of your favorite road-tripping tunes. The speakers are good for five hours on a single charge, so chances are you'll run out of energy before they do.

Get Ready for ROBOTS

School's out. It's been a long day, so you head home to relax. You're greeted by a pal who's happy to see you, listens to you talk about your day, and reminds you to text your cousin happy birthday. And that's before he helps you with your homework.

This is your future, and it all starts with a knee-high robot called NAO (pronounced NOW), which may be available by the year 2040. Representing the new generation of self-guided robots, these 'bots can sense, think, and act. Other robots might do two out of the three. For example, a robot might sense things using cameras and think using computers, but with no arms, wheels, or claws, it can't act. Other robots can move and sense things, but can't think for themselves. But NAO can do it all.

Teams of NAO robots play in the RoboCup, a yearly soccer competition among these self-guided robots.

ROBOT PERSONALITY

"You can program your computer to give NAO what could be called personality," says Natanel Dukan of Aldebaran Robotics, the French company that built NAO. The robot has cute, childlike features—a high voice, a small body, big eyes, and a large head. "These are things that are known to have an emotional appeal to people," robot expert Dan Kara says. NAO's friendly design helps in one of NAO's main functions—to teach people how useful personal robots can be. Someday one may help you ace a test!

3 COOL THINGS ABOUT GPS

Thanks to GPS, you may never get lost—or lose anything—again! Short for *global positioning system,* this superhelpful technology relies on satellites in space to collect and plot your position. You can use that info for everything from finding a friend's house to tracking down your dog. Here are some cool ways GPS can help you!

1. Find Your Pets

Forget hanging flyers around your neighborhood: When your pet goes missing, just check your phone! Thanks to GPS tracking devices that attach to your dog or cat's collar, you can find out exactly where your pet is from your phone or computer. Some products even send text messages to you if your pet wanders too far from home.

2. Locate Lost Items

Can't find your smartphone? You may be able to locate it with the help of GPS. Many laptops, mobile phones, and tablets are equipped with a built-in GPS receiver that can send out signals to show you its approximate location on a map.

3. Predict the Weather

Knowing the forecast for tomorrow is one thing. But what about the weather tomorrow exactly at 2:55 p.m.? Meteorologists and geodesists are drawing on data from GPS satellites, including atmospheric temperatures, to help generate more accurate—and up-to-the-minute—weather forecasts. How cool!

How GPS Works

A system of about 30 satellites is orbiting 12,550 miles (20,200 km) above the Earth, traveling at speeds of about 8,500 miles (13,800 km) an hour. As they orbit, the satellites transmit signals to GPS receivers on Earth. Once your GPS receiver picks up radio signals from at least four of these satellites, it can calculate their coordinates to pinpoint your exact position on Earth.

GPS units use satellites to determine your location.

ANIMAL KILLERS BUSTED!

The cool science behind solving wildlife mysteries

Like detectives, scientists at the U.S. National Fish and Wildlife Service (FWS) Forensics Laboratory examine evidence left behind at crime scenes to help solve mysteries. Here's how they use cutting-edge technology to help solve crimes against animals—and catch the crooks!

CRIME SCENE EVIDENCE

FINGERPRINT

THE VICTIMS: ELK
THE CRIME SCENE: COLORADO
THE EVIDENCE: FINGERPRINT

STICKY FINGERS

To passersby, the man was enjoying a campout. But he was really illegally sneaking into reserved hunting grounds to kill elk for their prized antlers. Instead of the permitted bow and arrow, he was using a gun.

The hunter couldn't move the large antler racks home during hunting season, so he wrapped them in duct tape and hid them in tree branches. He'd return for them after hunting season.

But the suspect left something else behind. After wardens found one of the racks, FWS lab technicians discovered a fingerprint on the duct tape. No two people have the same fingerprints. So the scientists searched a database, which matched the print with the suspect. They could confidently point their finger at the hunter, who pleaded guilty and went to jail.

BULLET
CRIME SCENE EVIDENCE

THE VICTIMS: **TIGERS**
THE CRIME SCENE: **ILLINOIS**
THE EVIDENCE: **BULLET**

SMOKING GUN

In an abandoned warehouse, two men shot and killed two endangered tigers that they had bought at a roadside zoo. They hoped to sell the hides, skulls, and meat. But the suspects did a sloppy cleanup job. When an undercover agent from the FWS bought a full-body tiger-skin rug from the ringleader, she found a bullet in the tiger's skull.

A gun leaves a pattern of marks on the bullet it fires, which can match it back to that particular weapon. At a lab, scientists fired a test round of bullets from the ringleader's gun and then used a microscope to compare the marks from the test round with the bullet they found. They matched. Now the ringleader is locked up—instead of the tigers that would have been his next victims.

MICROSCOPE

MEATBALLS

THE VICTIMS: **FOX, COYOTE, BIRDS**
THE CRIME SCENE: **IDAHO**
THE EVIDENCE: **DNA**

BAD MEAT

The meatball trail stretched two miles (3.2 km) in the snow. What should have been a tasty treat for any animal was actually poisoned with a pesticide. FWS agents found the bodies of a fox, coyote, and three magpies that had died after eating the tainted meat. Based on a tip that someone was using poisoned meatballs to kill wolves, agents searched a man's garage. They discovered a bloodstained tool and a bottle containing pesticide, which was identified as the same poison in the meatballs. All the agents had to do was prove the man made the meatballs, then they would know he had also tried to kill endangered wolves.

A geneticist gathered DNA samples from a meatball and from the tool. Found in the body's cells, DNA determines the traits of all living things. And no two living things have the same DNA. The DNA samples from the meatball and the tool matched, which proved the man had made the poisoned meatballs. The trail of evidence led straight to the killer.

DNA

151

STUMP YOUR PARENTS

SUPER SCIENCE QUIZ

Are your dad and mom mad about science? See how much they really know about the subject with this quiz! ANSWERS BELOW

1 **True or false?** There is real gold in the sun.

2 **How many carats is the Hope Diamond?**
a. 91.6
b. 12.4
c. 45.5
d. three bunches

3 **Your brain generates enough electricity to power which household object?**
a. TV
b. refrigerator
c. microwave
d. lightbulb

4 **Which one of the following is considered to be a mineral?**
a. quartz
b. ruby
c. iceberg
d. all of the above

5 **What is the planet CoRoT-7b made of?**
a. ice
b. lava
c. gas
d. chocolate

Not STUMPED yet? Check out the *National Geographic Kids Quiz Whiz* collection for more crazy SCIENCE questions!

ANSWERS:
1. True; 2. c; 3. d; 4. d; 5. b

Research Like a Pro

There is so much information on the Internet. How do you find what you need and make sure it's accurate?

Be Specific

To come up with the most effective keywords—words that describe what you want to know more about—write down what you're looking for in the form of a question, and then circle the most important words in that sentence. Those are the keywords to use in your search. And for best results use words that are specific rather than general.

Research

Research on the Internet involves "looking up" information using a search engine (see list below). Type one or two keywords, and the search engine will provide a list of websites that contain information related to your topic.

Use Trustworthy Sources

When conducting Internet research, be sure the website you use is reliable and the information it provides can be trusted. Sites produced by well-known, established organizations, companies, publications, educational institutions, or the government are your best bets.

Don't Copy

Avoid Internet plagiarism. Take careful notes and cite the websites you use to conduct research.

HELPFUL AND SAFE SEARCH ENGINES FOR KIDS

Google Safe Search	squirrelnet.com/search/Google_SafeSearch.asp
Yahoo! Kids	kids.yahoo.com
SuperKids	super-kids.com
Ask Kids	askkids.com
Kids Click	kidsclick.org
AOL Kids	kids.aol.com

FUN and GAMES

A-maze-ing Paris

Stay on the white paths and help the lost travelers find their way out of a crazy imaginary world underneath Paris, France.

ANSWER ON PAGE 338

Color Café

Some items in this scene have mysteriously changed color. Find at least 12 things that are the wrong color.

ANSWERS ON PAGE 338

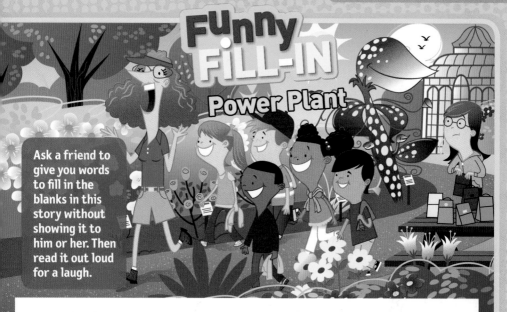

Funny FILL-IN
Power Plant

Ask a friend to give you words to fill in the blanks in this story without showing it to him or her. Then read it out loud for a laugh.

For our first field trip of the year, my class went to the arboretum to see all the

_____ plants. We dropped our _____ _____ lunches and followed
   adjective   adjective   noun

a(n) _____ through a(n) _____ forest, making sure not to _____
     type of job   adjective   verb

anything. But then I saw a rare _____ _____-eating plant that was as tall
                                      color   insect

as a(n) _____. I leaned in to _____ one of its flowers when I heard a
       noun   verb

_____. "_____!" I shouted. My _____ sandwich
  sound   silly expression   something gross

was being devoured by the plant! Still hungry, the plant reached out with its _____
                                                    large number

vines. I started to _____ for help. But then the plant _____ into
             verb   past-tense verb

my _____, pulled out a(n) _____, and put it in its _____.
   noun   favorite food   body part

Now that's what I call plant food!

159

SIGNS
OF THE TIMES

Seeing isn't always believing. Two of these funny signs are not real. Can you figure out which two are fake?

ANSWER ON PAGE 338

1

2

FOOT WEARING
NOT ALLOWED

3

Weigh Togo Road

4

DAN...
All Area Beyond
Sign Is Closed Because
Of Bear Danger

5

Zzyzx Rd

6

MULE
PARKING
ONLY
NO
MOTORIZED
VEHICLES
ALLOWED

Windy Jumble

A powerful wind has whipped through this neighborhood park. Some visitors' belongings have blown away and ended up with someone else. Figure out which items belong to the people listed on the right. Fill in the correct letter next to the names. We've done the first one for you.

ANSWERS ON PAGE 338

A Eleanor
____ Sam
____ Nicole
____ Steve
____ Carlos
____ Zak
____ Ava
____ Jill
____ Isabel
____ Daniel

161

What in the World?

COLOR YOUR WORLD
These photographs show close-up views of rainbow-colored objects. Unscramble the letters to identify what's in each picture.
Bonus: Use the highlighted letters to solve the puzzle below. ANSWERS ON PAGE 338

TWSASREE

_____

NBRWAOI

_____

ILPNRSKSE

_____

OODCLER ILSNECP

_____

LRBUEALM

_____

HOUSETRTBSHO

_____

RICCELOI

_____

ELOSTW

_____

AESHFRTE

_____

HINT: Leprechaun or not, anyone would be happy to find this under a rainbow.

ANSWER: ___ ___ ___ ___ ___ ___ G ___ ___ ___

Just Joking

Cheetah

KNOCK, KNOCK.

Who's there?
Aardvark.
Aardvark who?
Aardvark a million miles for you!

Q What did the **0** say to the **8**?

A Nice belt.

TOURIST: I'd like to purchase a ticket to the moon, please.
TOUR GUIDE: Sorry, sir. The moon is full tonight.

TONGUE TWISTER!

Say this fast three times:
Shelly is a selfish shellfish.

HA HA HA!

LARRY? ARE YOU IN THERE?

BONUS: Find 12 hearts in the scene.

NATIONAL GEOGRAPHIC
ANIMAL JAM ®

Twinkle Toes

In February, the *Animal Jam* crew meets at the dance club to celebrate a holiday called Friendship Festival. Can you guess what each character is thinking? Fill in the number that matches the correct animal.

1. "Put your hands in the air like you just don't care!"
2. "Robots have nothing on me."
3. "Let's do the bunny hop!"
4. "Aloha! Let's hula!"
5. "My moves really pack in the crowds."
6. "Too much dancing—time for a catnap."
7. "It's time for the fox trot!"

ANSWERS ON PAGE 338

EXPLORE!

NATIONAL GEOGRAPHIC KIDS' virtual world online: AnimalJam.com

Enter the special code **NGK2015** for a bonus!

The Funnies

"HE'D MAKE A FANTASTIC OUTFIELDER, COACH. HE'S GREAT AT CATCHING FLIES!"

"YOU'RE RIGHT. FROM UP HERE THEY ALL DO LOOK LIKE ANTS. HEY, I'M GETTING HUNGRY!"

"MAN, THIS BACKPACK GETS HEAVIER AND HEAVIER EVERY DAY."

"WHATEVER YOU DO, DON'T EVER CHALLENGE HIM TO A STARING CONTEST!"

"YOU KNOW, HALF THE FOOD THEY SPRINKLE IN HERE IS FOR ME!"

Funny FILL-IN
Spray 'n' Wash

Ask a friend to give you words to fill in the blanks in this story without showing it to him or her. Then read it out loud for a laugh.

CAR WASH! DONATIONS ACCEPTED

This weekend, my mother, sister, and I _____ our _____
                                        past-tense verb   adjective
_____ to a car wash. As a(n) _____ waved us in, we heard a(n)
type of transportation   type of job
_____ . A huge _____ was _____ cars! "_____ !"
funny sound   animal   verb ending in –ing   exclamation
we yelled. Using its _____ , it wiped the back of the _____ in front of us.
                      body part   noun
_____ dripped from a(n) _____ strapped to its hoof as it sprayed
something gross   noun
_____ with its trunk. Then the creature _____ the cars with its ears.
noun   past-tense verb
Everyone was covered in _____ . Who knows where that _____
                         type of liquid   same animal
came from—but our car has never been so _____ !
                                          adjective

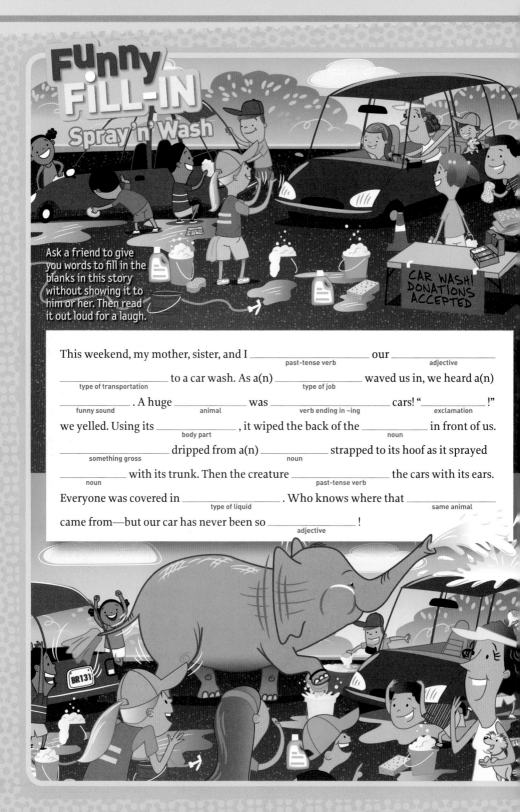

In Plane Sight

Can you name 10 items at this air show that rhyme with the word "plane"?

ANSWERS ON PAGE 338

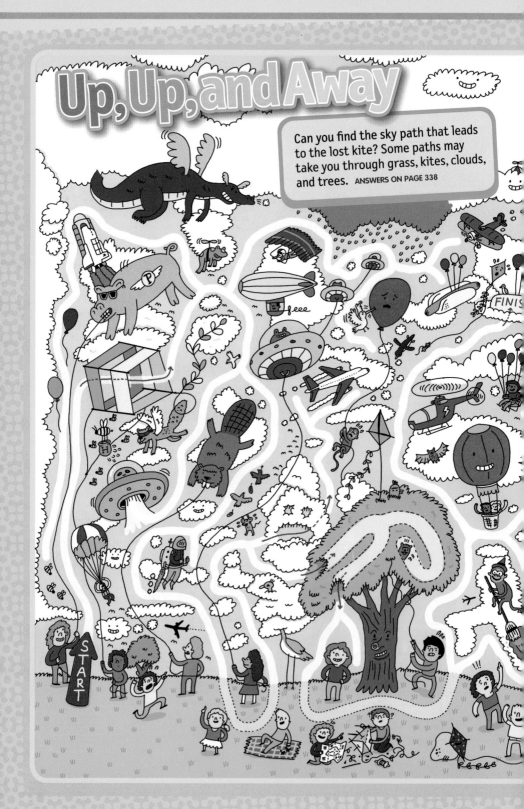

Up, Up, and Away

Can you find the sky path that leads to the lost kite? Some paths may take you through grass, kites, clouds, and trees. ANSWERS ON PAGE 338

FINISH

START

RAIN FOREST ROUNDUP

These photographs show close-up views of animals that live in the rain forest. Unscramble the letters to identify what's in each picture. **Bonus:** Use the highlighted letters to solve the puzzle below. ANSWERS ON PAGE 338

G R F O

_____

A B T

_____

O T S H L

_____

R G A A U J

_____

P R E V I

_____

A R P H N I A

_____

S P A G S R E H R O P

_____

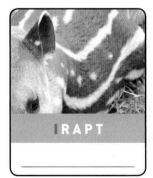

I R A P T

_____

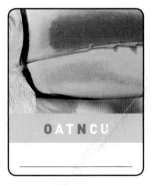

O A T N C U

_____

HINT: Where would you go to buy bananas from a loud primate?

ANSWER: _ H _ W _ _ R M _ K _ Y _ S _ E _

Just Joking

Guernsey Cow

KNOCK, KNOCK.

Who's there?
Olive.
Olive who?
Olive you.

Q How did the lion greet the impala?

A "Pleased to eat you!"

Q Why do birds fly south in the winter?

A It's easier than walking.

EMILY: Did you know you were built upside down?
ADAM: What do you mean?
EMILY: Your nose runs and your feet smell.

HA HA HA!

WAIT! I'M NOT NUTS! I'M JUST NUTS FOR YOU!

Funny Fill-In

Ka-ching!

Ask a friend to give you words to fill in the blanks in this story without showing it to him or her. Then read it out loud for a laugh.

_____ ! I just received _____ billion dollars from my _____
silly expression   large number   adjective

great-great-great-great-aunt for my birthday. I know exactly what I'll do with the _____ .
                                                                                    noun

First I'll buy the _____ . Maybe I could hire _____ to be my
                  favorite sports team   famous athlete

_____ ! I'm going to have all my _____ made of _____
type of job   article of clothing, plural   noun, plural

and build a roller coaster in my new _____ . I'll ride a (n) _____
                                     room of a house   verb ending in –ing

_____ to school—no more bus rides for me. And now I can get
type of transportation

_____ a(n) _____ like she always wanted. I think I'll even _____
female friend's name   noun   verb

a charity to save the _____ . I'm so rich, I can give my *parents* an allowance.
                      animal, plural

Cormorant fishermen light lanterns for night fishing on the Li River in Xingping, China. Instead of nets or lines, cormorant birds are used to catch fish.

Culture
Connection

20 CELEBRATIONS

① CHINESE NEW YEAR
February 19
Also called Lunar New Year, this holiday marks the new year according to the lunar calendar. Families celebrate with parades, feasts, and fireworks. Young people may receive gifts of money in red envelopes.

② HOLI
March 6
This festival in India celebrates spring and marks the triumph of good over evil. People cover one another with powdered paint, called *gulal*, and douse one another with buckets of colored water.

③ NYEPI
March 21
A national day of silence, this Hindu holiday marks Lunar New Year in Bali, Indonesia, and encourages meditation and reflection. Those who follow traditional customs do not talk, use electricity, travel, or eat for 24 hours.

④ QINGMING FESTIVAL
April 5
Also known as "grave sweeping day," this Chinese celebration calls on people to return to the graves of their deceased loved ones. There, they tidy up the grave, as well as light firecrackers, burn fake money, and leave food as an offer to the spirits.

⑤ EASTER
April 5
A Christian holiday that honors the resurrection of Jesus Christ, Easter is celebrated by giving baskets filled with gifts, decorated eggs, or candy to children.

⑥ VESAK DAY
May
Buddhists around the world observe Buddha's Birthday with special rituals including chanting and prayer, candlelight processions, and meditation.

⑦ BERMUDA DAY
May 25
The first day of the year that Bermudians take a dip in the ocean. It is also traditionally the first day on which Bermuda shorts are worn as business attire. To celebrate the holiday, there is a parade in Hamilton, and a road race from the west end of the island into Hamilton.

⑧ RAMADAN AND EID AL-FITR
June 18*–July 18**
A Muslim religious holiday, Ramadan is a month long, ending in the Eid Al-Fitr celebration. Observers fast during this month—eating only after sunset. Muslims pray for forgiveness and hope to purify themselves through observance.

⑨ ST. JOHN'S NIGHT
June 21
In Poland, people celebrate the longest day of the year—also known as the summer solstice—with rituals including making bonfires, floating flower wreaths down a stream, and releasing thousands of paper lanterns into the night sky.

⑩ BASTILLE DAY
July 14
The French call this day *La Fête Nationale*, or the celebration of the start of the French Revolution in 1789. In Paris, fireworks light up the night skies while dance parties spill into the streets.

*Begins at sundown.
**Dates may vary slightly by location.

Around the World

11 MELON DAY
August 9
Since 1994, people in the Asian nation Turkmenistan have taken a day—aptly named Melon Day—to celebrate the country's sweet muskmelons.

12 NAG PANCHAMI
August 19
In Nepal and India, Hindus worship snakes—and keep evil spirits out of their homes—by sticking images of serpents on their doors and making offerings to the revered reptiles.

13 ROSH HASHANAH
September 13*–15
A Jewish religious holiday marking the beginning of a new year on the Hebrew calendar. Celebrations include prayer, ritual foods, and a day of rest.

14 OKTOBERFEST
September 19–October 4
Originally celebrating the marriage of Bavarian royalty back in 1810, Oktoberfest is now a mega-festival celebrated all over the world. People enjoy food, drink, music, and merriment.

15 SUKKOT
September 27*–October 4
A Jewish holiday celebrating the fall harvest, when people build (and, often, eat and sleep) in outdoor temporary huts called Sukkahs.

16 GUY FAWKES DAY
November 5
Over 400 years ago, a man named Guy Fawkes plotted with other conspirators to blow up the British Parliament. He failed, and Brits still celebrate his demise by lighting bonfires and setting off fireworks.

17 DIWALI
November 11–15
India's largest and most important holiday. People light their homes with clay lamps to symbolize the inner light that protects against spiritual darkness.

18 HANUKKAH
December 6*–14
This Jewish holiday is eight days long. It commemorates the rededication of the Temple in Jerusalem. Hanukkah celebrations include the lighting of menorah candles for eight days and the exchange of gifts.

19 CHRISTMAS DAY
December 25
A Christian holiday marking the birth of Jesus Christ, Christmas is usually celebrated by decorating trees, exchanging presents, and having festive gatherings.

20 BOXING DAY
December 26
Some people think this national holiday in Great Britain, Australia, Canada, and New Zealand was initially designated as a day to box up donations for the poor. Today? It's all about shopping, parties, and playing soccer.

What's Your Chinese Horoscope?
Locate your birth year to find out.

In Chinese astrology the zodiac runs on a 12-year cycle, based on the lunar calendar. Each year corresponds to one of 12 animals, each representing one of 12 personality types. Read on to find out which animal year you were born in and what that might say about you.

RAT
1972, '84, '96, 2008
Say cheese! You're attractive, charming, and creative. When you get mad, you can have really sharp teeth!

RABBIT
1975, '87, '99, 2011
Your ambition and talent make you jump at opportunity. You also keep your ears open for gossip.

HORSE
1966, '78, '90, 2002, '14
Being happy is your "mane" goal. And while you're smart and hardworking, your teacher may ride you for talking too much.

ROOSTER
1969, '81, '93, 2005
You crow about your adventures, but inside you're really shy. You're thoughtful, capable, brave, and talented.

OX
1973, '85, '97, 2009
You're smart, patient, and as strong as an ... well, you know what. Though you're a leader, you never brag.

DRAGON
1976, '88, 2000, '12
You're on fire! Health, energy, honesty, and bravery make you a living legend.

SHEEP
1967, '79, '91, 2003, '15
Gentle as a lamb, you're also artistic, compassionate, and wise. You're often shy.

DOG
1970, '82, '94, 2006
Often the leader of the pack, you're loyal and honest. You can also keep a secret.

TIGER
1974, '86, '98, 2010
You may be a nice person, but no one should ever enter your room without asking—you might attack!

SNAKE
1977, '89, 2001, '13
You may not speak often, but you're very smart. You always seem to have a stash of cash.

MONKEY
1968, '80, '92, 2004
No "monkey see, monkey do" for you. You're a clever problem-solver with an excellent memory.

PIG
1971, '83, '95, 2007
Even though you're courageous, honest, and kind, you never hog all the attention.

ANNIVERSARIES

Annual	1 year
Biennial	2 years
Triennial	3 years
Quadrennial	4 years
Quinquennial	5 years
Sexennial	6 years
Septennial	7 years
Octennial	8 years
Novennial	9 years
Decennial	10 years
Undecennial	11 years
Duodecennial	12 years
Tredecennial	13 years
Quattuordecennial	14 years
Quindecennial	15 years
Vigintennial or vicennial	20 years
Semicentennial or quinquagenary	50 years
Semisesquicentennial	75 years
Centennial	100 years
Quasquicentennial	125 years
Sesquicentennial	150 years
Demisemiseptcentennial or quartoseptcentennial	175 years
Bicentennial	200 years
Semiquincentennial	250 years
Tercentennial or tricentennial	300 years
Semiseptcentennial	350 years
Quadricentennial or quatercentenary	400 years
Quincentennial	500 years
Sexcentennial	600 years
Septicentennial or septuacentennial	700 years
Octocentennial	800 years
Nonacentennial	900 years
Millennial	1,000 years
Bimillennial	2,000 years

CULTURE CONNECTION

2015 CALENDAR

JANUARY
S	M	T	W	T	F	S
				1	2	3
4	5	6	7	8	9	10
11	12	13	14	15	16	17
18	19	20	21	22	23	24
25	26	27	28	29	30	31

FEBRUARY
S	M	T	W	T	F	S
1	2	3	4	5	6	7
8	9	10	11	12	13	14
15	16	17	18	19	20	21
22	23	24	25	26	27	28

MARCH
S	M	T	W	T	F	S
1	2	3	4	5	6	7
8	9	10	11	12	13	14
15	16	17	18	19	20	21
22	23	24	25	26	27	28
29	30	31				

APRIL
S	M	T	W	T	F	S
			1	2	3	4
5	6	7	8	9	10	11
12	13	14	15	16	17	18
19	20	21	22	23	24	25
26	27	28	29	30		

MAY
S	M	T	W	T	F	S
					1	2
3	4	5	6	7	8	9
10	11	12	13	14	15	16
17	18	19	20	21	22	23
24	25	26	27	28	29	30
31						

JUNE
S	M	T	W	T	F	S
	1	2	3	4	5	6
7	8	9	10	11	12	13
14	15	16	17	18	19	20
21	22	23	24	25	26	27
28	29	30				

JULY
S	M	T	W	T	F	S
			1	2	3	4
5	6	7	8	9	10	11
12	13	14	15	16	17	18
19	20	21	22	23	24	25
26	27	28	29	30	31	

AUGUST
S	M	T	W	T	F	S
						1
2	3	4	5	6	7	8
9	10	11	12	13	14	15
16	17	18	19	20	21	22
23	24	25	26	27	28	29
30	31					

SEPTEMBER
S	M	T	W	T	F	S
		1	2	3	4	5
6	7	8	9	10	11	12
13	14	15	16	17	18	19
20	21	22	23	24	25	26
27	28	29	30			

OCTOBER
S	M	T	W	T	F	S
				1	2	3
4	5	6	7	8	9	10
11	12	13	14	15	16	17
18	19	20	21	22	23	24
25	26	27	28	29	30	31

NOVEMBER
S	M	T	W	T	F	S
1	2	3	4	5	6	7
8	9	10	11	12	13	14
15	16	17	18	19	20	21
22	23	24	25	26	27	28
29	30					

DECEMBER
S	M	T	W	T	F	S
		1	2	3	4	5
6	7	8	9	10	11	12
13	14	15	16	17	18	19
20	21	22	23	24	25	26
27	28	29	30	31		

HALLOWEEN PET PARADE

Some of the sweetest Halloween goodies come wrapped . . . in fur! Millions of pets will wear a disguise for the holiday. Check out these fetching trick-or-treaters.

These pets like wearing costumes, but yours may not. Never force your pet to do something it does not want to do.

I AM ONE CLASSY KITTY.

ELROY THE CAT SHOWS SOME STYLE DRESSED AS THE MAD HATTER FROM *ALICE'S ADVENTURES IN WONDERLAND.*

"MEOW." UM, I MEAN "RIBBIT."

ROSIE THE KITTEN HOPS INTO HAL-LOWEEN WITH HER FROG COSTUME.

TIME FOR MY CLOSE-UP.

DUTCHESS THE STANDARD POODLE SPORTS A PINK FROCK AND SHADES.

FETCHING COSTUMES

What were the HOTTEST pet costumes last Halloween? Take a look at some of the trendiest disguises.

1. pumpkin	4. bee
2. devil	5. cat
3. hot dog	6. witch

NATIONAL GEOGRAPHIC KIDS SCANNER

SCAN THIS PAGE!
GET BONUS MOBILE CONTENT! Download the free NG Kids scanner app. Directions on inside front cover.

Cool Carvings

Show your pumpkin's true personality with these wacky designs. Use a child-safe carving tool or ask an adult for help.

Express Yourself!◄

Let your jack-o'-lantern tell the world how it feels with emoticon smileys. It'll make your friends LOL!

Ahoy, Matey!

Pumpkins can wear costumes, too. Hats, inexpensive jewelry, and other accessories can create a pirate, cowboy, or even a baseball player.

Spell It Out ◄

Who says a jack-o'-lantern needs a face? Carve spooky messages into your pumpkins instead.

◄ Stack 'Em Up

Build a snowman by placing the biggest pumpkin at the bottom and the smallest one on top. Slant the knife when you cut off the tops, creating a ledge to support another pumpkin

CREATE THE PERFECT DESIGN

Before you start cutting, sketch your design on white paper. Tape the paper to your pumpkin where you want the design to be. Punch along the lines of the sketch with a pin, poking through the paper and into the pumpkin. Then carve along the dotted lines you've made on the pumpkin.

1

IN SPAIN, EATING **TWELVE GRAPES** AT THE STROKE OF MIDNIGHT ON NEW YEAR'S DAY BRINGS GOOD LUCK.

2

Believe it or not, in several cultures it's considered **good luck to be POOPED ON** by a bird.

3

IN ENGLAND, FINDING A SPIDER IN YOUR WEDDING DRESS IS CONSIDERED GOOD LUCK.

4

IN GERMANY, IT'S GOOD LUCK TO **TOUCH** A CHIMNEY SWEEP'S BRUSH.

15 COOL THINGS ABOUT

5

Many people believe **CROSSING THEIR FINGERS** brings good luck.

6

AROUND THE WORLD, PEOPLE BELIEVE **LADYBUGS ARE A SIGN OF GOOD LUCK.**

7

EIGHT IS A LUCKY NUMBER IN CHINA: MORE THAN 300,000 COUPLES IN CHINA **GOT MARRIED ON 8/o8/o8.**

8

WEARING **YELLOW UNDERWEAR** ON NEW YEAR'S DAY IN PERU IS CONSIDERED LUCKY.

9 FOR MORE THAN **2,600 YEARS,** PEOPLE IN WESTERN EUROPE HAVE CONSIDERED **THE FEET OF RABBITS TO BE LUCKY.**

10 THE PHRASE "**BREAK A LEG**" IS SUPPOSED TO BRING GOOD LUCK TO PERFORMERS ABOUT TO GO ONSTAGE.

11 Four-leaf clovers are considered LUCKY, but perhaps the most lucky clover is the WORLD RECORD HOLDER for **most leaves, 56.**

12 MANY CULTURES CONSIDER THE NUMBER 7 TO BE LUCKY: IN THE UNITED STATES, THE AVERAGE NUMBER OF WEDDINGS TRIPLED ON 7/07/07.

LUCK

13 IN THE U.S. SOUTH, EATING BLACK-EYED PEAS **ON NEW YEAR'S DAY** IS BELIEVED TO BRING GOOD LUCK.

14

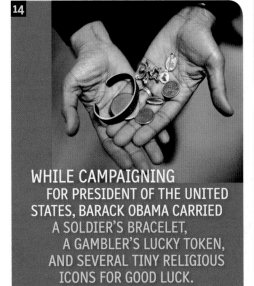

WHILE CAMPAIGNING FOR PRESIDENT OF THE UNITED STATES, BARACK OBAMA CARRIED A SOLDIER'S BRACELET, A GAMBLER'S LUCKY TOKEN, AND SEVERAL TINY RELIGIOUS ICONS FOR GOOD LUCK.

15 Hanging a horseshoe over a door is believed to bring good luck in the United States.

CHEETAH

WHISKERS CAN BE TRICKY.

The most useful tools? "A fine paintbrush and a steady hand," Daniele says. "My favorite is a cheetah because it was my first and brought me luck."

THE REAL ANIMAL CHEETAHS NEED TO DRINK ONLY ONCE EVERY THREE TO FOUR DAYS.

HANDIMALS

MACAW

"THE MOST IMPORTANT THING IS TO PAINT THE EYE

with the shape and expression of each animal," Daniele says. "It gives character and life to the art."

THE REAL ANIMAL

TO OPEN NUTS, A MACAW USES ITS BEAK, WHICH IS STRONG ENOUGH TO BREAK THROUGH A BROOMSTICK.

MOOSE

THE ARTIST USED THREE HANDS

to make the moose and 75 fingers for the grass. "The moose was the most complicated to build," Daniele says.

THESE ARE HUMAN FINGERS!

THE REAL ANIMAL

A MALE MOOSE'S SET OF ANTLERS CAN WEIGH MORE THAN 70 POUNDS (32 KG).

CHECK OUT THESE **WILD HANDMADE** CREATIONS.

What do you get when you cross a human hand with an animal? A "handimal"! Artist Guido Daniele, who lives in Milan, Italy, positions people's hands into animal shapes, and then paints them to create realistic works of art. He paints the animals onto the hands of models—usually his son or daughter. Check out these "handimals" and some of the secrets to Daniele's art. In this case, it's OK to "handle" the animals!

IGUANA

SMALL DETAILS CAN BE EASIER TO PAINT

while the hand is relaxed. Large features are painted while the hand is in the animal position. The iguana took the most time—between four and six hours. "It takes a lot of patience," Daniele says.

THE REAL ANIMAL

IGUANAS CAN LEAP INTO THE WATER FROM A TREE AND USE THEIR POWERFUL TAILS TO SWIM AWAY FROM PREDATORS.

Food That Fools You

SOAPY ORANGE JUICE

Bubbles in freshly poured juice disappear quickly. To keep this OJ looking fresh for the photo shoot, stylists created long-lasting bubbles by mixing two drops of soap with some juice in a separate container. These were then added on top of the drink with a spoon.

PIN THE BLUEBERRY ON THE PANCAKE

The fruit on top of this stack won't be rolling away anytime soon. A pin was pushed through each berry and into the pancakes to hold it in place. Some stylists use toothpicks to help position food, such as olives in a salad.

FRUIT COLORING

Sliced strawberries often have bright white insides that don't photograph well. To make the fruit camera-ready, stylists brush red food coloring over the white areas with a small paintbrush. White spots on a strawberry's skin can be colored with dabs of lipstick.

SNIP 'N' SPRAY

Your hair isn't the only thing that sometimes needs a trim. If a pancake isn't perfectly round, stylists will snip it into shape with scissors. A flapjack stack might also be coated with a spray people normally use to protect furniture from stains. The spray keeps the syrup from soaking in.

Your tummy may be rumbling, but if you sink your teeth into *this* chow, you'll get a surprise. The breakfast items are filled with dish soap, pins, cardboard, and other things you would never eat.

Even an amazing dish will start to look bad or lose shape if left out for too long. So food stylists and photographers have some pretty unappetizing techniques to make food appear tasty for things such as ads and cookbooks. A rolled-up tortilla might be glued so it doesn't unfold during a shoot. Or lemon juice could be added to a banana to keep it from turning brown. Feast your eyes on more secrets of food styling.

GOT GLUE?

This bowl isn't really brimming with cereal. A circular piece of cardboard was fitted inside the dish near the rim. That way, cereal pieces couldn't sink to the bottom. A thin layer of glue and flakes were added on top of the cardboard. Why glue? Unlike milk, glue won't make flakes soggy.

SIZZLING SYRUP

Stylists wanted to make this maple syrup look really thick. So before it was drizzled onto the pancakes, the syrup was heated in a saucepan to about 270°F (132°C). (That's more than twice as hot as warm syrup you'd eat.) As the temperature rose, water evaporated and the syrup thickened.

SHAPIN' BACON

To give bacon a wavy shape, stylists first mold a sheet of tinfoil into rows of ridges and fit the strips of raw meat over the foil. They then roast the bacon in an oven. As the meat cooks, its shape hardens.

187

CHEW ON THIS

TACOS!

The word "taco" hasn't always been on restaurant menus. In the 18th century, "tacos" were charges of gunpowder wrapped in paper used by Mexican miners. The wrap concept stuck when cooks started calling tortillas stuffed with meat and beans "tacos." Chow down on more filling facts.

Made from avocado, **GUACAMOLE** comes from the Aztec word *ahuacamolli* (ah-wah-kah-MOH-lee), or avocado sauce.

Natural **CHEDDAR CHEESE** has an almost white color. The bright orange color you see in grocery store cheddar comes from food coloring.

People in the United States spend more money on **SALSA** than on ketchup.

Crunchy corn **TACO** shells have been in U.S. cookbooks only since 1939. But soft tortillas have been around since the 13th century.

One type of **BLACK BEAN** tastes like mushrooms.

MAKE YOUR OWN TACOS

Tacos are crunchy sandwiches—the tortilla is like the bread, which you can stuff with anything you want! Get a parent's help to create a yummy taco.

 Warm a skillet over medium heat. Cook 1½ pounds (680 g) ground beef or turkey for 6 to 8 minutes.

 Add 1 teaspoon (5 mL) of cumin and ¾ teaspoon (4 mL) of salt. Stir occasionally for 2 to 3 minutes.

 Fill 8 taco shells with the meat and top with 1 diced avocado, sour cream, and salsa.

4 Sprinkle with cheddar cheese.

MUSHROOMS are some seriously freaky fungi. They've been grown in caves and buried in, um, excrement, and some even glow in the dark.

PIZZA!

Pizza may have originated 2,000 years ago when the ancient Greeks prepared round, flat breads covered with oil, herbs, and spices. In 1830, chefs in Naples, Italy, cooked their crust in an oven lined with rocks from a nearby volcano. Some say that could have been the first pizzeria. The restaurant is still open today. Gobble up these other tasty tidbits.

People in the United States eat about 250 million pounds (113 million kg) of **PEPPERONI** a year, more than any other pizza topping.

BELL PEPPERS are fruits, not vegetables.

Most **CHEESE** is made from cow's, goat's, or sheep's milk. The traditional way to make mozzarella is from water buffalo's milk.

TOMATOES can be red, orange, yellow, green, purple, and even striped.

MAKE YOUR OWN PIZZA

Created in Naples, Italy, the Margherita pizza represents the colors in the Italian flag: red tomatoes, green basil, and white cheese. **Get a parent's help to make your own.**

1 Bake premade pizza dough at 450°F (232°C) for about 5 minutes. Brush the crust lightly with olive oil.

2 Top dough with 4 or 5 thin tomato slices, and a pinch each of dried oregano, salt, and pepper. Sprinkle 1 cup (240 mL) of shredded mozzarella on top.

3 Bake until golden for 10 to 12 minutes. Sprinkle ½ cup (120 mL) of chopped fresh basil over the top.

12 Ways to Say Happy Birthday

1 **ARABIC** Eid milaad sa'eed
2 **FRENCH (CANADA)** Bonne Fête
3 **GERMAN** Alles Gute zum Geburtstag
4 **GREEK** Hronia polla
5 **HAWAIIAN** Hau'oli La Hanau
6 **HEBREW** Yom Huledet Sameakh
7 **HINDI** Janmadin mubarak ho
8 **MANDARIN** Shengrì kuàilè
9 **RUSSIAN** S dniom rojdeniya
10 **SPANISH** ¡Feliz cumpleaños!
11 **SWAHILI** Nakutakia mema kwa siku yako ya kuzaliwa!
12 **TURKISH** Dogum günün kutlu olsun

LANGUAGES IN PERIL

TODAY, there are more than 7,000 languages spoken on Earth. But by 2100, more than half of those may disappear. In fact, experts say one language dies every two weeks, due to the increasing dominance of larger languages, such as English, Spanish, and Mandarin. So what can be done to keep dialects from disappearing? Efforts like National Geographic's Enduring Voices Project are now tracking down and documenting the world's most threatened indigenous languages, such as Tofa, spoken by only 30 people in Siberia, and Magati Ke, from Aboriginal Australia. The hope is to preserve these languages— and the cultures they belong to.

10 LEADING LANGUAGES

Approximate population of first-language speakers (in millions)

Language	Population
1. Chinese*	1,213
2. Spanish	329
3. English	328
4. Arabic	221
5. Hindi	182
6. Bengali	181
7. Portuguese	178
8. Russian	144
9. Japanese	122
10. German	90

Some languages have only a few hundred speakers, while Chinese has some one billion two hundred thirteen million native speakers worldwide. That's more than triple the next largest group of language speakers. Colonial expansion, trade, and migration account for the spread of the other most widely spoken languages. With growing use of the Internet, English is becoming the language of the technology age.

*Includes all forms of the language.

Bet you didn't know

6 page-turning facts about **books**

1 *Percy Jackson and the Olympians* began as a bedtime story for author **Rick Riordan's son.**

2 In L. Frank Baum's *The Wonderful Wizard of Oz* Dorothy's **shoes** are described as **silver.**

3 **Each book** in R.L. Stine's *Goosebumps* series took about **8 days** to **write.**

4 *Treasure Island* was **inspired by a map** that author **Robert Louis Stevenson** drew with his **12-year-old** stepson.

5 In an early version, **Roald Dahl's** *James and the Giant Peach* featured a **giant cherry.**

6 **J.K. Rowling** considered calling the **final** *Harry Potter* book *Harry Potter and the Elder Wand.*

MONEY Around the World!

THE GREEK GODDESS ATHENA AND HER **SACRED OWL** APPEARED ON COINS MINTED OVER 2,000 YEARS AGO.

A CAMBODIAN LEADER **ONCE ABOLISHED THE USE OF MONEY.**

THE SOUTHERN CROSS CONSTELLATION APPEARS ON **BRAZILIAN COINS.**

BOTSWANA'S CURRENCY IS NAMED *PULA,* OR RAIN, WHICH IS VALUABLE IN THIS DESERT NATION.

THIS WILL BUY YOU A LOT OF DOG TREATS.

BELGIUM ISSUED A COIN FEATURING THE CARTOON **HERO TINTIN** AND HIS DOG, **SNOWY.**

FIBERS FROM THE ABACA PLANT, A CLOSE RELATIVE OF THE BANANA PLANT, ARE USED IN **JAPANESE BANKNOTES.**

IN THE NETHERLANDS IN 1636, **TULIPS** WERE SO VALUABLE THAT SOME COST AS MUCH AS **A HOUSE.**

CANADIAN BANKNOTES COME WITH **RAISED DOT PATTERNS** FOR VISUALLY IMPAIRED PEOPLE.

IN INDIA, THE SLANG TERM FOR THE AMOUNT OF **100,000** RUPEES IS *PETI,* OR SUITCASE. YOU MIGHT NEED ONE TO CARRY THAT MUCH MONEY!

The PERTH MINT
in Australia recently minted a 2.2-pound (1-kg) solid-gold coin worth
$62,950.

Peru's currency is named the NUEVO SOL, which is Spanish for "NEW SUN."

A MINT ERROR ADDED AN EXTRA HUMP to the bison on some of the 2005 KANSAS STATE, USA, QUARTERS.

IT'S GONNA BE HARD FITTING ME INTO A WALLET.

A Korean artist is known for his "moneygami"— origami made out of banknotes.

USING A METAL DETECTOR, TWO ENGLISH MEN UNCOVERED 206 ROMAN COINS DATING BACK **2,200 YEARS.**

A 1922 German banknote is called the
"VAMPIRE NOTE"
because some claim that a vampire is biting the neck of the worker on the bill.

VAMPIRE BITE?

THE U.S. MINT employs full-time sculptors to create models FOR COINS.

The U.S. Bureau of Engraving and Printing uses
8.5 TONS (7.7 MT) **OF INK** each day to print money.

KING TUT appears on the Egyptian one-pound coin.

MONEY TIP!
ANYTIME YOU BUY SOMETHING **ON SALE**, PUT WHAT YOU SAVED IN YOUR PIGGY BANK.

MYTHOLOGY

GREEK

The ancient Greeks believed that many gods and goddesses ruled the universe. According to this mythology, the Olympians lived high atop Greece's Mount Olympus. Each of these 12 principal gods and goddesses had a unique personality that corresponded to particular aspects of life, such as love or death.

THE OLYMPIANS

Aphrodite was the goddess of love and beauty.

Apollo, Zeus's son, was the god of the sun, music, and healing. Artemis was his twin.

Ares, Zeus's son, was the god of war.

Artemis, Zeus's daughter and Apollo's twin, was the goddess of the hunt and of childbirth.

Athena, born from the forehead of Zeus, was the goddess of wisdom and crafts.

Demeter was the goddess of fertility and nature.

Hades, Zeus's brother, was the god of the underworld and the dead.

Hephaestus, the son of Hera, was the god of fire.

Hera, the wife and older sister of Zeus, was the goddess of women and marriage.

Hermes, Zeus's son, was the messenger of the gods.

Poseidon, the brother of Zeus, was the god of the sea and earthquakes.

Zeus was the most powerful of the gods and the top Olympian. He wielded a thunderbolt and was the god of the sky and thunder.

EGYPTIAN

Egyptian mythology is based on a creation myth that tells of an egg that appeared on the ocean. When the egg hatched, out came Ra, the sun god. As a result, ancient Egyptians became worshippers of the sun and of the nine original deities, most of whom were the children and grandchildren of Ra.

THE NINE DEITIES

Geb, son of Shu and Tefnut, was the god of the Earth.

Isis (Ast), daughter of Geb and Nut, was the goddess of fertility and motherhood.

Nephthys (Nebet-Hut), daughter of Geb and Nut, was protector of the dead.

Nut, daughter of Shu and Tefnut, was the goddess of the sky.

Osiris (Usir), son of Geb and Nut, was the god of the afterlife.

Ra (Re), the sun god, is generally viewed as the creator. He represents life and health.

Seth (Set), son of Geb and Nut, was the god of the desert and chaos.

Shu, son of Ra, was the god of air.

Tefnut, daughter of Ra, was the goddess of rain.

All cultures around the world have unique legends and traditions that have been passed down over generations. Many myths refer to gods or supernatural heroes who are responsible for occurrences in the world. For example, Norse mythology tells of the red-bearded Thor, the god of thunder, who is responsible for creating lightning and thunderstorms. And many creation myths, especially from some of North America's native cultures, tell of an earth-diver represented as an animal that brings a piece of sand or mud up from the deep sea. From this tiny piece of earth, the entire world takes shape.

NORSE

ROMAN

Norse mythology originated in Scandinavia, in northern Europe. It was complete with gods and goddesses who lived in a heavenly place called Asgard that could be reached only by crossing a rainbow bridge.

While Norse mythology is lesser known, we use it every day. Most days of the week are named after Norse gods, including some of these major deities.

NORSE GODS

Balder was the god of light and beauty.

Freya was the goddess of love, beauty, and fertility.

Frigg, for whom Friday was named, was the queen of Asgard. She was the goddess of marriage, motherhood, and the home.

Heimdall was the watchman of the rainbow bridge and the guardian of the gods.

Hel, the daughter of Loki, was the goddess of death.

Loki, a shape-shifter, was a trickster who helped the gods—and caused them problems.

Skadi was the goddess of winter and of the hunt. She is often represented as "The Snow Queen."

Thor, for whom Thursday was named, was the god of thunder and lightning.

Tyr, for whom Tuesday was named, was the god of the sky and war.

Wodan, for whom Wednesday was named, was the god of war, wisdom, death, and magic.

Much of Roman mythology was adopted from Greek mythology, but the Romans also developed a lot of original myths as well. The gods of Roman mythology lived everywhere, and each had a role to play. There were thousands of Roman gods, but here are a few of the stars of Roman myths.

ANCIENT ROMAN GODS

Ceres was the goddess of the harvest and motherly love.

Diana, daughter of Jupiter, was the goddess of hunting and the moon.

Juno, Jupiter's wife, was the goddess of women and fertility.

Jupiter, the patron of Rome and master of the gods, was the god of the sky.

Mars, the son of Jupiter and Juno, was the god of war.

Mercury, the son of Jupiter, was the messenger of the gods and the god of travelers.

Minerva was the goddess of wisdom, learning, and the arts and crafts.

Neptune, the brother of Jupiter, was the god of the sea.

Venus was the goddess of love and beauty.

Vesta was the goddess of fire and the hearth. She was one of the most important of the Roman deities.

World Religions

A round the world, religion takes many forms. Some belief systems, such as Christianity, Islam, and Judaism, are monotheistic, meaning that followers believe in just one supreme being. Others, like Hinduism, Shintoism, and most native belief systems, are polytheistic, meaning that many of their followers believe in multiple gods.

All of the major religions have their origins in Asia, but they have spread around the world. Christianity, with the largest number of followers, has three divisions—Roman Catholic, Eastern Orthodox, and Protestant. Islam, with about one-fifth of all believers, has two main divisions—Sunni and Shiite. Hinduism and Buddhism account for almost another one-fifth of believers. Judaism, dating back some 4,000 years, has more than 13 million followers, less than one percent of all believers.

CHRISTIANITY

Based on the teachings of Jesus Christ, a Jew born some 2,000 years ago in the area of modern-day Israel, Christianity has spread worldwide and actively seeks converts. Followers in Switzerland (above) participate in an Easter season procession with lanterns and crosses.

BUDDHISM

Founded about 2,400 years ago in northern India by the Hindu prince Gautama Buddha, Buddhism spread throughout East and Southeast Asia. Buddhist temples have statues, such as the Mihintale Buddha (above) in Sri Lanka.

HINDUISM

Dating back more than 4,000 years, Hinduism is practiced mainly in India. Hindus follow sacred texts known as the Vedas and believe in reincarnation. During the festival of Navratri, which honors the goddess Durga, the Garba dance is performed (above).

CLOSE-UP

Now that's a
BIG crowd!

It has been 1,200 years since the bishop of Rome became known as the pope. Today, the pope is still the head of the Roman Catholic Church. Every Easter Sunday about 100,000 people gather in St. Peter's Square in Vatican City to receive his blessing.

ISLAM

Muslims believe that the Koran, Islam's sacred book, records the words of Allah (God) as revealed to the Prophet Muhammad beginning around A.D. 610. Believers (above) circle the Kaaba in the Haram Mosque in Mecca, Saudi Arabia, the spiritual center of the faith.

JUDAISM

The traditions, laws, and beliefs of Judaism date back to Abraham (the Patriarch) and the Torah (the first five books of the Old Testament). Followers pray before the Western Wall (above), which stands below Islam's Dome of the Rock in Jerusalem.

STUMP YOUR PARENTS

CULTURE CONNECTION QUIZ

Give your 'rents a crash course in culture by testing their knowledge of happenings around the world. ANSWERS BELOW

1 During the holiday of Sukkot, where do people eat and sleep?
a. their cars
b. restaurants
c. outdoor huts
d. their bedroom

2 **True or false?** Hinduism dates back more than 100,000 years.

3 Aside from being Zeus's son, Ares is also the Greek god of _____?

ZEUS

4 How many languages are spoken on Earth?
a. too many to count
b. 20
c. 50,000
d. more than 7,000

5 According to the Chinese Horoscope, 2015 is the year of the _____?

Not **STUMPED** yet?
Check out the *National Geographic Kids*
Quiz Whiz collection for more
crazy **CULTURE** questions!

ANSWERS:
1. c; 2. False. It dates back more than 4,000 years; 3. War; 4. d; 5. Sheep

HOMEWORK HELP

Explore a New Culture

INDIAN STAMP

5-RUPEE COIN

INDIAN FLAG

You're a student, but you're also a citizen of the world. Writing a report on a foreign nation or your own country is a great way to better understand and appreciate how people in other parts of the world live. Pick the country of your ancestors, one that's been in the news, or one that you'd like to visit someday.

Passport to Success

A country report follows the format of an expository essay because you're "exposing" information about the country you choose.

Simple Steps

1. RESEARCH Gathering information is the most important step in writing a good country report. Look to Internet sources, encyclopedias, books, magazine and newspaper articles, and other sources to find important and interesting details about your subject.

2. ORGANIZE YOUR NOTES Put the information you gathered into a rough outline. For example, sort everything you found about the country's system of government, climate, etc.

3. WRITE IT UP Follow the basic structure of good writing: introduction, body, and conclusion. Remember that each paragraph should have a topic sentence that is then supported by facts and details. Incorporate the information from your notes, but make sure it's in your own words. And make your writing flow with good transitions and descriptive language.

4. ADD VISUALS Include maps, diagrams, photos, and other visual aids.

5. PROOFREAD AND REVISE Correct any mistakes, and polish your language. Do your best!

6. CITE YOUR SOURCES Be sure to keep a record of your sources.

Wonders of
Nature

Weather and Climate

Weather is the condition of the atmosphere—temperature, precipitation, humidity, and wind—at a given place at a given time. Climate, however, is the average weather for a particular place over a long period of time. Different places on Earth have different climates, but climate is not a random occurrence. It is a pattern that is controlled by factors such as latitude, elevation, prevailing winds, the temperature of ocean currents, and location on land relative to water. Climate is generally constant, but evidence indicates that human activity is causing a change in the patterns of climate.

WEATHER EXTREMES

MOST SNOW RECORDED IN ONE SEASON: 1,140 inches (29 m) in Mount Baker, Washington, U.S.A.

FASTEST TEMPERATURE RISE: 49˚F (27.2˚C) in 15 minutes, in Rapid City, South Dakota, U.S.A.

MOST DAYS IN A ROW ABOVE 100˚F (37.8˚C): 160 days in Marble Bar, Western Australia

GLOBAL CLIMATE ZONES

Climatologists, people who study climate, have created different systems for classifying climates. One often-used system is called the Köppen system, which classifies climate zones according to precipitation, temperature, and vegetation. It has five major categories—Tropical, Dry, Temperate, Cold, and Polar—with a sixth category for locations where high elevations override other factors.

ARCTIC OCEAN

ARCTIC CIRCLE

TROPIC OF CANCER

ATLANTIC OCEAN

PACIFIC OCEAN

EQUATOR

PACIFIC OCEAN

INDIAN OCEAN

TROPIC OF CAPRICORN

ANTARCTIC CIRCLE

Climate

Tropical   Dry   Temperate   Cold   Polar

WEATHER COMPARISONS

Weather events can be so big and widespread that it's sometimes hard to comprehend them. For example, a single hurricane can cover hundreds of miles; its eye alone can be up to 200 miles (320 km) wide. That's about as far as Paris, France, is from London, England, U.K. But weather is also a part of daily life. Let's think about weather in terms of some everyday objects and events.

Is It Hot Enough to Fry an Egg on a Sidewalk?

It's possible for sidewalks to get hot enough (158°F/70°C), but once an egg hits the surface, the sidewalk cools. The sun alone can't cook the egg thoroughly.

How Fast Is a Hurricane?

A powerful hurricane can reach wind speeds of more than 155 miles an hour (249 kph). That's about as fast as some Indy cars speed around the track.

How Much Rain Is in a Snowfall?

Snowflakes come in many different shapes and sizes, so each snowfall contains a different amount of moisture. Rule of thumb: 10 inches (25 cm) of snow is equal to an inch (2.5 cm) of rain.

1
The largest hurricanes can measure ten miles (16 km) from top to bottom.

2
RAINDROPS are shaped more like hamburger buns than like teardrops!

3
A RAINDROP'S top speed is 18 mph (29 kph).

4
TORNADOES SPIN COUNTERCLOCKWISE IN THE NORTHERN HEMISPHERE AND CLOCKWISE IN THE SOUTHERN HEMISPHERE.

15 COOL THINGS ABOUT

5
The world's largest snowball fight had 5,387 participants.

6
THE HIGHEST WEATHER STATION ON EARTH IS LOCATED AT 26,000 FEET (7,925 M) ON MOUNT EVEREST.

7
In a double rainbow, the inner rainbow has the red on top. The outer one has the red on the bottom!

8 The lifetime of a typical fluffy cotton-ball-looking cumulus cloud is 5 to 40 minutes.

9 A LIGHTNING FLASH IS NO MORE THAN ONE INCH (2.5 CM) WIDE.

10 SOME PEOPLE THINK IT WILL BE A SEVERE WINTER IF SQUIRRELS HAVE BUSHY TAILS IN FALL, BUT SCIENTISTS HAVE NOT FOUND EVIDENCE TO SUPPORT THIS THEORY.

11 PINECONES can predict the weather! In dry weather, the scales open, and when rain is on the way, they close.

WEATHER

12 Satellites up to 1,000 miles (1,609 km) above Earth keep track of the weather below.

13 The world's **tallest snowman** **was a girl!** She measured 122 feet, 1 inch (37.21 m).

14 All snowflakes have six sides.

15 THERE IS FOG ON MARS.

Natural Disasters

Every world region has its share of natural disasters—the mix just varies from place to place. The Ring of Fire—grinding tectonic plate boundaries that follow the coasts of the Pacific Ocean—shakes with volcanic eruptions and earthquakes. Lives and livelihoods here and along other oceans can be swept away by tsunamis. North America's heartland endures blizzards in winter and tornadoes that can strike in spring, summer, or fall. Tropical cyclones batter many coastal areas in Asia and Australia with ripping winds, torrents of rain, and huge storm surges along their deadly paths.

HURRICANES IN 2015

HELLO, MY NAME IS . . .

Hurricane names come from six official international lists. The names alternate between male and female. When a storm becomes a hurricane, a name from the list is used, in alphabetical order. Each list is reused every six years. A name "retires" if that hurricane caused a lot of damage or many deaths.

Ana
Bill
Claudette
Danny
Erika
Fred
Grace
Henri
Ida
Joaquin
Kate
Larry
Mindy
Nicholas
Odette
Peter
Rose
Sam
Teresa
Victor
Wanda

A monster storm with 150-mile-an-hour (241-kph) winds churns west across the Atlantic Ocean. Scientists at the National Hurricane Center in Miami have tracked it for days using satellite images. Now they're worried it may threaten the United States.

It's time for the "hurricane hunters" to go to work! All ships and airplanes have been warned away from this monster. But two four-engine airplanes head toward the storm. Their mission? To collect data inside the hurricane that will tell meteorologists where the storm is going, when it will get there, and how violent it will be.

The word "hurricane" comes from Huracan, the god of big winds and evil spirits once worshipped by the Maya people of Central America. These superstrong storms—which usually last about nine days—are the most destructive during their first 12 hours onshore, when high winds can topple homes and cause major flooding.

To help people prepare for a hurricane that's hustling to shore, the U.S. National Oceanic and Atmospheric Administration (NOAA) sends out the hurricane hunters, who fly straight into the storm to determine characteristics such as temperature, air pressure, wind speed, and wind direction. It's a dangerous job, but by mission's end, the hunters' work will help to keep everyone in the hurricane's path safe.

Scale of Hurricane Intensity

CATEGORY	ONE	TWO	THREE	FOUR	FIVE
DAMAGE	Minimal	Moderate	Extensive	Extreme	Catastrophic
WINDS	74–95 mph (119–153 kph)	96–110 mph (154–177 kph)	111–129 mph (178–208 kph)	130–156 mph (209–251 kph)	157 mph or higher (252+ kph)
(DAMAGE refers to wind and water damage combined.)					

Wildfire!

During the summer of 2013, a fire erupted in Stanislaus National Forest in northern California, U.S.A., eventually spreading into nearby Yosemite National Park. Within days, over 250,000 acres (101,100 ha) had been charred, making it one of the worst wildfires in California's history. In some spots, the fire burned so intensely that it wiped out trees and other vegetation, leaving an eerie, barren moonscape.

How do wildfires start? Often, they're sparked by a careless act by a human, such as leaving a campfire unattended or irresponsibly disposing of a cigarette. Some are deliberately set, or are ignited by lightning strikes or fallen power lines. However they begin, wildfires can quickly rage out of control.

Highly trained forest firefighters are equipped and experienced to fight huge forest fires. Some even parachute into a remote area to battle the blaze. In addition to the work of skilled firefighters, a break in the weather can also help in beating a wildfire. Rain assisted in containing the Yosemite fire.

Flood!

The Danube River, which usually peacefully flows through cities and towns in Austria, Hungary, Germany, and other parts of central Europe, swelled to epic levels the spring of 2013. In Budapest, the river hit a record high of 29 feet (8.9 m) before finally receding a few days later.

Although flash floods can occur quickly and be quite dangerous, most floods develop slowly, giving residents time to prepare. In Europe, crews of volunteers placed millions of sandbags along the Danube's banks in an attempt to prevent the water from spilling into the streets, and thousands of people in the affected areas were evacuated. Still, the flood caused serious problems. The Danube's flooding stalled road and subway traffic, submerged small towns and farmland, and racked up several billion dollars in damages.

How to Survive Lightning

Caught off guard by a sudden thunderstorm? Avoid becoming a human glow stick with these easy tips.

SEEK SHELTER

If you see lightning and can't count to 30 before you hear thunder, get into an enclosed structure or vehicle as soon as you can. Remain there for 30 minutes after the last thunderclap.

DON'T BE A TREE HUGGER

Lightning often strikes the tallest thing around, so don't look for shelter under tall trees. That goes double for telephone or electrical poles.

GO SWIMMING LATER

Water is conductive, meaning it can transfer the lightning's electricity to you. Stay away from bodies of water, even puddles. If you're in the pool, get out!

LIGHTEN THE LOAD

Metal is also conductive. If you're wearing anything with metal in it—a backpack, a belt, jewelry—now's the time to get rid of it.

SHORTEN IT UP

If you're out in the open, make yourself as small as possible. Crouch with your head between your knees. Not being the tallest object around may protect you from a direct strike.

BECOME A LONER

If you're with a bunch of people, space yourselves more than 15 feet (4.6 m) apart so that lightning won't jump from person to person.

Tsunami Heroes

RESCUED OR REUNITED, ANIMALS AND PEOPLE PULL TOGETHER AFTER A HUGE NATURAL DISASTER.

When a 9.0-magnitude earthquake struck off the coast of Honshu, Japan, in 2011, it knocked people off their feet and made tall buildings sway. Then things got even worse. Miles offshore, the massive movement created a series of huge waves called a tsunami, which rushed toward the island nation. Walls of water as tall as 30 feet (9 m) crashed into the coast and wiped out everything in the way—and separated humans from their pets. Many animal lovers went out of their way to help animals in need after the tsunami. Here are two stories of survival and hope.

DOG AT SEA

SAFE ON LAND

PUP RESCUED FROM ROOF

Three weeks after the disaster, a helicopter crew spots a dog pacing across the roof of a wrecked house floating more than a mile (1.6 km) offshore. A rescue team reaches the canine by canoe, carrying her aboard a larger boat on a stretcher. A woman from a nearby town sees the rescue on the local news and instantly recognizes her missing pet, a two-year-old mixed breed named Ban. Dog and owner are happily reunited—safe and on dry land.

RESCUED

PORPOISE SURVIVES STRANDING

A tiny porpoise is spotted in a flooded rice field, more than a mile (1.6 km) away from the shore. Pet shop owner Ryo Taira wades into the water, grabs the three-foot (1-m)-long animal and cradles it in his arms. He then wraps the exhausted porpoise in wet towels and drives it to a nearby beach. As soon as it's placed into the sea, the porpoise springs back to life and energetically swims away.

THE WATER CYCLE

RISING UP

Some of the water and spray from the waterfall in this picture will **evaporate** into the air. In other bodies of water, heat from the sun causes some water to evaporate, or turn into water vapor, or gas. This water vapor rises from the stream, river, or lake and goes into the air.

HANGING OUT

Water covers more than 70 percent of Earth's surface in the form of oceans, lakes, and rivers. When water ends up on land from rain, snow, or hail, it may soak into the earth, becoming part of the ground-water and leaving the water cycle for a while.

Scientists think that the water we drink, bathe in, and use to grow crops today has been here on Earth since long before the time of the dinosaurs. It has just been moving around and around in the atmosphere in a nearly endless cycle. But there's not much water in the air. In fact, if all of the atmosphere's water rained down at once, it would cover the globe only to a depth of one inch (2.5 cm). It's a good thing, then, that we have the water cycle—Earth's original recycling project. Here's how it works:

CHILLING OUT

As water vapor cools in the air, it **condenses.** This means that it changes back into liquid form. You will notice the same kind of thing happening if you pour a cold glass of water on a hot day. Water forms on the outside of the glass. The water vapor in the warm air touches the cold glass and turns to liquid.

FALLING DOWN

After so much water has condensed that the air can't hold it anymore, it falls as **precipitation**—rain, hail, sleet, or snow—into Earth's oceans, lakes, and rivers.

RUNNING OFF

Melted snow and rain that run downhill eventually end up in large bodies of water. The transfer of land water to the ocean is called **runoff.**

LOCATED AT THE BORDER OF CHINA AND VIETNAM, THE DETIAN WATERFALL IS ONE OF THE LARGEST WATERFALLS IN ASIA. ITS NAME MEANS "VIRTUOUS HEAVEN."

THE OC

PACIFIC OCEAN

STATS

Surface area
65,436,200 sq mi (169,479,000 sq km)

Portion of Earth's water area
47 percent

Greatest depth
Challenger Deep
(in the Mariana Trench)
-36,070 ft (-10,994 m)

Surface temperatures
Summer high: 90°F (32°C)
Winter low: 28°F (-2°C)

Tides
Highest: 30 ft (9 m) near Korean peninsula
Lowest: 1 ft (0.3 m) near Midway Islands

Cool creatures: giant Pacific octopus,
bottlenose whale, clownfish, great
white shark

ATLANTIC OCEAN

STATS

Surface area
35,338,500 sq mi (91,526,300 sq km)

Portion of Earth's water area
25 percent

Greatest depth
Puerto Rico Trench
-28,232 ft (-8,605 m)

Surface temperatures
Summer high: 90°F (32°C)
Winter low: 28°F (-2°C)

Tides
Highest: 52 ft (16 m)
Bay of Fundy, Canada
Lowest: 1.5 ft (0.5 m)
Gulf of Mexico and Mediterranean Sea

Cool creatures: blue whale, Atlantic spotted
dolphin, sea turtle

GREAT WHITE SHARK

GREEN SEA TURTLE

EANS

INDIAN OCEAN

STATS

Surface area
28,839,800 sq mi (74,694,800 sq km)

Portion of Earth's water area
21 percent

Greatest depth
**Java Trench
-23,376 ft (-7,125 m)**

Surface temperatures
**Summer high: 93°F (34°C)
Winter low: 28°F (-2°C)**

Tides
**Highest: 36 ft (11 m)
Lowest: 2 ft (0.6 m)
Both along Australia's west coast**

Cool creatures: humpback whale, Portuguese man-of-war, dugong (sea cow)

DUGONG

ARCTIC OCEAN

STATS

Surface area
5,390,000 sq mi (13,960,100 sq km)

Portion of Earth's water area
4 percent

Greatest depth
**Molloy Deep
-18,599 ft (-5,669 m)**

Surface temperatures
**Summer high: 41°F (5°C)
Winter low: 28°F (-2°C)**

Tides
**Less than 1 ft (0.3 m) variation
throughout the ocean**

Cool creatures: beluga whale, orca, harp seal, narwhal

ORCA

To see the major oceans and bays in relation to landmasses, look at the map on pages 260 and 261.

Coral Reefs

Just below the surface of the Caribbean Sea's crystal-clear water, miles (km) of vivid corals grow in fantastic shapes that shelter tropical fish of every color. Coral reefs account for a quarter of all life in the ocean and are often called the rain forests of the sea. Like big apartment complexes for sea creatures, coral reefs provide a tough limestone skeleton for fish, clams, and other organisms to live in— and plenty of food for them to eat, too.

And how does the coral get its color? It's all about the algae that cling to its limestone polyps. Algae and coral live together in a mutually helpful relationship. The coral provides a home to the algae and helps the algae convert sunlight to food that the corals consume. But as beautiful as coral reefs are, they are also highly sensitive. A jump of even 2°F (1.1°C) in water temperature makes the reef rid itself of the algae, leaving the coral with a sickly, bleached look. Pollution is another threat; it can poison the sensitive corals. Humans pose a threat, too: One clumsy kick from a swimmer can destroy decades of coral growth.

QUEEN ANGELFISH

MANTA RAY

SEA STAR
ON A SPONGE

NO TWO
GIANT
CLAMS
HAVE
THE SAME
COLORING.

GIANT BUMPHEAD
PARROTFISH

MORAY EEL

BY THE NUMBERS

50 million years ago, some of Earth's coral reefs began growing.

2,300 feet (700 m) is the depth at which some deep-sea coral will grow.

90 percent of coral reefs are in danger of disappearing by 2030.

NATIONAL
GEOGRAPHIC
KIDS
SCANNER

SCAN THIS PAGE!
GET BONUS MOBILE
CONTENT! Download
the free NG Kids
scanner app. Directions
on inside front cover.

HOW DOES YOUR GARDEN GROW?

Three characteristics make plants distinct:

1. Most have chlorophyll (a green pigment that makes photosynthesis work and turns sunlight into energy), while some are parasitic.

2. They cannot change their location on their own.

3. Their cell walls are made from a stiff material called cellulose.

The plant kingdom is more than 300,000 species strong, growing all over the world: on top of mountains, in the sea, in frigid temperatures—everywhere. Without plants, life on Earth would not be able to survive. Plants provide food and oxygen for animals and humans.

Photosynthesis

Plants are lucky—they don't have to hunt or shop for food. Most use the sun to produce their own food. In a process called photosynthesis, the plant's chloroplast (the part of the plant where the chemical chlorophyll is located) captures the sun's energy and combines it with carbon dioxide from the air and nutrient-rich water from the ground to produce a sugar called glucose. Plants burn the glucose for energy to help them grow. As a waste product, plants emit oxygen, which humans and other animals need to breathe. When we breathe, we exhale carbon dioxide, which the plants then use for more photosynthesis—it's all a big, finely tuned system. So the next time you pass a lonely houseplant, give it thanks for helping you live.

Try This!
FOOD FOR YOUR GARDEN!

Grow a healthy garden and reduce waste by using leftovers to make your own compost, which is organic material that adds nutrients to the soil.

RECYCLE THE NATURAL WAY

By composting you reduce the need for chemical fertilizers in your yard, and you send less waste to landfills. Yard trimmings and food scraps make up about 25 percent of the trash from cities and towns in the United States. So put that banana peel to good use. Turn it—and a lot of other things in your trash can—into environmentally helpful compost. By making natural fertilizer you will help the environment *and* have a great excuse to play with your food!

GROW VEGGIES AND FLOWERS

HOW TO MAKE COMPOST

1. Choose a dry, shady spot to create your compost pile.

2. Use a bin with a tight-fitting lid and plenty of airholes to hold your compost ingredients. In the bin, start with a 6-inch (15-cm) layer of dry "brown" material (see examples in the list below right). Break down large pieces before you place them in the bin.

3. Add a 3-inch (8-cm) layer of "green" materials (see list). Add a little bit of soil to this layer.

4. Mix the brown and green layers.

5. Finish with another 3-inch (8-cm) layer of brown materials.

6. Add water until the contents are moist. If you accidentally add too much water, just add more brown materials to the bin. Mix your compost pile every week or two.

7. After one to four months, the compost will be almost ready. When it is dark brown and moist, and you can't identify the original ingredients, wait two more weeks. Then add your finished compost to your garden.

COMPOST THESE

"BROWN" MATERIALS
Dead leaves
Eggshells
Twigs
Shredded newspaper
Nutshells

"GREEN" MATERIALS
Grass clippings
Fruit and vegetable scraps
Coffee grounds
Tea bags

217

Biomes

A BIOME, OFTEN CALLED A MAJOR LIFE ZONE, is one of the natural world's major communities where plants and animals adapt to their specific surroundings. Biomes are classified depending on the predominant vegetation, climate, and geography of a region. They can be divided into six major types: forest, fresh water, marine, desert, grassland, and tundra. Each biome consists of many ecosystems.

Biomes are extremely important. Balanced ecological relationships among biomes help to maintain the environment and life on Earth as we know it. For example, an increase in one species of plant, such as an invasive one, can cause a ripple effect throughout the whole biome.

Because biomes can be fragile in this way, it is important to protect them from negative human activity, such as deforestation and pollution. We must work to conserve these biomes and the unique organisms that live within them.

FOREST

The forest biomes have been evolving for about 420 million years. Today, forests occupy about one-third of Earth's land area. There are three major types of forests: tropical, temperate, and boreal (taiga). Forests are home to a diversity of plants, some of which may hold medicinal qualities for humans, as well as thousands of animal species, some still undiscovered. Forests can also absorb carbon dioxide, a green-house gas, and give off oxygen.

FRESH WATER

Most water on Earth is salty, but freshwater ecosystems—including lakes, ponds, wetlands, rivers, and streams—usually contain water with less than one percent salt concentration. The countless animal and plant species that live in a freshwater biome vary from continent to continent, but include algae, frogs, turtles, fish, and the larvae of many insects. Throughout the world, people use food, medicine, and other resources from this biome.

MARINE

The marine biome covers almost three-fourths of Earth's surface, making it the largest habitat on our planet. The four oceans make up the majority of the saltwater marine biome. Coral reefs are considered to be the most biodiverse of any of the biome habitats. The marine biome is home to more than one million plant and animal species. Some of the largest animals on Earth, such as the blue whale, live in the marine biome.

DESERT

Covering about one-fifth of Earth's surface, deserts are places where precipitation is less than 10 inches (25 cm) per year. Although most deserts are hot, there are other kinds as well. The four major kinds of deserts in the world are hot, semiarid, coastal, and cold. Far from being barren wastelands, deserts are biologically rich habitats with a vast array of animals and plants that have adapted to the harsh conditions there.

GRASSLAND

Biomes called grasslands are characterized by having grasses instead of large shrubs or trees. Grasslands generally have precipitation for only about half to three-fourths of the year. If it were more, they would become forests. Widespread around the world, grasslands can be divided into two types: tropical (savannas) and temperate. Grasslands are home to some of the largest land animals on Earth, such as elephants, hippopotamuses, rhinoceroses, and lions.

TUNDRA

The coldest of all biomes, a tundra is characterized by an extremely cold climate, simple vegetation, little precipitation, poor nutrients, and a short growing season. There are two types of tundra: arctic and alpine. A very fragile environment, a tundra is home to few kinds of vegetation. Surprisingly, though, there are quite a few animal species that can survive the tundra's extremes, such as wolves, caribou, and even mosquitoes.

STUMP YOUR PARENTS

WONDERS OF NATURE QUIZ

Are your folks one with nature? Test them to see how much they know about the great outdoors. ANSWERS BELOW

1 **True or false?** You can fry an egg on a sidewalk.

2 **Which is not a hurricane name in 2015?**
a. Wanda
b. George
c. Rose
d. Joaquin

3 **What's the best way to protect yourself from a lightning strike?**
a. get out of the pool
b. remove your belt
c. seek shelter
d. all of the above

4 **In which ocean would you find a Portuguese man-of-war?**
a. Atlantic Ocean
b. Arctic Ocean
c. Indian Ocean
d. Pacific Ocean

5 **How much of the Earth's surface is covered by deserts?**
a. One-fifth
b. Half
c. One-tenth
d. Two-thirds

Not **STUMPED** yet?
Check out the *National Geographic Kids Quiz Whiz* collection for more crazy **NATURE** questions!

ANSWERS:
1. False. While it can get hot enough, the sidewalk would cool too quickly to actually fry the egg; 2. b; 3. d; 4. c; 5. a

SPEAK NATURALLY

Oral Reports Made Easy

Does the thought of public speaking start your stomach churning like a tornado? Would you rather get caught in an avalanche than give a speech?

Giving an oral report does not have to be a natural disaster. The basic format is very similar to a written essay. There are two main elements that make up a good oral report—the writing and the presentation. As you write your oral report, remember that your audience will be hearing the information as opposed to reading it. Follow the guidelines below, and there will be clear skies ahead.

> **TIP:**
> Make sure you practice your presentation a few times. Stand in front of a mirror or have a parent record you so you can see if you need to work on anything, such as eye contact.

Writing Your Material

Follow the steps in the "How to Write a Perfect Essay" section on p. 116, but prepare your report to be spoken rather than written. Try to keep your sentences short and simple. Long, complex sentences are harder to follow. Limit yourself to just a few key points. You don't want to overwhelm your audience with too much information. To be most effective, hit your key points in the introduction, elaborate on them in the body, and then repeat them once again in your conclusion.

An oral report has three basic parts:

- **Introduction**—This is your chance to engage your audience and really capture their interest in the subject you are presenting. Use a funny personal experience or a dramatic story, or start with an intriguing question.

- **Body**—This is the longest part of your report. Here you elaborate on the facts and ideas you want to convey. Give information that supports your main idea, and expand on it with specific examples or details. In other words, structure your oral report in the same way you would a written essay so that your thoughts are presented in a clear and organized manner.

- **Conclusion**—This is the time to summarize the information and emphasize your most important points to the audience one last time.

Preparing Your Delivery

1 Practice makes perfect.
Practice! Practice! Practice! Confidence, enthusiasm, and energy are key to delivering an effective oral report, and they can best be achieved through rehearsal. Ask family and friends to be your practice audience and give you feedback when you're done. Were they able to follow your ideas? Did you seem knowledgeable and confident? Did you speak too slowly or too fast, too softly or too loudly? The more times you practice giving your report, the more you'll master the material. Then you won't have to rely so heavily on your notes or papers, and you will be able to give your report in a relaxed and confident manner.

2 Present with everything you've got.
Be as creative as you can. Incorporate videos, sound clips, slide presentations, charts, diagrams, and photos. Visual aids help stimulate your audience's senses and keep them intrigued and engaged. They can also help to reinforce your key points. And remember that when you're giving an oral report, you're a performer. Take charge of the spotlight and be as animated and entertaining as you can. Have fun with it.

3 Keep your nerves under control.
Everyone gets a little nervous when speaking in front of a group. That's normal. But the more preparation you've done—meaning plenty of researching, organizing, and rehearsing—the more confident you'll be. Preparation is the key. And if you make a mistake or stumble over your words, just regroup and keep going. Nobody's perfect, and nobody expects you to be.

History Happens

Completed in 1894, Tower Bridge spans the Thames River in London, England, U.K.

PACKING FOR THE
AFTERLIFE

BOATS

Egyptians believed the sun god traveled to the afterlife each night by boat. Entombed model boats—and even full-size versions—helped the dead make that same voyage.

IMAGINE HOW YOU'D

FEEL IF YOU BOARDED A PLANE FOR A LONG TRIP

and realized you forgot to pack. To the ancient Egyptians, who viewed death as the start of a great journey, passing into the afterlife unprepared was equally unsettling. That's why family and friends filled the tombs of their dearly departed with everything they would need in the hereafter.

Graves of poor Egyptians were packed with just the essentials: food, cosmetics, and clothes. The ornate burial chambers of pharaohs overflowed with treasures and art. Browse these grave goodies recovered from ancient Egyptian tombs.

FOOD

Family members left food offerings outside a tomb to nourish their loved one's spirit. Paintings of feasts on tomb walls or sculptures of food trays were thought to provide magical bottomless buffets.

GAMES

Board games like Senet provided eternal entertainment.

CLOTHES

Most tombs were stocked with chests of clothes, fine linens, sandals, and other attire. It would be unseemly to spend eternity naked, after all.

COFFINS

Coffins were carved in the likeness of the deceased so that spirits could recognize their own bodies.

SERVANTS

Summoned to life by a spell, carved figures known as shabtis served as laborers in the afterlife. One pharaoh's tomb contained nearly a thousand of these ancient action figures.

JEWELRY

The adage "You can't take it with you" would have horrified wealthy Egyptians, who packed their tombs with their favorite jewelry.

225

Ancient World ADVENTURE

ANGKOR WAT

WHERE: Cambodia
BUILT: A.D. 1113 to A.D.1150

COOL FACT: Created to honor the Hindu god Vishnu, Angkor Wat remains the largest religious complex in the world. It's still protected by a 4-mile (6.4-km)-long moat!

BOROBUDUR

WHERE: Indonesia
BUILT: About A.D. 778 to A.D. 850

COOL FACT: The world's largest Buddhist monument, this temple is made from two million rocks and took about 75 years to build.

FORBIDDEN CITY

WHERE: China
BUILT: Between A.D. 1406 and A.D. 1420

COOL FACT: The 180-acre (73-ha) imperial compound in Beijing is rumored to have more than 9,999 rooms and was home to 24 Chinese emperors over a nearly 500-year span.

*E*ver wonder what it was like on Earth thousands of years ago? Check out these amazing ancient sites. Visiting them is like taking a time machine into the past!

PYRAMIDS AT GIZA

WHERE: Egypt
BUILT: About 2500 B.C.

COOL FACT: These massive pyramids—built as tombs for Egypt's pharaohs—are part of a complex that included a palace, temples, and boat pits. The largest pyramid is 481 feet (147 m) tall and is made from 2.3 million stone blocks.

PALENQUE

TIMBUKTU

WHERE: Mexico
BUILT: About A.D. 500

COOL FACT: This ancient Maya city-state's buildings, including temples and tombs, were built without the use of metal tools, pack animals, or even the wheel.

WHERE: Mali
BUILT: About A.D. 1100

COOL FACT: Once known as the fabled "City of Gold," Africa's Timbuktu was a center of learning and culture in the 15th and 16th centuries and is home to a still standing university.

The ancient Olmec gave the cocoa tree, used to make chocolate, its earliest known name: KAKAWA.

ACCORDING TO A CHINESE LEGEND, TEA DRINKING ORIGINATED WHEN DRIED TEA LEAVES FELL INTO A CUP OF WATER SERVED TO AN EMPEROR.

People have lived in **the world's oldest neighborhood**—Iraq's the Citadel—for at least 7,000 years.

15 COOL THINGS ABOUT

ANCIENT EGYPTIAN KIDS PLAYED HOCKEY WITH STICKS MADE FROM PALM BRANCHES.

Roads built by the ancient Romans are still intact and in use today, from Europe to the Middle East.

People in ancient India **stitched up wounds** with hair and plants such as flax and hemp.

An Inca burial site was found 20,702 feet (6,310 m) high in the Andes Mountains.

8

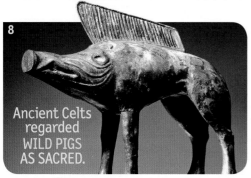

Ancient Celts regarded WILD PIGS AS SACRED.

9

IN ANCIENT GREECE, COINS WERE DECORATED WITH IMAGES OF BEES.

10

IN CHINA, the earliest writing—about 1200 B.C.—was inscribed on the BONES OF ANIMALS.

11

Bright red skeletal remains of the ancient Maya reveal they coated their dead in the red mineral CINNABAR.

ANCIENT CULTURES

12

Horse riding began about 6,000 years ago in Central Asia.

13

CITIZENS OF THE ANCIENT GREEK CITY-STATE OF SPARTA—SPARTANS— VOTED BY POUNDING ON THEIR SHIELDS.

14

Australian Aborigines, the world's oldest living culture, have existed for at least 50,000 years.

15

The Romans believed cinnamon was sacred. Wreaths made from the plant's leaves often decorated Roman temples.

Knight Life

Protector of the Castle

It started with a childhood full of boring chores and ended at age 21 with a ceremonial smack to the head that knocked some men on their tails. The road to knighthood was long and rough, but the journey was often worth the trouble. Successful knights found fortune and glory.

In times of war and peace, knights led a dangerous life. These professional warriors were charged with protecting the lord's land from invaders, leading the castle's men-at-arms during sieges, and fighting on behalf of the church. Between battles, they competed in deadly games called tournaments to sharpen their skills.

In exchange for military service, knights were granted their own lands—along with peasants to farm it—and noble titles. The mightiest knights rose to rival lords in power and property. Sir Ulrich von Liechtenstein, one of the 13th century's most famous knights, owned three castles.

Not just anyone could become a knight. Armor, weapons, and warhorses cost more than a typical peasant might earn in a lifetime, so knights often hailed from noble families. They started their training early in life—at the age most kids today begin first grade.

Lord Lore
England's royal family still grants knighthood to actors, scientists, and other accomplished citizens.

How to Become a Knight

1. Serve as a Page

A boy destined for knighthood left home at age 7 to become a servant in a great lord's castle. The page learned courtly manners, received a basic education, and played rough with other pages.

2. Squire for a Knight

Once he turned 14, a page became a squire for a knight. He learned about armor by cleaning his master's suit and helping him dress for battle. He practiced fighting with swords, shields, and other weaponry. Most important of all, he learned to attack from the saddle of a huge warhorse—the type of mounted combat knights were famous for.

3. Get Dubbed

By age 21, a squire was ready for his dubbing ceremony. He knelt before his lord or lady and received a hard slap to help him remember his oath. (This brutal blow later evolved into a friendlier sword tap on the shoulders.) The newly dubbed knight was given the title "sir" and could seek service at a lord's castle.

Knightly Num

55	pounds (25 kg) of a weighed down a kn the battlefield.
45	years was the life expectancy of most knights.
45	days per year was t typical term of serv knight owed his lorc

Good knights acted chivalrously, which meant they protected the weak, treated women with respect, served the church, and were generous and humble.

MYSTERY of the BURIED TREASURE

TRUE STORY

AN ANCIENT STASH OF GOLD AND SILVER WORTH MILLIONS OF DOLLARS IS UNCOVERED IN A FARMER'S FIELD.

Beep! The man stops suddenly as his metal detector sounds off. Something is buried under the English field he's been exploring. Is it a worthless piece of junk—or something far more valuable?

The man's discovery turns out to be more than 3,500 pieces of gold and silver treasure buried by ancient warriors at least 1,300 years ago. Archaeologists uncovered sword handles, helmet pieces, and shield decorations. Some were studded with jewels or engraved with animals.

The treasure is worth about $5.5 million. But archaeologists are more excited about what it could tell us about these ancient warriors.

MYSTERIOUS PEOPLE

The treasure was buried by people called the Anglo-Saxons, who settled in England after arriving from Germany starting around A.D. 410. Archaeologists think it may have belonged to the Anglo-Saxon ruler, King Penda of Mercia.

The Anglo-Saxons lived in the Dark Ages, once believed to be a time when little was happening in art or culture. But the treasure helps confirm that the Anglo-Saxon period was a time of great change and amazing artistry.

SECRETS OF THE TREASURE

Anglo-Saxons were considered fierce warriors, and they cared about their weapons. But the quality of the metalwork shows they were also artists. Craftsmen created tiny, detailed engravings without magnifying lenses.

The treasure may also shed new light on where Anglo-Saxons lived. Because it was found in western England, rather than in the south or east, where archaeologists believed early Anglo-Saxons settled, this may mean the people had traveled farther than once thought.

Still, archaeologists may have more questions than answers. Why weren't there any items belonging to women? Was the treasure buried for safekeeping, or to mark a victory?

The answers to these mysteries may come with further study, but more than anything, this discovery has brought the people of the Anglo-Saxon era to life.

CHEEK PIECE
This helmet fragment protected a warrior during battle.

POMMEL
This knob formed the very top of a hilt, or handle, of a knife.

PIECES FROM THE PAST
Scientists have tried to identify the real-life uses of the mysterious treasure. Here's how they match up in this artist's rendering of an Anglo-Saxon warrior.

HILT FITTING
Decorated with red gemstones, this piece was the bottom part of the handle.

THE AMAZING HOUDINI!
Death-Defying Magic Tricks
REVEALED

Throughout history, many magicians have wowed audiences with their amazing illusions. But there has only been one Harry Houdini. Known for his death-defying magic tricks, Houdini, who died in 1926, was one of the most fearless illusionists of all time. Here is the scoop about two of his most legendary stunts.

VANISHING ELEPHANT

The Trick: Houdini promises to make Jenny, a 4,000-pound (1,814-kg) elephant, disappear.

What You See: Houdini coaxes Jenny into an enormous wooden box and closes its front curtain. A moment later, he reopens it and she's gone.

What You Don't See: The box has a secret back door. Houdini closes the curtain and Jenny is lured out the back exit by the smell of her favorite food.

SUSPENDED STRAITJACKET

The Trick: Hanging by his feet from a building while wearing a straitjacket, Houdini vows to free himself—without falling!

What You See: Houdini wriggles against the straps of his straitjacket, freeing one arm at a time. Pulling the jacket over his head, he drops to the ground below.

What You Don't See: Legend has it that Houdini took a deep breath to expand his chest and keep the straitjacket loose. Then he used his flexibility to help him wriggle free.

Secrets of the

SCIENTISTS USE CUTTING-EDGE TECHNOLOGY TO UNCOVER NEW EVIDENCE ABOUT HOW THE SHIP SANK.

Sunday, April 14, 1912: The R.M.S. *Titanic* steams across the North Atlantic Ocean. The 882-foot (269-m)-long passenger ship carries 2,208 people on its maiden voyage from Southampton, England, to New York City, in the United States of America.

Suddenly, a dark shape appears. An iceberg scrapes the ship, and within three hours, the *Titanic* sinks. Almost 1,500 people lose their lives.

Scientists have closely studied the *Titanic*'s wreck on the ocean floor since it was discovered in 1985. Recently, National Geographic Explorer-in-Residence James Cameron—the director of the movie *Titanic*—assembled a team of experts to examine the shipwreck anew. Using 3-D modeling and state-of-the-art technology, the experts reveal new clues about how the *Titanic* sank.

FLOODING

It might have been possible for the ship to sink more slowly, allowing more people to survive. Many of the ship's portholes were found open—most likely because passengers were airing out their rooms and never closed them. This caused the ship to take on water faster.

Something similar also may have happened in one of the grand lobbies, where a large door was found open. "The size of the door is twice the size of the original iceberg damage," Cameron says. "This would have sped up the sinking of the ship."

BREAKING

As the *Titanic* took on water, the front of the ship, called the bow, sank below the surface, causing the back, or stern, to lift into the air. The great stress broke the ship in half. "When the *Titanic* broke in half and the bow pulled away, the bottom likely remained attached to the back of the ship until it, too, was pulled apart," Cameron says.

EXPLORER JAMES CAMERON PILOTS AN UNDERWATER VEHICLE CALLED A SUBMERSIBLE.

SINKING

In its final resting place, the bow looks remarkably intact. But the stern looks like a bomb destroyed it. Why? The bow was filled with water when it sank, so the pressure was the same on the inside as the outside. The stern, however, sank with lots of air inside and imploded from the pressure.

FINAL IMPACT

The sinking ship created a massive trail of water that followed it downward at 20 to 25 miles an hour (32 to 40 kph). Experts think that this water trail pummeled the *Titanic* after it hit bottom. "Millions of gallons of water came pushing down on it," Cameron says. With all this new information, is our understanding of the *Titanic* tragedy complete? "I think we have a very good picture of what happened," Cameron says. "But there will always be mysteries."

Titanic

TITANIC
19 ○ 12
LONDON

SUPERSIZE SHIP
The *Titanic* was almost as long as three football fields. With its smokestacks, the ship was as tall as a 17-story building.

NATIONAL GEOGRAPHIC KiDS
SCANNER

SCAN THIS PAGE!
GET BONUS MOBILE CONTENT! Download the free NG Kids scanner app. Directions on inside front cover.

TITANIC

WHAT IF...
Scientists know a lot about how the *Titanic* sank, but other factors contributed as well.

SAILING SCHEDULE
The *Titanic* set sail more than three weeks behind schedule. If the ship had left on time, an iceberg probably wouldn't have been in its path.

FROM CALM TO CHAOS
The sea was unusually calm on April 14, 1912. Waves would have made the iceberg easier to spot.

MISSED MESSAGES
Two messages were telegraphed from other ships to warn the *Titanic* of icebergs, but they never reached the captain.

We asked oceanographer and National Geographic Explorer-in-Residence Robert Ballard, who led the team that discovered the *Titanic* in 1985, what it felt like to make the discovery of the century.

"**My first reaction** was one of excitement and celebration. But we were at the **very spot** on the **cold North Atlantic Ocean** where it all happened. So then we had **a quiet moment of remembrance.**"

WAR!

Since the beginning of time, different countries, territories, and cultures have feuded with each other over land, power, and politics. Major military conflicts include the following wars:

1095–1291 THE CRUSADES
Starting late in the 11th century, these wars over religion were fought in the Middle East for nearly 200 years.

1337–1453 HUNDRED YEARS' WAR
France and England battled over rights to land for more than a century before the French eventually drove the English out in 1453.

1754–1763 FRENCH AND INDIAN WAR (part of Europe's Seven Years' War)
A nine-year war between the British and French for control of North America.

1775–1783 AMERICAN REVOLUTION
Thirteen British colonies in America united to reject the rule of the British government and to form the United States of America.

1861–1865 AMERICAN CIVIL WAR
Occurred when the northern states (the Union) went to war with the southern states, which had seceded, or withdrawn, to form the Confederate States of America. Slavery was one of the key issues in the Civil War.

1910–1920 MEXICAN REVOLUTION
The people of Mexico revolted against the rule of dictator President Porfirio Díaz, leading to his eventual defeat and to a democratic government.

1914–1918 WORLD WAR I
The assassination of Austria's Archduke Ferdinand by a Serbian nationalist sparked this wide-spreading war. The U.S. entered after Germany sunk the British ship *Lusitania*, killing more than 120 Americans.

1918–1920 RUSSIAN CIVIL WAR
Following the 1917 Russian Revolution, this conflict pitted the Communist Red Army against the foreign-backed White Army. The Red Army won, leading to the establishment of the Union of Soviet Socialist Republics (U.S.S.R.) in 1922.

1936–1939 SPANISH CIVIL WAR
Aid from Italy and Germany helped the Nationalists gain victory over the Communist-supported Republicans. The war resulted in the loss of more than 300,000 lives and increased tension in Europe leading up to World War II.

1939–1945 WORLD WAR II
This massive conflict in Europe, Asia, and North Africa involved many countries that aligned with the two sides: the Allies and the Axis. After the bombing of Pearl Harbor in Hawaii in 1941, the U.S. entered the war on the side of the Allies. More than 50 million people died during the war.

1946–1949 CHINESE CIVIL WAR
Also known as the "War of Liberation," this pitted the Communist and Nationalist parties in China against each other. The Communists won.

1950–1953 KOREAN WAR
Kicked off when the Communist forces of North Korea, with backing from the Soviet Union, invaded their democratic neighbor to the south. A coalition of 16 countries from the United Nations stepped in to support South Korea.

Remembering Anne Frank
70 Years Later

1950s–1975 VIETNAM WAR
Fought between the Communist North, supported by allies including China, and the government of South Vietnam, supported by the United States and other anticommunist nations.

1967 SIX-DAY WAR
A battle for land between Israel and the states of Egypt, Jordan, and Syria. The outcome resulted in Israel's gaining control of coveted territory, including the Gaza Strip and the West Bank.

1991–PRESENT
SOMALI CIVIL WAR
Began when Somalia's last president, a dictator named Mohamed Siad Barre, was overthrown. The war has led to years of fighting and anarchy.

2001–2014
WAR IN AFGHANISTAN
After attacks in the United States by the terrorist group al Qaeda, a coalition that eventually included more than 40 countries invaded Afghanistan to find Osama bin Laden and other al Qaeda members and to dismantle the Taliban. Bin Laden was killed in a U.S. covert operation in 2011. The North Atlantic Treaty Organization (NATO) took control of the coalition's combat mission in 2003. That combat mission ended in 2014.

2003–2011 WAR IN IRAQ
A coalition led by the U.S., and including Britain, Australia, and Spain, invaded Iraq over suspicions that Iraq had weapons of mass destruction.

Imagine one day you're just a regular, happy kid living in a normal home with your normal family. And the next, you're in hiding from German Nazi soldiers in a secret attic apartment where you'll stay for two years before you're found and sent to a concentration camp. This is the story of Anne Frank, one of the many tragic tales to emerge from World War II. For two years, while Anne and her family hid in an attic in Amsterdam, Netherlands, she documented her everyday thoughts as well as her frustration about the war. In diaries that were later shared by her father—the only family member to survive their horrific ordeal—Anne offered insight into what it was like to be persecuted for being Jewish and to endure the constant fear of being discovered. Her work, *The Diary of a Young Girl*, has since been read by millions.

Now, 70 years since Anne's untimely death in 1945 at age 15, we remember this amazing girl and the other victims of the Holocaust, which claimed the lives of nearly six million people. Even today, it is difficult to comprehend the magnitude of this tragedy. That's why, no matter how much time passes, it is important that we never, ever forget.

O Canada!

Canada is a federation of 13 mainly self-governing provinces and territories. There are three levels of government within Canada: the federal government, which deals with matters that affect all Canadians, such as defense and foreign policy; the provincial and territorial governments; and the local, or municipal, governments. Each province has its own capital, government, and premier. The national capital is Ottawa.

The federal government is a parliamentary democracy. It is formed by the political party that wins the most seats in parliament. The leader of the governing party serves as prime minister. Although the people of Canada wield the authority through representation in parliament, there is also a monarch—currently Queen Elizabeth II—who is the head of state. All governmental acts are done in her name. Her power is referred to as the crown. While the queen is sovereign, she rarely exercises her power and is mainly represented in the country by the governor general, whom she appoints. The duties of the governor general are mostly ceremonial.

The governor general in council appoints members of the judicial branch, but once appointed, these judges operate independently.

The Constitution

The Constitution of Canada is the highest law in the land.
Some of its most influential documents include:
Constitution Act of 1867, Constitution Act of 1871,
Statute of Westminster of 1931, and Constitution Act of 1982.

At a meeting in London (circa 1866),
the Fathers of Confederation
frame the British North America Act.

Constitution Act of 1867

Formerly known as the British North America Act, it granted Canada self-government and laid out how the government would operate.

Constitution Act of 1871

Also an act of the British Parliament, it described how new provinces and territories could join what was then the Dominion of Canada.

Statute of Westminster of 1931

This law granted Canada full powers over its foreign policy, making Canada legislatively independent from Great Britain.

Constitution Act of 1982

Unlike those before it, this act was a totally Canadian-born amendment, giving Canada its first constitution. The act gave Canada complete independence from Britain. It also laid out a Charter of Rights and Freedoms for every Canadian citizen. These inalienable rights include the freedoms of religion, expression, and peaceable assembly, as well as the right to vote and move freely in the country; the right to life, liberty, and security of person; and the right to not be arbitrarily detained or imprisoned.

Until 1982, all acts, of which there were many more, were seen as part of the British North America Act. The 1982 Constitution Act changed the names of all documents that came before, bringing them together to form Canada's Constitution.

HOW THE GOVERNMENT WORKS

QUEEN
Represented in Canada by the governor general

Executive Branch

Legislative Branch

Judicial Branch

PRIME MINISTER

PARLIAMENT

SUPREME COURT
Nine judges appointed by the governor general

CABINET
Appointed by the prime minister

SENATE
105 members appointed by the prime minister

HOUSE OF COMMONS
308 members elected by voters

COURTS
Federal court, courts of appeal, & provincial courts

The Royal Family

The Royal Family is led by Queen Elizabeth II, who has served as the sovereign of Canada's government since 1952, making her one of the longest-reigning British monarchs. In her six decades as the Queen, she has seen enormous political and social change. Other members of the Royal Family carry out a variety of official duties. These include her husband, His Royal Highness Prince Philip, Duke of Edinburgh, as well as their four children and eight grandchildren. The Queen's son Prince Charles, the Prince of Wales, is heir to the throne. The Duke and Duchess of Cambridge, Prince William and Catherine (formerly Middleton), welcomed their first child, Prince George of Cambridge, on July 22, 2013.

Executive Branch

The prime minister heads the executive branch and serves as the cabinet chair. He or she organizes the cabinet and provides leadership and direction to the government. The prime minister appoints cabinet members, who are usually members of his or her own party and who are responsible for setting policies and priorities for the federal government.

House of Commons (legislative branch)

Senate (legislative branch)

Legislative Branch

The parliament of Canada is the legislative branch of the government, which means it makes the laws for the country. It consists of two parts—the Senate and the House of Commons.

The House of Commons is the most powerful body of parliament. Its 308 members are elected by the people for up to five years. The 105 members of the Senate are appointed by the prime minister and may serve until the age of 75. The directive of the parliament is "to make laws for the peace, order and good government of Canada."

Judicial Branch

The judicial branch, which interprets and enforces the law, is composed of the courts—the supreme court, the federal courts, and the provincial/territorial superior courts. The judges of the courts are appointed by the governor general in council.

Supreme Court (judicial branch)

The prime minister of Canada,

head of the Canadian government, is also known as the minister of the crown, the *premier ministre*, the chair of the cabinet, *Le Très Honorable*, and the head of the executive branch.

The prime ministership is the most politically powerful position in the Canadian government. While not elected directly, the prime minister is chosen by constitutional convention, and the ministership is given to the leader of the political party that occupies the largest number of seats in the House of Commons.

The prime minister does not have a fixed term limit because he or she serves at the pleasure of Her Majesty, the Queen. Therefore, the prime minister serves in the office until he or she resigns, is dismissed, or passes away. To date, there have been 22 Canadian prime ministers.

JOHN JOSEPH CALDWELL ABBOTT
3rd Prime Minister of Canada
BORN: March 12, 1821
St.-André-Est, Quebec
TERM: 1891–1892
POLITICAL PARTY: Liberal-Conservative
DIED: October 30, 1893

SIR JOHN ABBOTT was once in the railway business.

JOHN SPARROW DAVID THOMPSON
4th Prime Minister of Canada
BORN: November 10, 1844
Halifax, Nova Scotia
TERM: 1892–1894
POLITICAL PARTY: Liberal-Conservative
DIED: December 12, 1894

JOHN ALEXANDER MACDONALD
1st Prime Minister of Canada
BORN: January 11, 1815
Glasgow, Scotland
TERMS: 1867–1873; 1878–1891
POLITICAL PARTY: Liberal-Conservative
DIED: June 6, 1891

MACKENZIE BOWELL
5th Prime Minister of Canada
BORN: December 27, 1823
Rickinghall, Suffolk, England
TERM: 1894–1896
POLITICAL PARTY: Conservative
DIED: December 10, 1917

ALEXANDER MACKENZIE
2nd Prime Minister of Canada
BORN: January 28, 1822
Logierait, Perthshire, Scotland
TERM: 1873–1878
POLITICAL PARTY: Liberal
DIED: April 17, 1892

CHARLES TUPPER
6th Prime Minister of Canada
BORN: July 2, 1821
Amherst, Nova Scotia
TERM: 1896
POLITICAL PARTY: Conservative
DIED: October 30, 1915

WILFRID LAURIER
7th Prime Minister of Canada

BORN: November 20, 1841
Saint-Lin, Quebec
TERM: 1896–1911
POLITICAL PARTY: Liberal
DIED: February 17, 1919

RICHARD BEDFORD BENNETT
11th Prime Minister of Canada

BORN: July 3, 1870
Hopewell, New Brunswick
TERM: 1930–1935
POLITICAL PARTY: Conservative
DIED: June 26, 1947

ROBERT LAIRD BORDEN
8th Prime Minister of Canada

BORN: June 26, 1854
Grand Pré, Nova Scotia
TERM: 1911–1920
POLITICAL PARTY: Conservative
DIED: June 10, 1937

LOUIS STEPHEN ST.-LAURENT
12th Prime Minister of Canada

BORN: February 1, 1882
Compton, Quebec
TERM: 1948–1957
POLITICAL PARTY: Liberal
DIED: July 25, 1973

ARTHUR MEIGHEN
9th Prime Minister of Canada

BORN: June 16, 1874
Anderson, Ontario
TERMS: 1920–1921; 1926
POLITICAL PARTY: Conservative
DIED: August 5, 1960

JOHN GEORGE DIEFENBAKER
13th Prime Minister of Canada

BORN: September 18, 1895
Neustadt, Ontario
TERM: 1957–1963
POLITICAL PARTY: Progressive
Conservative
DIED: August 16, 1979

WILLIAM LYON MACKENZIE KING
10th Prime Minister of Canada

BORN: December 17, 1874
Berlin, Ontario
TERMS: 1921–1926; 1926–1930;
1935–1948
POLITICAL PARTY: Liberal
DIED: July 22, 1950

JOHN DIEFENBAKER SOLD NEWSPAPERS WHEN HE WAS A KID.

WILLIAM LYON MACKENZIE KING OWNED THREE IRISH TERRIERS IN HIS LIFETIME, AND NAMED THEM ALL PAT.

LESTER BOWLES PEARSON
14th Prime Minister of Canada

BORN: April 23, 1897
Newton Brook, Ontario
TERM: 1963–1968
POLITICAL PARTY: Liberal
DIED: December 27, 1972

PIERRE ELLIOTT TRUDEAU
15th Prime Minister of Canada

BORN: October 18, 1919
Montreal, Quebec

TERMS: 1968–1979; 1980–1984

POLITICAL PARTY: Liberal

DIED: September 28, 2000

KIM CAMPBELL
19th Prime Minister of Canada

BORN: March 10, 1947
Port Alberni,
British Columbia

TERM: 1993

POLITICAL PARTY: Progressive
Conservative

DIED: —

PIERRE TRUDEAU RARELY APPEARED IN PUBLIC WITHOUT WEARING A RED ROSE IN HIS LAPEL.

JOSEPH JACQUES JEAN CHRÉTIEN
20th Prime Minister of Canada

BORN: January 11, 1934
Shawinigan, Quebec

TERM: 1993–2003

POLITICAL PARTY: Liberal

DIED: —

CHARLES JOSEPH CLARK
16th Prime Minister of Canada

BORN: June 5, 1939
High River, Alberta

TERM: 1979–1980

POLITICAL PARTY: Progressive
Conservative

DIED: —

At the age of 79, Jean Chrétien learned to wakeboard.

JOHN NAPIER TURNER
17th Prime Minister of Canada

BORN: June 7, 1929
Richmond, Surrey, England

TERM: 1984

POLITICAL PARTY: Liberal

DIED: —

PAUL EDGAR PHILIPPE MARTIN
21st Prime Minister of Canada

BORN: August 28, 1938
Windsor, Ontario

TERM: 2003–2006

POLITICAL PARTY: Liberal

DIED: —

MARTIN BRIAN MULRONEY
18th Prime Minister of Canada

BORN: March 20, 1939
Baie-Comeau, Quebec

TERM: 1984–1993

POLITICAL PARTY: Progressive
Conservative

DIED: —

STEPHEN JOSEPH HARPER
22nd Prime Minister of Canada

BORN: April 30, 1959
Toronto, Ontario

TERM: 2006 to present

POLITICAL PARTY: Conservative

DIED: —

Canada's Political Parties

As in many democratic countries, numerous political parties vie for representation in Canada's government, but only a few really achieve it. There are also many provincial and territorial parties that are distinct from the federal parties. The following parties are those likely to be represented in parliament in the coming years.

Bloc Québécois

Bloc Québécois, known as The Bloc, was founded in 1991. It is a federal political party devoted to the separation of Quebec from the rest of the country.

Conservative Party

The Conservative Party of Canada, known as the Tories, is a group that was founded in 2003. It is one of the largest political parties in Canada. The CP was formed by the merger of the Canadian Alliance Party and the Progressive Conservative Party.

Green Party

The Green Party of Canada was launched in 1983. This left-wing party focuses on issues like the environment, social justice, and nonviolence. Elizabeth May has led the Green Party since 2006.

Liberal Party

The Liberal Party of Canada, known as the Grits, was founded in 1867. This moderate party is a dominant player in Canadian politics, having held power longer than any other party.

New Democratic Party

The New Democratic Party of Canada is a social democratic political party that was founded in 1961. It is considered to be the most liberal of Canada's major parties.

HAPPY BIRTHDAY!

The unmistakable maple leaf flag celebrates a major milestone in 2015: It turns 50! On February 15, 1965, the red and white flag was raised above Parliament Hill in Ottawa, officially replacing the Canadian Red Ensign.

Canadian Heroes

ALICE MUNRO 1931 (Wingham, Ontario)–

A writer specializing in short stories, Munro is one of the world's most well-known authors. Her books and collection of stories, which include *Dance of the Happy Shades*, have sold millions of copies around the world. Known as the "master of the contemporary short story," Munro is the first Canadian woman and just the 13th woman to earn the Nobel Prize in literature, a CAD $1.3 million award. **Did you know?** In 1963, Munro opened a bookstore in Victoria, British Columbia, which still stands today.

LAURA SECORD 1775 (Great Barrington, Massachusetts colony, America)–1868 (Niagara Falls, Ontario)

By being in the right place at the right time during the War of 1812, Secord was instrumental in the First Nations and British forces' defeat of American troops at the Battle of Beaver Dams. Legend has it that Secord overheard Americans talking about surprising the British at Beaver Dams and capturing an officer. She then walked 20 treacherous miles (32 km) through woods and streams in sweltering temperatures to warn the troops and save them from ambush. **Did you know?** Secord wasn't recognized for her impressive deed for decades, but was finally honored as a national hero when she was 85 years old.

JOHN McCRAE 1872 (Guelph, Ontario)–1918 (Boulogne, France)

A doctor with a flair for creativity, John McCrae is best remembered for penning the poem "In Flanders Fields," which he wrote in 1915 while serving as an officer and a surgeon for the Canadian Army during World War I. McCrae, who had previously taught pathology and medicine at several Canadian universities, wrote the poem on a pad while sitting on the back of an ambulance mere feet from the site of the bloody Battle of Ypres, in France. It remains one of the most memorable war poems ever written. **Did you know?** McCrae didn't just write poems. He also wrote short stories and scientific articles, and he was a talented artist as well.

CHIEF POUNDMAKER circa 1842 (Battleford Region, Western Saskatchewan)–1886 (Blackfoot Crossing, Alberta)

Chief Poundmaker, also called Pitikwahanapiwiyin, was a visionary Cree leader known as a peacemaker and guardian of his people. When the Canadian government did not live up to its treaties to the First Nations, Poundmaker became their critic. A gifted public speaker, Poundmaker defended his beliefs and his people. He helped negotiate with the Canadian government to get agricultural supplies and disaster relief for the First Nations. **Did you know?** The name Pitikwahanapiwiyin means "The One Who Sits at the Pound." Pound refers to the corrals into which buffalo were herded.

CLARA HUGHES 1972 (Winnipeg, Manitoba)–

The only woman in history to win medals at both Summer and Winter Olympic Games, Clara Hughes is one of Canada's greatest athletes. The cyclist and speed skater, who competed in a total of six Olympic Games, has earned six medals, including Canada's first ever medals in women's road cycling. An active humanitarian, Hughes has raised thousands of dollars for children's charities, including Right to Play, which encourages and establishes youth sports in underprivileged areas. **Did you know?** Hughes carried the Canadian flag into the opening ceremonies of the 2010 Winter Olympics in Vancouver, British Columbia.

Bet you didn't **know**

6 Sporty Canadian facts

1 LACROSSE, once known as "baggataway," was first played over 600 years ago by Iroquois in Ontario and New York, U.S.A.

2 Canadian-born JAMES NAISMITH, a gym teacher, INVENTED BASKETBALL in 1891.

3 Some EARLY HOCKEY PUCKS were made from chunks of FROZEN COW DUNG.

4 The FIRST FEMALE HOCKEY PLAYERS played in long skirts and dresses.

5 ONTARIO'S Mike Weir is the FIRST CANADIAN ever to WIN the Masters golf tournament.

6 Each February, Quebec City hosts canoe races across the icy St. Lawrence River, a tradition dating back more than 150 years.

ABORIGINAL

THE NATION'S FIRST INHABITANTS

Saamis Teepee is the world's largest teepee and was constructed for the 1988 Winter Olympics in Calgary. It now stands in Medicine Hat, Alberta.

A Blackfoot Blood First Nations dancer poses atop a cliff in Indian Battle Provincial Park, Lethbridge, Alberta.

Before European colonists arrived in North America, First Nations and Inuit people lived for thousands of years on the land that is now called Canada. The cultures of these aboriginal, or indigenous, people were diverse. From coast to coast they lived in harmony with nature: the Inuit in the Arctic; Tlingit, Haida, and Salish on the Pacific Coast; Blackfoot, Okanagan, and Nakoda on the Plains; Cree and Dene in the western subarctic; and Algonquin, Mohawk, and Iroquois in the St. Lawrence River Valley.

CANADA

Here Come the Europeans

In the 17th century, European settlers began to establish permanent settlements on aboriginal land in North America. For First Nations this was a cause for concern and occasionally led to conflict. To resolve the tension, First Nations signed treaties with the crown, which gave settlers access to some land. In exchange, the crown would provide services such as education and health care. The treaties also gave rights to both First Nations and Europeans, and made the founding of Canada possible.

As the number of settlers grew, they failed to honor their obligations to the native peoples. Laws were imposed on aboriginal peoples, strictly limiting them, forcing them to move onto small areas of land called reserves, and trying to force them to assimilate.

Today, Canada has a unique cultural heritage infused with the First Nations influence, including the name of Canada, which is believed to come from the Huron-Iroquois word *kanata*, meaning "village."

Inuit boy on a wooden sledge in Baker Lake, Nunavut

The Aboriginal Groups

There are more than one million aboriginal people in Canada, generally divided into three groups: First Nations, Inuit, and Métis.

First Nations is the largest group, composed of some 850,000 people. These people include a range of diverse groups who originally occupied Canadian land, such as the Dakota, the Iroquois, and the Innu, among many others. This means that among First Nations there are numerous individual tribal nations and languages.

The Inuit live mainly in northern Canada, particularly the Arctic regions. They share a common language and culture and number some 60,000.

The Métis are an ethnic group of mixed First Nation and European ancestry. There are some 452,000 Métis in Canada. They see themselves as the first true Canadians.

Members of the First Nations are the only aboriginal people who are recognized under the Indian Act, which means they receive treaty benefits and have reservations provided for them by the government.

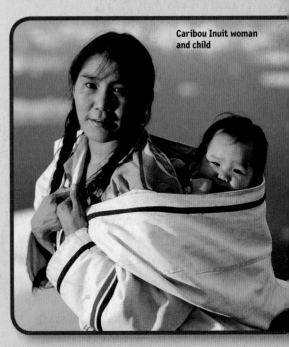

Caribou Inuit woman and child

249

W🍁MEN

Fighting for Equality

Prominent women activists gather in Ottawa for the Women's War Conference in 1918. Delegates determined how women could support the nation during World War I.

There was a time when Canadian women could not vote, serve in public office, practice law, or even enroll in universities. What's more, women lost almost all of their rights—including the ability to own land—once they were married.

Things began to change at the beginning of the 20th century when women started speaking up about the importance of equality. In the early 1900s, voting rights were granted in many provinces. By 1919, most women throughout the country were given the right to vote. It took another 42 years to extend that right to all women, regardless of race.

A landmark moment came in 1928 when a group of equality pioneers (later called the "Famous Five") petitioned for the right to be appointed to the Senate. The Constitution stated that "qualified persons" could serve in the Senate, but many people assumed that this did not include women. The Supreme Court even ruled that the word "person" in section 24 of the British North America Act did not include female persons. The Famous Five disagreed, and took their case to the Judicial Committee of the Privy Council, in London, England, where the Supreme Court's ruling was overturned, allowing women to become senators. The first female senator, Cairine Reay Wilson, was appointed four months later.

Today, the women's rights movement has enabled women to achieve success in many aspects of Canadian life. Women represent the majority of students at most universities, and there are 76 female representatives in the House of Commons, an all-time high. And as women continue to make great strides throughout Canada's society, they will always look back and thank those who sparked such an important change a century ago.

An International Women's Day march and rally in Toronto

Key Events in Women's Rights

1887: **Clara Brett Martin** becomes Canada's first female lawyer and the first woman to practice law in the entire British Empire.

1919: **Most women are given the right to vote** in federal elections.

1921: **Agnes McPhail becomes Canada's first female member of parliament.** She is elected to the House of Commons in the first federal election in which women are able to vote and run for parliament.

1928: **Canada's Olympic Team includes women** for the first time. The 4 x 100 meter relay team wins gold on the track, setting a world record in the process.

1929: **The Judicial Committee of the Privy Council** overturns the Supreme Court of Canada's decision that women cannot be appointed to the Senate. Canada's first female senator is appointed four months later.

1940: **Quebec becomes the final province** to give women the right to vote in provincial elections.

1956: **The passing of the Female Employees Equal Pay Act** ensures that women make the same amount in wages as men.

1971: **The federal government amends the Canada Labour Code** to prohibit discrimination based on sex and to reinforce equal pay for equal work.

1977: **March 8 is deemed International Women's Day** in Canada.

1980: **Nova Scotia's Alexa McDonough** is the first woman to be elected leader of a provincial political party holding seats in a legislature.

1982: **Women's groups fight** to ensure that the Charter of Rights and Freedoms in the Canadian Constitution of 1982 includes gender equality.

2000: **Beverly McLachlin** is the first woman to become Chief Justice of Canada.

Roberta Bondar

As a child growing up in Sault Ste. Marie, Ontario, Roberta Bondar used to daydream about exploring the skies above. In 1992, that dream came true when Bondar became the first Canadian woman to go into space.

Medicine was Bondar's first passion, and she studied to become a doctor. She also earned her pilot's license, learning to fly a plane before she could drive a car.

ROBERTA BONDAR

After submitting an application, Bondar was chosen as a member of the first Canadian Astronaut Program in 1983. Her experience as a doctor primed her for her role as an astronaut, as she conducted studies on the effects of weightlessness on the human body. After years of training, Bondar flew on the space shuttle *Discovery* in January 1992.

Lisa LaFlamme

One of Canada's most intrepid broadcast journalists, Lisa LaFlamme has crisscrossed the globe to cover the biggest breaking news stories. No stranger to danger, LaFlamme has dodged bullets in war zones such as Afghanistan and escaped violence during a political uprising in Egypt in 2012.

LISA LAFLAMME

A native of Kitchener-Waterloo, LaFlamme began her broadcasting career in 1989 and spent the next 20 years covering major news stories including the Royal Wedding, the Olympics, Hurricane Katrina, and the Haiti earthquake. LaFlamme's unflappable spirit and professionalism has allowed her to soar to the top of the industry. She succeeded Lloyd Robertson as chief anchor of CTV News in 2011.

STUMP YOUR PARENTS

HISTORY HAPPENS QUIZ

Test your parents to see if they're well-read on the past— or if it's time to hit the books. ANSWERS BELOW

1 What did the Anglo-Saxons bury under an English field 1,300 years ago?

a. 3,500 pieces of gold and silver
b. diamond necklaces
c. dinosaur bones
d. a time capsule

2 **True or false?** Boys began training for knighthood when they were ten years old.

3 Where is Borobudur, the world's largest Buddhist monument?

a. Indonesia
b. Indiana
c. Malaysia
d. Cambodia

4 How tall was the *Titanic*?

a. 13 stories
b. 17 stories
c. 70 stories
d. as tall as 13 giraffes

5 Which of the following has not been recovered from an Egyptian tomb?

a. clothes
b. games
c. jewelry
d. popcorn

Not STUMPED yet?
Check out the *National Geographic Kids Quiz Whiz* collection for more crazy HISTORY questions!

Brilliant Biographies

A biography is the story of a person's life. It can be a brief summary or a long book. Biographers—those who write biographies— use many different sources to learn about their subjects. You can write your own biography of a famous person whom you find inspiring.

How to Get Started

Choose a subject you find interesting. If you think Cleopatra is cool, you have a good chance of getting your reader interested, too. If you're bored by ancient Egypt, your reader will be snoring after your first paragraph.

Your subject can be almost anyone: an author, an inventor, a celebrity, a politician, or a member of your family. To find someone to write about, ask yourself these simple questions:

1. Whom do I want to know more about?
2. What did this person do that was special?
3. How did this person change the world?

Do Your Research

- Find out as much about your subject as possible. Read books, news articles, and encyclopedia entries. Watch video clips and movies, and search the Internet. Conduct interviews, if possible.
- Take notes, writing down important facts and interesting stories about your subject.

Write the Biography

- Come up with a title. Include the person's name.
- Write an introduction. Consider asking a probing question about your subject.
- Include information about the person's childhood. When was this person born? Where did he or she grow up? Whom did he or she admire?
- Highlight the person's talents, accomplishments, and personal attributes.
- Describe the specific events that helped to shape this person's life. Did this person ever have a problem and overcome it?
- Write a conclusion. Include your thoughts about why it is important to learn about this person.
- Once you have finished your first draft, revise and then proofread your work.

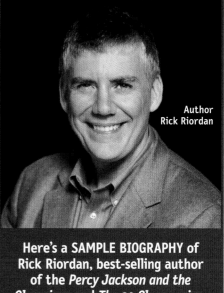

Author Rick Riordan

Here's a SAMPLE BIOGRAPHY of Rick Riordan, best-selling author of the *Percy Jackson and the Olympians* and *The 39 Clues* series. Of course, there is so much more for you to discover, and write about on your own!

Rick Riordan—Author

Rick Riordan was born on June 5, 1964, in San Antonio, Texas, U.S.A. Born into a creative family—his mom was a musician and artist and his dad was a ceramicist— Riordan began writing in middle school, and he published his first short stories while attending college.

After graduating from University of Texas at Austin, Riordan went on to teach English to middle schoolers, spending his summers as a music director at a summer camp. Writing adult mysteries on the side, Riordan soon discovered his knack for writing for younger readers and published *The Lightning Thief*, the first book in the Percy Jackson series, in 2005. *The Sea of Monsters* soon followed. Before long, Riordan quit his teaching job to become a full-time writer.

Today Riordan has penned more than 35 books, firmly establishing himself as one of the most accomplished and well-known authors of our time. When he's not writing, Riordan—who lives with his wife, Becky, and their sons Haley and Patrick— likes to read, swim, play guitar, and travel with his family.

Geography
Rocks

KINDS OF MAPS

Maps are special tools that geographers use to tell a story about Earth. Maps can be used to show just about anything related to places. Some maps show physical features, such as mountains or vegetation. Maps can also show climates or natural hazards and other things we cannot easily see. Other maps illustrate different features on Earth—political boundaries, urban centers, and economic systems.

AN IMPERFECT TOOL

Maps are not perfect. A globe is a scale model of Earth with accurate relative sizes and locations. Because maps are flat, they involve distortions of size, shape, and direction. Also, cartographers—people who create maps—make choices about what information to include. Because of this, it is important to study many different types of maps to learn the complete story of Earth. Three commonly found kinds of maps are shown on this page.

PHYSICAL MAPS. Earth's natural features—landforms, water bodies, and vegetation—are shown on physical maps. The map above uses color and shading to illustrate mountains, lakes, rivers, and deserts of western Africa. Country names and borders are added for reference, but they are not natural features.

POLITICAL MAPS. These maps represent characteristics of the landscape created by humans, such as boundaries, cities, and place-names. Natural features are added only for reference. On the map above, capital cities are represented with a star inside a circle, while other cities are shown with black dots.

THEMATIC MAPS. Patterns related to a particular topic or theme, such as population distribution, appear on these maps. The map above displays the region's climate zones, which range from tropical wet (bright green) to tropical wet and dry (light green) to semiarid (dark yellow) to arid or desert (light yellow).

GEOGRAPHIC FEATURES

From roaring rivers to parched deserts, from underwater canyons to jagged mountains, Earth is covered with beautiful and diverse environments. Here are examples of the most common types of geographic features found around the world.

DESERT

Deserts are land features created by climate, specifically by a lack of water. Here, a camel caravan crosses the Sahara in North Africa.

VALLEY	RIVER	MOUNTAIN
Valleys, cut by running water or moving ice, may be broad and flat or narrow and steep, such as the Indus River Valley in Ladakh, India (above).	As a river moves through flatlands, it twists and turns. Above, the Rio Los Amigos winds through a rain forest in Peru.	Mountains are Earth's tallest landforms, and Mount Everest (above) rises highest of all, at 29,035 feet (8,850 m) above sea level.

GLACIER	CANYON	WATERFALL
Glaciers—"rivers" of ice—such as Alaska's Hubbard Glacier (above) move slowly from mountains to the sea. Global warming is shrinking them.	Steep-sided valleys called canyons are created mainly by running water. Buckskin Gulch in Utah (above) is the deepest slot canyon in the American Southwest.	Waterfalls form when a river reaches an abrupt change in elevation. Above, Kaieteur Falls, in Guyana, has a sheer drop of 741 feet (226 m).

THE POLITICAL WORLD

Earth's land area is made up of seven continents, but people have divided much of the land into smaller political units called countries. Australia is a continent made up of a single country, and Antarctica is set aside for scientific research. But the other five continents include almost 200 independent countries. The political map shown here depicts boundaries—imaginary lines created by treaties—that separate countries. Some boundaries, such as the one between the United States and Canada, are very stable and have been recognized for many years.

See Europe map for more detail.

Winkel Tripel Projection

Other boundaries, such as the one between Ethiopia and Eritrea in northeast Africa, are relatively new and still disputed. Countries come in all shapes and sizes. Russia and Canada are giants; others, such as Luxembourg, are small. Some countries are long and skinny—look at Chile in South America! Still other countries—such as Indonesia and Japan in Asia—are made up of groups of islands. The political map is a clue to the diversity that makes Earth so fascinating.

OCEAN

Svalbard (Norway)
Barents Sea
Kara Sea
Severnaya Zemlya
New Siberian Islands
Laptev Sea
East Siberian Sea
Novaya Zemlya

NORWAY
SWEDEN
FINLAND
DEN.
GERMANY
LATV.
EST.
LITH.
POLAND
BELARUS
UKRAINE
MOLD.
ROMANIA
BULGARIA
ITALY
ALBANIA
GREECE
TUNISIA
Mediterranean Sea
CYPRUS
LEBANON
ISRAEL
GEORGIA
ARM. AZERB.
TURKEY
SYRIA
IRAQ
JORDAN
Caspian Sea
UZBEK.
TURKMEN.
KYRGYZSTAN
TAJIKISTAN
AFGHAN.
KAZAKHSTAN

R U S S I A

Sea of Okhotsk
Lake Baikal
MONGOLIA
NORTH KOREA
SOUTH KOREA
Bering Sea
JAPAN

C H I N A

TAIWAN
The People's Republic of China claims Taiwan as its 23rd province. Taiwan's government (Republic of China) maintains that there are two political entities.

Taiwan

ALGERIA
LIBYA
EGYPT
IRAN
PAKISTAN
NEPAL
BHUTAN
BANGLADESH
INDIA
MYANMAR (BURMA)
LAOS
VIETNAM
THAILAND
CAMBODIA
South China Sea
Philippine Sea
PHILIPPINES
Northern Mariana Islands (U.S.)
Guam (U.S.)
PACIFIC OCEAN
MARSHALL ISLANDS

NIGER
CHAD
SUDAN
ERITREA
YEMEN
DJIBOUTI
OMAN
SAUDI ARABIA
BAHRAIN
QATAR
U.A.E.
KUWAIT
Arabian Sea
Bay of Bengal
SRI LANKA
MALDIVES
BENIN
NIGERIA
TOGO
CAMEROON
C.A.R.
SOUTH SUDAN
ETHIOPIA
SOMALIA
UGANDA
KENYA
BRUNEI
MALAYSIA
SINGAPORE
PALAU
FEDERATED STATES OF MICRONESIA
KIRIBATI

GABON
CONGO
DEM. REP. OF THE CONGO
RWANDA
BURUNDI
TANZANIA
SEYCHELLES
COMOROS
Cabinda (Angola)
ANGOLA
ZAMBIA
MALAWI
ZIMBABWE
MOZAMBIQUE
MADAGASCAR
NAMIBIA
BOTSWANA
Réunion (France)
MAURITIUS

INDIAN OCEAN

INDONESIA
New Guinea
PAPUA NEW GUINEA
TIMOR-LESTE (EAST TIMOR)
SOLOMON ISLANDS
TUVALU
EQUATOR
NAURU
VANUATU
Coral Sea
FIJI

SOUTH AFRICA
SWAZILAND
LESOTHO

Kerguelen Islands (France)

AUSTRALIA

Great Australian Bight
Tasman Sea
Tasmania
NEW ZEALAND
North Island
South Island
New Caledonia (France)

CIRCLE

ARCTICA

Ross Sea

THE PHYSICAL WORLD

Earth is dominated by large landmasses called continents—seven in all—and by an interconnected global ocean that is divided into four parts by the continents. More than 70 percent of Earth's surface is covered by oceans, and the remaining 30 percent is made up of land areas.

Different landforms give variety to the surface of the continents. The Rockies and the Andes mark the western edge of the Americas, and the Himalaya tower above southern Asia. The Plateau of Tibet forms the rugged core of Asia, while the Northern European Plain extends from the North Sea to the Ural Mountains. Much of Africa is a plateau, and dry plains cover large areas of Australia. Mountains rise more than 16,000 feet (4,877 m) above Antarctica's massive ice sheets. Mountains and trenches make the ocean floors as varied as any continent. A mountain chain called the Mid-Atlantic Ridge runs the length of the Atlantic Ocean. In the western Pacific, trenches drop deep into the ocean floor.

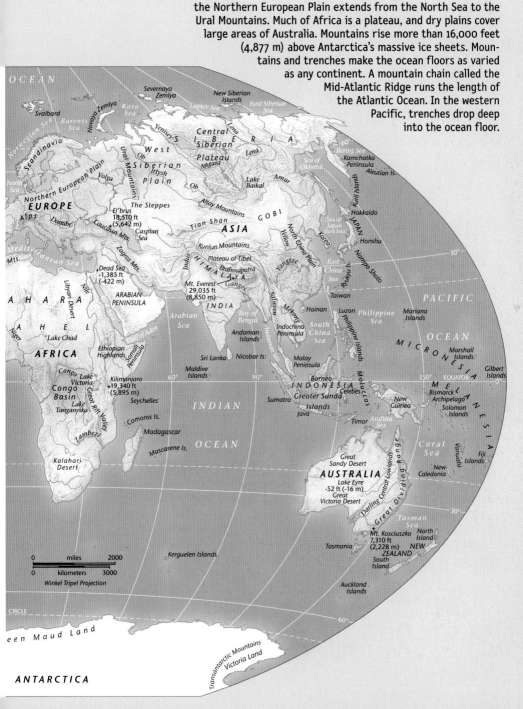

SPOTLIGHT ON
AFRICA

SCANNER

SCAN THIS PAGE!
GET BONUS MOBILE
CONTENT! Download
the free NG Kids
scanner app. Directions
on inside front cover.

African lion
and cub

A lion's roar
can be heard
up to 5 miles
(8 km) away.

In legends from
Tanzania, Africa,
witches ride on
hyenas, not
broomsticks.

The massive continent of Africa, where humankind began millions of years ago, is second to only Asia in size. Stretching nearly as far from west to east as it does from north to south, Africa is home to both the longest river in the world (the Nile) and the largest hot desert on Earth (Sahara).

Zulu woman in native costume

Beautiful Baskets

Young girls and women weave brightly colored baskets from grass and straw that have become a trademark of African cultures. The baskets are used for decoration and to store food.

Dry Land

One-third of Africa is covered in sand, bedrock, and stone. In the Sahara, there's only about 1 person per square mile (0.4 sq km), one of the lowest population densities on Earth.

Great Lakes

Three of the world's ten biggest lakes are in Africa. Lake Victoria, Lake Tanganyika, and Lake Malawi are found in the Great Rift Valley, which stretches from Ethiopia to Mozambique.

Unique Animals

Ninety percent of the animals found on the island of Madagascar evolved there and nowhere else. Many are endangered, including some of the numerous species of lemurs.

Top 5 Largest Animals

1. African elephant
   up to 14,000 pounds (6,350 kg)

2. Hippopotamus
   up to 8,000 pounds (3,630 kg)

3. White rhinoceros
   up to 7,920 pounds (3,600 kg)

4. Black rhinoceros
   up to 3,080 pounds (1,400 kg)

5. Giraffe
   up to 2,800 pounds (1,270 kg)

Downtown Johannesburg in South Africa

AFRICA

PHYSICAL

LAND AREA
11,608,000 sq mi
(30,065,000 sq km)

HIGHEST POINT
Kilimanjaro,
Tanzania
19,340 ft (5,895 m)

LOWEST POINT
Lake Assal, Djibouti
-512 ft (-156 m)

LONGEST RIVER
Nile
4,241 mi (6,825 km)

LARGEST LAKE
Victoria
26,800 sq mi
(69,500 sq km)

POLITICAL

POPULATION
1,099,579,000

LARGEST COUNTRY
Algeria
919,595 sq mi
(2,381,741 sq km)

LARGEST METROPOLITAN AREA
Lagos, Nigeria
Pop. 11,223,000

MOST DENSELY POPULATED COUNTRY
Mauritius 1,646 people
per sq mi (636 per sq km)

ASIA

EUROPE

Atlantic
Ocean

Azores
(Portugal)

Madeira Islands
(Portugal)

Canary Islands
(Spain)

Strait of Gibraltar

Rabat
Casablanca ⊛
MOROCCO
Marrakech •
Fez •

Oran ⊛
Algiers ⊛
Constantine •

Tunis ⊛
TUNISIA
Tripoli ⊛
Benghazi •

Mediterranean Sea

Alexandria •
Port
Said • Africa–Asia
boundary
Cairo ⊛
Nile
River

Red Sea

EGYPT

LIBYA

ALGERIA

Western
Sahara
(Morocco)

MAURITANIA
⊛ Nouakchott

CAPE
VERDE
•

Dakar ⊛
SENEGAL
Banjul • GAMBIA

MALI

Tombouctou
(Timbuktu) •

BURKINA
FASO

NIGER

Niamey
⊛

CHAD

SUDAN

Omdurman •
Khartoum •

DARFUR

ERITREA
⊛ Asmara

TROPIC OF CANCER

SOMALIA

ETHIOPIA

SOUTH SUDAN

CENTRAL AFRICAN REPUBLIC

DJIBOUTI

Mogadishu (historic capital; no central government since 1991)

Addis Ababa

Djibouti

Lake Assal (-156 m) -512 ft. ▼

Gulf of Aden

10°N

0°

SEYCHELLES

Victoria ⊛

MAURITIUS
Port Louis ⊛
Réunion ○ (France)

MADAGASCAR

Antananarivo ⊛

COMOROS
Moroni ⊛

Mombasa

Dar es Salaam

Mozambique Channel

Indian Ocean

30°S

10°S

50°E

60°E

40°E

KENYA

Nairobi ⊛

Kilimanjaro
19,340 ft
(5,895 m) ▲

TANZANIA

Dodoma ⊛

Lake Victoria

MALAWI

Lilongwe ⊛

MOZAMBIQUE

SWAZILAND

Maputo ⊛
Lobamba

LESOTHO

Durban

Maseru ⊛

Port Elizabeth

Juba •

UGANDA

Kampala ⊛

RWANDA

Kigali ⊛

BURUNDI
Bujumbura ⊛

DEMOCRATIC REPUBLIC OF THE CONGO

Kisangani •

Mbuji-Mayi •

Kananga •

Kinshasa ⊛

Bangui ⊛

Lubumbashi •

Kolwezi •

Kitwe •

ZAMBIA

Lusaka ⊛

Harare •

ZIMBABWE

BOTSWANA

Gaborone ⊛

NAMIBIA

Windhoek ⊛

Pretoria (Tshwane)

Mbabane

Johannesburg •

Bloemfontein ⊛

SOUTH AFRICA

Cape Town ⊛

N'Djamena ⊛

CAMEROON

Yaoundé ⊛

Douala •

Malabo ⊛

EQUATORIAL GUINEA

São Tomé

SAO TOME & PRINCIPE

GABON

Libreville ⊛

CONGO

Brazzaville ⊛

Pointe-Noire •

Cabinda (Angola)

Luanda ⊛

ANGOLA

NIGERIA

Kano •

Abuja ⊛

Ogbomosho •

Lagos •

Porto-Novo ⊛

Cotonou •

BENIN

TOGO

Lomé ⊛

Accra ⊛

GHANA

Ouagadougou ⊛

Bamako ⊛

CÔTE D'IVOIRE (IVORY COAST)

Yamoussoukro ⊛

Abidjan •

LIBERIA

Monrovia ⊛

SIERRA LEONE

Freetown ⊛

Conakry ⊛

GUINEA

GUINEA-BISSAU

Bissau ⊛

Ascension (U.K.)

St. Helena (U.K.)

Atlantic Ocean

EQUATOR

TROPIC OF CAPRICORN

20°W

10°W

0°

10°S

20°S

30°S

800 Miles

800 Kilometers

0

0

Azimuthal Equal-Area Projection

Map Key

⊛ National capital
• Other city
▲ Highest point
▼ Lowest point

SPOTLIGHT ON
ANTARCTICA

Elephant seals living along the coast can stay underwater for up to two hours.

Winds in Antarctica can gust to more than 200 miles an hour (322 kph).

Elephant seal

This frozen continent may be a cool place to visit, but unless you're a penguin, you probably wouldn't want to hang out in Antarctica for long. The fact that it's the coldest, windiest, and driest continent helps explain why humans never colonized this ice-covered land surrounding the South Pole.

A seasonal Argentine scientific research station, Almirante Brown is also a popular stop for tourists.

Bare Ground

Just 2 percent of the continent is not covered by ice. In Dry Valleys, a 1,500-square-mile (3,885-sq-km) area of bare land, high winds blast away snow and prevent an ice buildup.

Warm Waters

Deception Island's geothermal pools are a popular spot for the 15,000 tourists who visit Antarctica each year. Activity from an underwater active volcano keeps the waters warm.

Stealth Seals

Native to Antarctica, Weddell seals are the world's southernmost animal. The rarely seen animals spend most of their time below ice, and they breathe through holes in the ice's surface.

Cool Blooms

Yes, flowers do grow on Antarctica! Two species of flowering plants, including the Antarctic pearlwort, grow along the Antarctic Peninsula and on some islands.

Extreme Antarctica

Highest recorded temperature
59°F (15°C), 1974

Lowest recorded temperature
-135.8°F (-93.2°C), 2010

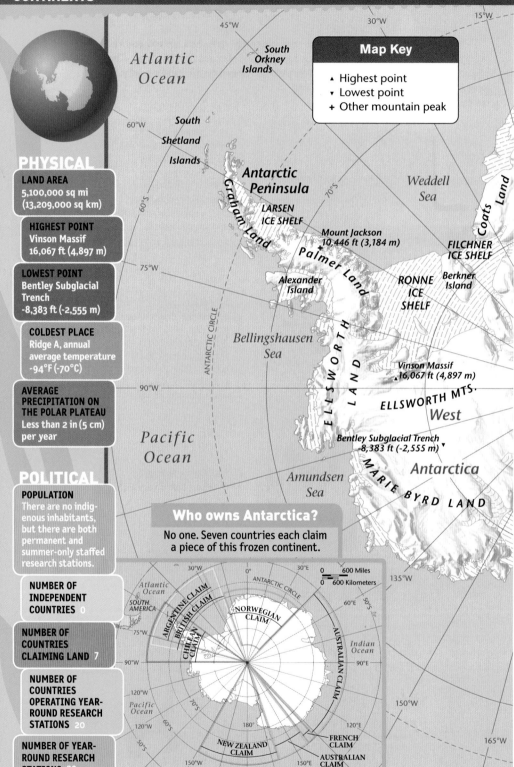

Map Key

▲ Highest point
▼ Lowest point
+ Other mountain peak

Atlantic Ocean

South Orkney Islands

South Shetland Islands

Graham Land

Antarctic Peninsula

LARSEN ICE SHELF

Mount Jackson
10,446 ft (3,184 m)

Palmer Land

Alexander Island

Weddell Sea

Coats Land

FILCHNER ICE SHELF

RONNE ICE SHELF

Berkner Island

Bellingshausen Sea

E L L S W O R T H   L A N D

Vinson Massif
▲16,067 ft (4,897 m)

ELLSWORTH MTS.

West

Bentley Subglacial Trench
-8,383 ft (-2,555 m) ▼

Antarctica

Pacific Ocean

Amundsen Sea

M A R I E   B Y R D   L A N D

ANTARCTIC CIRCLE

PHYSICAL

LAND AREA
5,100,000 sq mi
(13,209,000 sq km)

HIGHEST POINT
Vinson Massif
16,067 ft (4,897 m)

LOWEST POINT
Bentley Subglacial Trench
-8,383 ft (-2,555 m)

COLDEST PLACE
Ridge A, annual average temperature -94°F (-70°C)

AVERAGE PRECIPITATION ON THE POLAR PLATEAU
Less than 2 in (5 cm) per year

POLITICAL

POPULATION
There are no indigenous inhabitants, but there are both permanent and summer-only staffed research stations.

NUMBER OF INDEPENDENT COUNTRIES 0

NUMBER OF COUNTRIES CLAIMING LAND 7

NUMBER OF COUNTRIES OPERATING YEAR-ROUND RESEARCH STATIONS 20

NUMBER OF YEAR-ROUND RESEARCH STATIONS 39

Who owns Antarctica?

No one. Seven countries each claim a piece of this frozen continent.

Atlantic Ocean

SOUTH AMERICA

ARGENTINE CLAIM

BRITISH CLAIM

CHILEAN CLAIM

NORWEGIAN CLAIM

ANTARCTIC CIRCLE

AUSTRALIAN CLAIM

Indian Ocean

Pacific Ocean

FRENCH CLAIM

AUSTRALIAN CLAIM

NEW ZEALAND CLAIM

0   600 Miles
0   600 Kilometers

ANTARCTICA

FIMBUL
ICE SHELF

0° 15°E 30°E 45°E

RIISER-LARSEN
ICE SHELF

60°E

Q U E E N   M A U D   L A N D

ENDERBY
LAND

*Indian
Ocean*

Valkyrie
Dome

MacKenzie Bay 75°E

Lambert
Glacier

AMERY ICE SHELF

AMERICAN

HIGHLAND

Ridge A +

WEST
ICE SHELF

POLAR PLATEAU

East

90°E

● South Pole

Antarctica

SHACKLETON
ICE SHELF

T R A N S A N T A R C T I C   M O U N T A I N S

80°S

105°E

ROSS
ICE
SHELF

W I L K E S   L A N D

Roosevelt
Island

Taylor
Glacier

Ross Island

Mount Erebus
12,448 ft
(3,794 m)

70°S

*Ross
Sea*

V I C T O R I A   L A N D

120°E

Talos
Dome

180°

60°S

● South
Magnetic
Pole (2013)

*Indian
Ocean*

0   600 Miles
0   600 Kilometers

Azimuthal Equidistant Projection

150°E 135°E

269

SPOTLIGHT ON
ASIA

Shwedagon Pagoda in
Yangon (Rangoon), Myanmar
(Burma)

The
Shwedagon
Pagoda (right) is
topped with 5,448
diamonds and 2,317
rubies, sapphires,
and other gems.

Archery
is the national
sport of Bhutan,
a country in
southern Asia.

Made up of 46 countries, Asia is the world's largest continent. And just how big is it? From western Turkey to the eastern tip of Russia, Asia spans nearly half the globe! Home to four billion citizens—that's three out of five people on the planet—Asia's population is bigger than that of all the other continents combined.

Rare Breed

Native to Indonesia, Southeast Asia, and Malaysia, the rare binturong—or bear cat—has a cat's face, a bear's body, and a tail that's as long as its body.

Kuala Lumpur, Malaysia

Popular Passage

Each year about 70,000 merchant ships cross the Strait of Malacca between Malaysia and Indonesia. The most direct route between India and China, this channel serves as an important shipping lane.

Go Bananas

Bananas have grown in Southeast Asia for over 7,000 years. Today, the Philippines is one of the world's largest exporters of the fruit.

On the Move

About a third of the population of Mongolia moves seasonally, living in portable huts called ger while traveling up to 70 miles (112 km) on foot to find food sources for their livestock.

Asia's Tallest Buildings

Burj Khalifa	Makkah Clock Royal Tower	Taipei 101	Shanghai World Financial Center	International Commerce Centre
Dubai, U.A.E. 2,717 feet (828 m)	Mecca, Saudi Arabia 1,972 feet (601 m)	Taiwan 1,667 feet (508 m)	Shanghai, China 1,614 feet (492 m)	Hong Kong, China 1,588 feet (484 m)

Komodo dragon in Indonesia

ASIA

PHYSICAL

LAND AREA
17,208,000 sq mi
(44,570,000 sq km)

HIGHEST POINT
Mount Everest,
China–Nepal
29,035 ft (8,850 m)

LOWEST POINT
Dead Sea,
Israel–Jordan
-1,385 ft (-422 m)

COLDEST PLACE
Yangtze, China
3,880 mi (6,244 km)

**LARGEST LAKE
ENTIRELY IN ASIA**
Lake Baikal, Russia
12,200 sq mi
(31,500 sq km)

POLITICAL

POPULATION
4,302,088,000

**LARGEST
METROPOLITAN AREA**
Tokyo, Japan
Pop. 37,217,000

**LARGEST COUNTRY
ENTIRELY IN ASIA**
China
3,705,405 sq mi
(9,596,960 sq km)

**MOST DENSELY
POPULATED COUNTRY**
Singapore
21,349 people
per sq mi
(8,248 per sq km)

EUROPE

Mediterranean Sea

Dardanelles
Bosporus
İzmir
TURKEY
Ankara
ARMENIA
GEORGIA
Tbilisi
Yerevan
Baku
AZERBAIJAN
LEBANON
Beirut
SYRIA
Damascus
Jerusalem
Amman
ISRAEL
Dead Sea
-1,385 ft
(-422 m)
JORDAN
Baghdad
IRAQ
Basra
Tehran
IRAN
Mashhad
Medina
KUWAIT
Kuwait City
Jeddah
SAUDI ARABIA
Mecca
Manama
Riyadh
BAHRAIN
Doha
QATAR
Dubai
Abu Dhabi
Muscat
Sanaa
YEMEN
OMAN
Aden
UNITED ARAB
EMIRATES

Nizhniy Tagil
Tyumen'
Yekaterinburg
Magnitogorsk
Chelyabinsk
Omsk
Astana
TURKMENISTAN
Qaraghandy
KAZAKHSTAN
Ashgabat
UZBEKISTAN
Tashkent
Bishkek
Almaty
Samarqand
KYRGYZSTAN
Dushanbe
TAJIKISTAN
AFGHANISTAN
Hotan
Kabul
Islamabad
Rawalpindi
Faisalabad
Lahore
PAKISTAN
Delhi
New Delhi
NEPAL
Karachi
Jaipur
Kanpur
Indore
Bhopal
Surat
Mumbai
(Bombay)
INDIA
Pune
Hyderabad
Bangalore
(Bengaluru)
Chennai
(Madras)
SRI
LANKA
Colombo
Sri Jayewardenepura Kotte
Male
MALDIVES

Europe
Asia
R U

AFRICA

Arabian
Sea

EQUATOR

0
800 Miles
0
800 Kilometers
Two-point Equidistant Projection

Indian Ocean

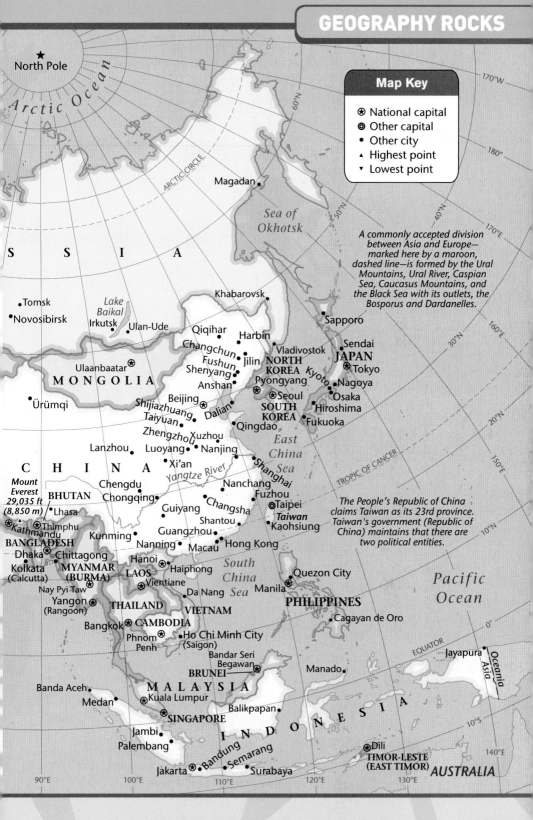

★ North Pole

Arctic Ocean

Map Key

⊛ National capital
◎ Other capital
• Other city
▲ Highest point
▼ Lowest point

R S S I A

•Tomsk
•Novosibirsk
Lake Baikal
Irkutsk• •Ulan-Ude

Magadan

Sea of Okhotsk

ARCTIC CIRCLE

Khabarovsk

Sapporo

A commonly accepted division between Asia and Europe—marked here by a maroon, dashed line—is formed by the Ural Mountains, Ural River, Caspian Sea, Caucasus Mountains, and the Black Sea with its outlets, the Bosporus and Dardanelles.

Qiqihar   Harbin
Changchun Jilin   Vladivostok
Fushun   Sendai
•Ulaanbaatar ⊛ Shenyang NORTH KOREA JAPAN
Anshan   Pyongyang Kyoto •Tokyo
M O N G O L I A   ⊛Seoul Nagoya
•Ürümqi   Beijing⊛ SOUTH Osaka
Shijiazhuang• •Dalian KOREA •Hiroshima
Taiyuan Qingdao• •Fukuoka
Zhengzhou •Xuzhou
Lanzhou• •Luoyang •Nanjing East China Sea
C H I N A •Xi'an Shanghai
Yangtze River   TROPIC OF CANCER
Mount Everest 29,035 ft (8,850 m) ▲ Chengdu• Nanchang
BHUTAN Chongqing• Changsha• Fuzhou
•Lhasa   Guiyang• •Taipei The People's Republic of China claims Taiwan as its 23rd province. Taiwan's government (Republic of China) maintains that there are two political entities.
⊛Kathmandu •Thimphu Shantou• Taiwan
BANGLADESH Kunming• Guangzhou• •Kaohsiung
•Dhaka ⊛Chittagong Nanning• •Macau •Hong Kong
Kolkata (Calcutta)• Hanoi⊛ South China Sea
MYANMAR (BURMA) Haiphong• •Quezon City
Nay Pyi Taw⊛ LAOS ⊛Vientiane Manila⊛ Pacific Ocean
Yangon (Rangoon)•⊛ Da Nang• PHILIPPINES
THAILAND VIETNAM
Bangkok⊛ •CAMBODIA Ho Chi Minh City (Saigon) •Cagayan de Oro
Phnom Penh⊛ Bandar Seri Begawan⊛ EQUATOR Jayapura•
Banda Aceh• BRUNEI Manado• Oceania Asia
Medan• M A L A Y S I A
•Kuala Lumpur Balikpapan•
⊛SINGAPORE I N D O N E S I A
Jambi•
Palembang• •Bandung •Dili
Jakarta⊛ •Semarang TIMOR-LESTE (EAST TIMOR) AUSTRALIA
Surabaya•

SPOTLIGHT ON
AUSTRALIA,
NEW ZEALAND, AND OCEANIA

More kangaroos than people live in Australia.

In Papua New Guinea, sunken ships from World War II are popular attractions for scuba divers.

Ifalik Island in Papua New Guinea

G'day, mate! This vast region, covering almost 3.3 million square miles (8.5 million sq km), includes Australia—the world's smallest and flattest continent—and New Zealand, as well as a fleet of mostly tiny islands scattered across the Pacific Ocean. Also known as "down under," all of the countries in this region are in the Southern Hemisphere, and below the Equator.

Aborigine children in ceremonial dress

Sporty Citizens

There's no doubt Australians are athletic: 70 percent of people over age 15 participate in sports more than once a week. Rugby, football, and cricket are fan favorites.

Don't Look Down!

Auckland, New Zealand's SkyJump offers daring visitors a wild ride. You can bungee jump off a 630-foot (192-m) -high platform on New Zealand's tallest man-made structure.

Cow Country

Australia, a top cattle producer, is home to about 29 million cows. Anna Creek Cattle Station in South Australia is the world's largest cattle ranch. It's slightly larger than Israel!

Giant Reef

The Great Barrier Reef, found off the east coast of Australia, is big enough to be seen from space. It's teeming with sea life, like whales, dolphins, sea turtles, snakes, coral, and fish.

Australia: Continent or Island?

Greenland: 836,330 sq mi (2,166,086 sq km)

Australia: 2,969,606 sq mi (7,692,024 sq km)

How does Australia compare to Greenland, the world's largest island?

Numbat

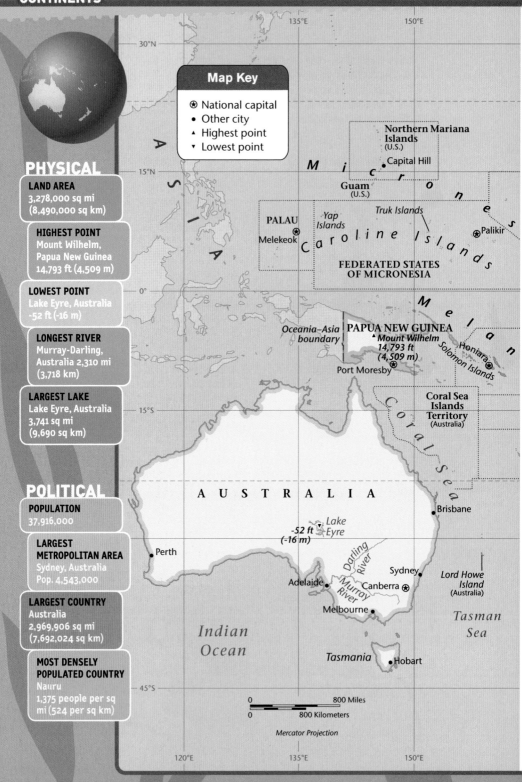

Map Key

- ⊛ National capital
- • Other city
- ▲ Highest point
- ▼ Lowest point

PHYSICAL

LAND AREA
3,278,000 sq mi
(8,490,000 sq km)

HIGHEST POINT
Mount Wilhelm,
Papua New Guinea
14,793 ft (4,509 m)

LOWEST POINT
Lake Eyre, Australia
-52 ft (-16 m)

LONGEST RIVER
Murray-Darling,
Australia 2,310 mi
(3,718 km)

LARGEST LAKE
Lake Eyre, Australia
3,741 sq mi
(9,690 sq km)

POLITICAL

POPULATION
37,916,000

**LARGEST
METROPOLITAN AREA**
Sydney, Australia
Pop. 4,543,000

LARGEST COUNTRY
Australia
2,969,906 sq mi
(7,692,024 sq km)

**MOST DENSELY
POPULATED COUNTRY**
Nauru
1,375 people per sq
mi (524 per sq km)

A S I A

M i c r o n e s i a

Northern Mariana
Islands
(U.S.)
• Capital Hill

Guam
(U.S.)

PALAU
Melekeok ⊛

Yap
Islands

Truk Islands

Caroline Islands

Palikir ⊛

FEDERATED STATES
OF MICRONESIA

M e l a n

Oceania–Asia
boundary

PAPUA NEW GUINEA
▲ Mount Wilhelm
14,793 ft
(4,509 m)
Port Moresby ⊛

Solomon Islands

Honiara ⊛

Coral Sea
Islands
Territory
(Australia)

Coral Sea

A U S T R A L I A

Brisbane

Lake
Eyre
-52 ft
(-16 m)

Darling River

Murray River

Sydney •

Canberra ⊛

Adelaide •

Melbourne •

Perth •

Lord Howe
Island
(Australia)

Indian
Ocean

Tasman
Sea

Tasmania

Hobart •

0   800 Miles
0   800 Kilometers

Mercator Projection

165°E · 180° · 165°W · 150°W · 135°W

North Pacific Ocean

Midway Is. (U.S.)

TROPIC OF CANCER

Monday | Sunday

Date Line

15°N

•Honolulu
Hawai'i •Hilo
(U.S.)

Wake Island (U.S.)

Johnston Atoll (U.S.)

Bikini Atoll

MARSHALL ISLANDS

Ratak Chain

Ralik Chain

⊛ Majuro

Kingman Reef (U.S.)

Palmyra Atoll (U.S.)

Howland Island (U.S.)

Kiritimati

Line Islands

EQUATOR

0°

Tarawa (Bairiki)

Baker Island (U.S.)

Gilbert Islands

⊛ Yaren
NAURU

Jarvis I. (U.S.)

Phoenix Is.

K I R I B A T I

Marquesas Islands

SOLOMON ISLANDS
Santa Cruz Islands

TUVALU
Funafuti ⊛

Tokelau (N.Z.)

VANUATU

Wallis and Futuna Is. (France)

SAMOA
Apia ⊛

American Samoa (U.S.)
Pago Pago

Cook Islands (N.Z.)

Papeete•

Tuamotu Archipelago

15°S

Port Vila•

⊛ Suva
FIJI

TONGA

Society Is.

French Polynesia (France)

•Nouméa

Nuku'alofa ⊛

Niue (N.Z.)

Avarua•

Austral Is.

TROPIC OF CAPRICORN

New Caledonia (France)

Norfolk Island (Australia)

South Pacific Ocean

Pitcairn Island (U.K.)

30°S

Kermadec Islands (N.Z.)

Auckland•

NEW ZEALAND ⊛ Wellington

AUSTRALIA, NEW ZEALAND, AND OCEANIA

Christchurch•

Chatham Island (N.Z.)

Date Line

45°S

165°E · 180° · 165°W · 150°W · 135°W

SPOTLIGHT ON
EUROPE

The Louvre first opened as a museum during the French Revolution in 1793.

The Rubik's Cube was invented in Hungary, a country in Europe.

Louvre Museum in Paris, France

A cluster of islands and peninsulas jutting west from Asia, Europe is bordered by the Atlantic and Arctic Oceans and more than a dozen seas. Here you'll find a variety of scenery, from mountains to countryside to coastlines. Europe is also known for its rich culture and fascinating history, which make it one of the most-visited continents on the planet.

Bagpiper in Scotland, U.K.

Name Game

The origin of Europe's name is often attributed to Europa, a princess in Greek mythology. It may also be based on the Greek, Phoenician, or Semitic words describing the land to the west.

Europa on euro coin

Spot On

Dalmatians get their name from Dalmatia, a region of Croatia along the Adriatic Sea. The spotted canines have served as border guard dogs during conflicts in the region.

Rock Monkeys

Macaques are the only nonhuman primates found in Europe. They have been living on Gibraltar, a narrow peninsula at the southern edge of Spain, for centuries.

Great Big Sea

About the same size as Japan, the Caspian Sea is the world's biggest body of water that's surrounded by land. It's home to sturgeon, endangered fish whose eggs (roe) are used to make caviar.

Europe's 6 Most Visited Cities*

1. **London, England**
   15.96 million visitors
2. **Paris, France**
   13.92 million visitors
3. **Istanbul, Turkey**
   10.37 million visitors
4. **Barcelona, Spain**
   8.41 million visitors
5. **Milan, Italy**
   6.83 million visitors
6. **Rome, Italy**
   6.71 million visitors

*2013

Brandenburg Gate in Berlin, Germany

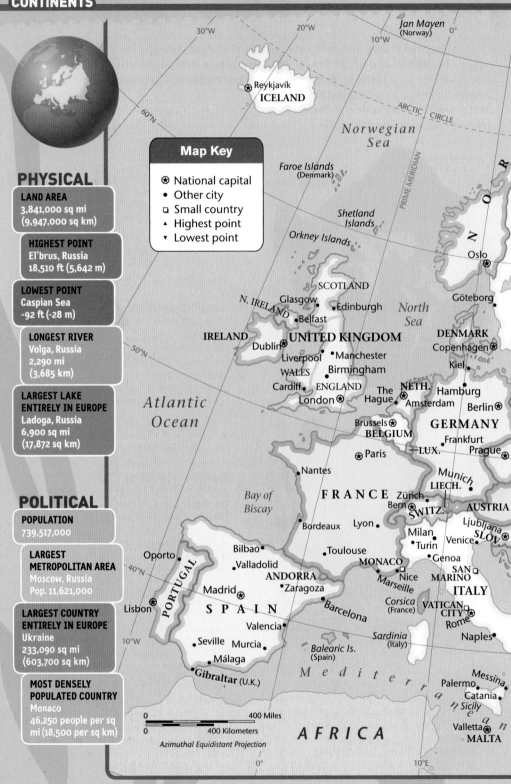

Map Key

- ⊛ National capital
- • Other city
- ▫ Small country
- ▲ Highest point
- ▾ Lowest point

PHYSICAL

LAND AREA
3,841,000 sq mi
(9,947,000 sq km)

HIGHEST POINT
El'brus, Russia
18,510 ft (5,642 m)

LOWEST POINT
Caspian Sea
-92 ft (-28 m)

LONGEST RIVER
Volga, Russia
2,290 mi
(3,685 km)

**LARGEST LAKE
ENTIRELY IN EUROPE**
Ladoga, Russia
6,900 sq mi
(17,872 sq km)

POLITICAL

POPULATION
739,517,000

**LARGEST
METROPOLITAN AREA**
Moscow, Russia
Pop. 11,621,000

**LARGEST COUNTRY
ENTIRELY IN EUROPE**
Ukraine
233,090 sq mi
(603,700 sq km)

**MOST DENSELY
POPULATED COUNTRY**
Monaco
46,250 people per sq
mi (18,500 per sq km)

Reykjavík
ICELAND

Norwegian Sea

Faroe Islands
(Denmark)

Jan Mayen
(Norway)

ARCTIC CIRCLE

PRIME MERIDIAN

Shetland Islands

Orkney Islands

N O R

Oslo

SCOTLAND

Glasgow
Edinburgh

N. IRELAND

Belfast

North Sea

Göteborg

DENMARK

Copenhagen

IRELAND

Dublin

UNITED KINGDOM

Liverpool
Manchester

WALES
Birmingham

Cardiff
ENGLAND

London

The Hague

NETH.

Amsterdam

Kiel

Hamburg

Berlin

Atlantic Ocean

Brussels
BELGIUM

Paris

Nantes

Bay of Biscay

FRANCE

Bordeaux
Lyon

LUX.

Frankfurt

GERMANY

Prague

Munich
LIECH.

Zürich
Bern
SWITZ.

AUSTRIA

Ljubljana
SLOV.

Milan
Turin

Venice

Oporto

Bilbao

Toulouse

Valladolid

ANDORRA

Madrid
Zaragoza

Lisbon
PORTUGAL

S P A I N

Barcelona

Valencia

Seville
Murcia

Málaga

Gibraltar (U.K.)

MONACO

Marseille

Nice

Corsica
(France)

Genoa

SAN
MARINO

ITALY

VATICAN
CITY

Rome

Naples

Sardinia
(Italy)

Balearic Is.
(Spain)

M e d i t e r r a n e a n

Palermo

Messina

Catania
Sicily

Valletta

MALTA

A F R I C A

0   400 Miles
0   400 Kilometers
Azimuthal Equidistant Projection

30°W   20°W   10°W   0°

60°N

50°N

40°N

10°W

0°

10°E

EUROPE

Barents Sea

Murmansk

SWEDEN

NORWAY

FINLAND

Arkhangel'sk

RUSSIA

ASIA

Asia
Europe

Lake Ladoga

Helsinki

Tallinn ⊛ Stockholm

ESTONIA

Baltic Sea

Riga

LATVIA

St. Petersburg

Volga River

Kazan'

Ufa

Tver'

Yaroslavl'

Nizhniy Novgorod

Samara Orenburg

⊛ Moscow

Ryazan'

LITHUANIA

Vitsyebsk

Smolensk

Penza

Kaliningrad
(Russia)

Kaunas

Vilnius

Saratov

Gdańsk

⊛ Minsk

Bryansk

KAZAKHSTAN

POLAND

⊛ Warsaw

BELARUS

Homyel'

Kursk

Bydgoszcz

Łódź

Volgograd

Wrocław

Kraków

Kiev

Kharkiv

Astrakhan'

CZECH REP.
(CZECHIA)

L'viv

UKRAINE

Poltava

Donets'k

Rostov

Vienna

SLOVAKIA

Vinnytsya

Dnipropetrovs'k

-92 ft
(-28 m)

⊛ Bratislava

MOLDOVA

Caspian Sea

⊛ Budapest

Chişinău

HUNGARY

Odesa

El'brus

Groznyy

Zagreb

ROMANIA

Simferopol'

(5,642 m) 18,510 ft

CROATIA

Belgrade

Bucharest

Sevastopol'

Sochi

Baku

BOSNIA &
HERZEGOVINA

SERBIA

GEORGIA

AZERBAIJAN

Sarajevo

KOSOVO

Prishtina

BULGARIA

Varna

Black Sea

MONTENEGRO

Podgorica

Sofia

Bosporus

Tirana

Skopje

MACED.

Istanbul

ALBANIA

Thessaloníki

TURKEY

Dardanelles

GREECE

Sea

Athens

Crete

Nicosia ⊛

CYPRUS

A commonly accepted division
between Asia and Europe—
marked here by a maroon,
dashed line—is formed by the
Ural Mountains, Ural River, Caspian
Sea, Caucasus Mountains, and
the Black Sea with its outlets, the
Bosporus and Dardanelles.

SPOTLIGHT ON
NORTH AMERICA

In the summer, the amount of water pouring over Niagara Falls each second could fill 13,000 bathtubs.

North America is home to only one marsupial, the opossum, which is active at night.

A nightly light show at Niagara Falls—on the border of Ontario, Canada, and New York, U.S.A.

From the Great Plains of the United States and Canada to the rain forests of Panama, North America stretches 5,500 miles (8,850 km) from north to south. The third largest continent, North America can be divided into five regions: the mountainous west (including parts of Mexico and Central America's western coast), the Great Plains, the Canadian Shield, the varied eastern region (including Central America's lowlands and coastal plains), and the Caribbean.

Mexican children perform mariachi music.

Coast to Coast

North America's 150,000-mile (241,402-km) coastline is the longest of any continent's. Canada alone claims 15 percent of the world's coastline—the most of any country.

Early Animals

Even though camels are associated with the Middle East, they actually originated in North America 45 million years ago. Dogs and horses also evolved on the continent.

Colossal Crystals

Mexico's Cave of Crystals contains some of the world's largest known natural crystals. They measure as long as 37.4 feet (11.4 m). That's almost as long as a school bus!

All Kinds of Climates

North America features all climate types, from the frozen tundra of Canada's Yukon Territory to the temperate rain forest of the Pacific Northwest coast to the Baja California desert.

5 Most Visited National Parks*

1. Great Smoky Mountains, U.S.A. 9,685,829
2. Grand Canyon, U.S.A. 4,421,352
3. Yosemite, U.S.A. 3,853,404
4. Yellowstone, U.S.A. 3,447,729
5. Banff, Canada 3,306,203**

Monarch butterfly

*2012 (National Park Service); **2012–2013 (Parks Canada)

PHYSICAL

LAND AREA
9,449,000 sq mi
(24,474,000 sq km)

HIGHEST POINT
Mount McKinley, Alaska
20,320 ft (6,194 m)

LOWEST POINT
Death Valley, California
-282 ft (-86 m)

LONGEST RIVER
Mississippi–Missouri,
United States
3,710 mi (5,970 km)

LARGEST LAKE
Lake Superior,
U.S.–Canada
31,700 sq mi
(82,100 sq km)

POLITICAL

POPULATION
556,558,000

LARGEST COUNTRY
Canada
3,855,103 sq mi
(9,984,670 sq km)

LARGEST METROPOLITAN AREA
Mexico City, Mexico
Pop. 20,446,000

MOST DENSELY POPULATED COUNTRY
Barbados / 1,524 people
per sq mi (588 per sq km)

Map Key

⊛ National capital
• Other city
▲ Highest point
▼ Lowest point

EUROPE

ASIA

Greenland
(Denmark)

North Pole

Arctic Ocean

C A N A D A

Alaska
(U.S.)

Mount McKinley ▲
(6,194 m) 20,320 ft

Anchorage

Edmonton

Calgary

Vancouver

Victoria

Seattle

Winnipeg

Thunder Bay

Montréal

ARCTIC CIRCLE

80°N

60°N

40°N

40°N

180°

160°W

20°W

40°W

40°W

800 Miles

800 Kilometers

Azimuthal Equidistant Projection

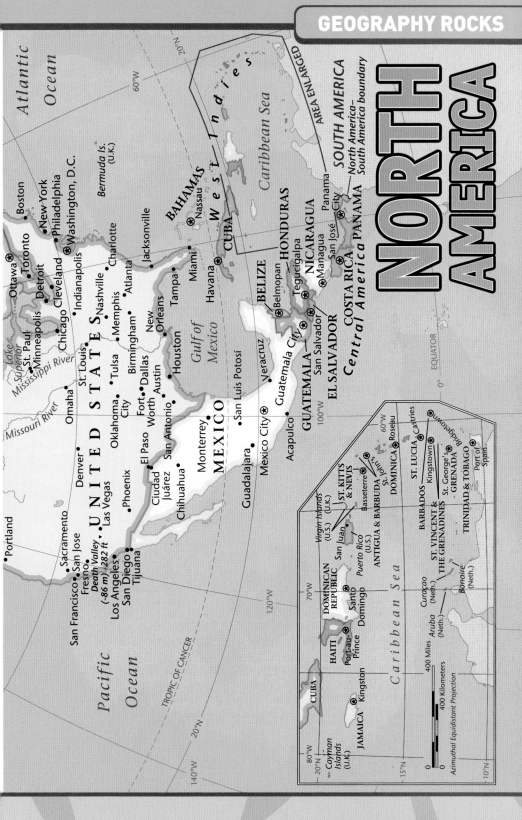

NORTH AMERICA

Atlantic Ocean

Pacific Ocean

Caribbean Sea

Gulf of Mexico

West Indies

Lake Superior

Mississippi River

Missouri River

UNITED STATES

Portland
San Francisco
San Jose
Fresno
Sacramento
Los Angeles
San Diego
Tijuana
Death Valley (–86 m) –282 ft ▼
Las Vegas
Phoenix
Denver
Omaha
Oklahoma City
Tulsa
St. Louis
Chicago
Minneapolis
St. Paul
Ottawa
Toronto
Detroit
Cleveland
Indianapolis
Nashville
Memphis
Birmingham
Dallas
Fort Worth
Austin
San Antonio
El Paso
Ciudad Juárez
Chihuahua
Atlanta
New Orleans
Houston
Tampa
Jacksonville
Charlotte
Boston
New York
Philadelphia
Washington, D.C.

MEXICO

Monterrey
Guadalajara
San Luis Potosí
Mexico City ⊛
Veracruz
Acapulco

Bermuda Is. (U.K.)

BAHAMAS
Nassau ⊛

CUBA
Havana ⊛
Miami

Caribbean Sea

BELIZE
Belmopan ⊛

GUATEMALA
Guatemala City ⊛

HONDURAS
Tegucigalpa ⊛

EL SALVADOR
San Salvador ⊛

NICARAGUA
Managua ⊛

COSTA RICA
San José ⊛

PANAMA
Panama City ⊛

Central America

SOUTH AMERICA

North America–South America boundary

AREA ENLARGED

20°N
60°W
80°W
100°W
120°W
140°W
40°W
20°N
EQUATOR
0°
TROPIC OF CANCER

Inset map: Caribbean Sea / West Indies

CUBA

JAMAICA
Kingston

Cayman Islands (U.K.)

HAITI
Port-au-Prince

DOMINICAN REPUBLIC
Santo Domingo

Puerto Rico (U.S.)
San Juan

Virgin Islands (U.S.) (U.K.)

ST. KITTS & NEVIS
Basseterre

ANTIGUA & BARBUDA
St. John's

DOMINICA
Roseau

ST. LUCIA
Castries

BARBADOS
Bridgetown

ST. VINCENT & THE GRENADINES
Kingstown

GRENADA
St. George's

TRINIDAD & TOBAGO
Port of Spain

Aruba (Neth.)
Curaçao (Neth.)
Bonaire (Neth.)

Caribbean Sea

70°W
60°W
15°N
10°N
20°N

400 Miles
400 Kilometers
0
0

Azimuthal Equidistant Projection

SPOTLIGHT ON
SOUTH AMERICA

A sloth would take a month to travel a single mile (1.6 km).

About two-thirds of the world's emeralds come from Colombia, South America.

A southern two-toed sloth hangs from a branch in Brazil's Amazon rain forest.

South America is bordered by three major bodies of water—the Caribbean Sea, Atlantic Ocean, and Pacific Ocean. The world's fourth largest continent extends over a range of climates from tropical in the north to subarctic in the south. South America produces a rich diversity of natural resources, including nuts, fruits, sugar, grains, coffee, and chocolate.

A boy celebrates Carnival in Rio de Janeiro, Brazil

Up in the Air

Brazil, which makes up half of South America in area, is an airline industry leader. São Paulo–based company Embraer designs and builds commercial airplanes flown all around the world.

No Bones About It

In Peru, scientists discovered the remains of a megalodon, a 60-foot (18-m)-long whale-eating prehistoric shark. Another team unearthed 41-million-year-old rodent fossils.

Big Bird

The Andean condor, which lives exclusively in the mountains and valleys of the Andes, is the largest raptor in the world and the largest flying bird in South America.

Awesome Eruptions

There are several active volcanoes in South America. Tungurahua in Ecuador recently erupted with ash plumes as tall as 45,000 feet (13,716 m). They were spotted over 80 miles (129 km) away.

World's Tallest Waterfalls

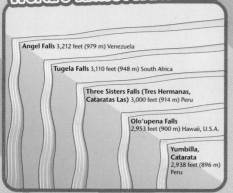

Angel Falls 3,212 feet (979 m) Venezuela

Tugela Falls 3,110 feet (948 m) South Africa

Three Sisters Falls (Tres Hermanas, Cataratas Las) 3,000 feet (914 m) Peru

Olo'upena Falls 2,953 feet (900 m) Hawaii, U.S.A.

Yumbilla, Catarata 2,938 feet (896 m) Peru

Casa Rosada in Buenos Aires, Argentina

PHYSICAL

LAND AREA
6,880,000 sq mi
(17,819,000 sq km)

HIGHEST POINT
Cerro Aconcagua,
Argentina
22,831 ft (6,959 m)

LOWEST POINT
Laguna del Carbón,
Argentina
-344 ft (-105 m)

LONGEST RIVER
Amazon
4,150 mi (6,679 km)

LARGEST LAKE
Lake Maracaibo,
Venezuela;
5,127 sq mi
(13,280 sq km)

POLITICAL

POPULATION
401,139,000

LARGEST COUNTRY
Brazil
3,287,612 sq mi
(8,514,877 sq km)

LARGEST METROPOLITAN AREA
São Paulo, Brazil
Pop. 19,924,000

MOST DENSELY POPULATED COUNTRY
Ecuador / 144 people per
sq mi (56 per sq km)

Map Key

⊛ National capital
• Other city
▲ Highest point
▼ Lowest point

Central
America

Caribbean
Sea

South America–
North America
boundary

Barranquilla
Maracaibo
Lake
Maracaibo
Medellín
Bogotá
Cali
COLOMBIA
Quito
ECUADOR
Guayaquil

Caracas
Valencia
Barquisimeto
VENEZUELA

Georgetown
Paramaribo
GUYANA
SURINAME
Cayenne
French Guiana
(France)

Belém

Manaus
Amazon River

P E R U
Trujillo
Lima
Cusco

BOLIVIA

B R A Z I L

Brasília

Fortaleza
Natal
Recife
Salvador
(Bahia)

EQUATOR

288

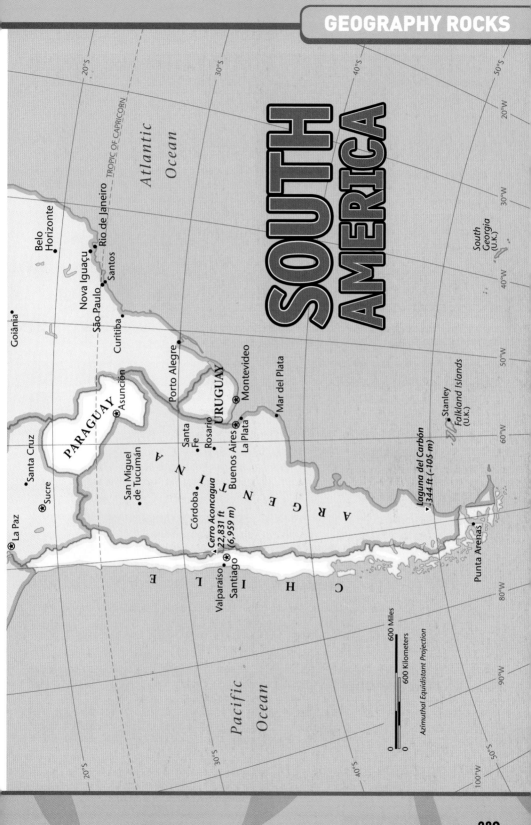

SOUTH AMERICA

Atlantic Ocean

Pacific Ocean

TROPIC OF CAPRICORN

Belo Horizonte

Goiânia

Nova Iguaçu
Rio de Janeiro
São Paulo
Santos

Curitiba

Porto Alegre

PARAGUAY
Asunción

Santa Cruz

Sucre

La Paz

URUGUAY
Montevideo
Mar del Plata

Santa Fe
Rosario
Buenos Aires
La Plata

San Miguel de Tucumán

Córdoba

Cerro Aconcagua
22,831 ft (6,959 m)

Valparaíso
Santiago

ARGENTINA

CHILE

Laguna del Carbón
-344 ft (-105 m)

Stanley
Falkland Islands (U.K.)

South Georgia (U.K.)

Punta Arenas

600 Miles

600 Kilometers

Azimuthal Equidistant Projection

20°S
30°S
40°S
50°S

20°W
30°W
40°W
50°W
60°W
80°W
90°W
100°W

30°S
40°S
50°S
20°S

289

COUNTRIES OF THE WORLD

The following pages present a general overview of all 195 independent countries recognized by the National Geographic Society, including the newest nation, South Sudan, which gained independence in 2011.

The flags of each independent country symbolize diverse cultures and histories. The statistical data cover highlights of geography and demography and provide a brief overview of each country. They present general characteristics and are not intended to be comprehensive. For example, not every language spoken in a specific country can be listed. Thus, languages shown are the most representative of that area. This is also true of the religions mentioned.

A country is defined as a political body with its own independent government, geographical space, and, in most cases, laws, military, and taxes.

Disputed areas such as Northern Cyprus and Taiwan, and dependencies of independent nations, such as Bermuda and Puerto Rico, are not included in this listing.

Note the color key at the bottom of the pages and the locator map below, which assign a color to each country based on the continent on which it is located. All information is accurate as of press time.

Color Key by Continent

Afghanistan

Area: 251,773 sq mi (652,090 sq km)
Population: 30,552,000
Capital: Kabul, pop. 3,097,000
Currency: afghani
Religions: Sunni Muslim, Shiite Muslim
Languages: Afghan Persian (Dari), Pashto, Turkic languages (primarily Uzbek and Turkmen), Baluchi, 30 minor languages (including Pashai)

Albania

Area: 11,100 sq mi (28,748 sq km)
Population: 2,774,000
Capital: Tirana, pop. 419,000
Currency: lek
Religions: Muslim, Albanian Orthodox, Roman Catholic
Languages: Albanian, Greek, Vlach, Romani, Slavic dialects

Algeria

Area: 919,595 sq mi (2,381,741 sq km)
Population: 38,290,000
Capital: Algiers, pop. 2,916,000
Currency: Algerian dinar
Religion: Sunni Muslim
Languages: Arabic, French, Berber dialects

Andorra

Area: 181 sq mi (469 sq km)
Population: 74,000
Capital: Andorra la Vella, pop. 23,000
Currency: euro
Religion: Roman Catholic
Languages: Catalan, French, Castilian, Portuguese

Angola

Area: 481,354 sq mi (1,246,700 sq km)
Population: 21,635,000
Capital: Luanda, pop. 5,068,000
Currency: kwanza
Religions: indigenous beliefs, Roman Catholic, Protestant
Languages: Portuguese, Bantu, and other African languages

Antigua and Barbuda

Area: 171 sq mi (442 sq km)
Population: 88,000
Capital: St. John's, pop. 27,000
Currency: East Caribbean dollar
Religions: Anglican, Seventh-day Adventist, Pentecostal, Moravian, Roman Catholic, Methodist, Baptist, Church of God, other Christian
Languages: English, local dialects

Argentina

Area: 1,073,518 sq mi (2,780,400 sq km)
Population: 41,267,000
Capital: Buenos Aires, pop. 13,528,000
Currency: Argentine peso
Religion: Roman Catholic
Languages: Spanish, English, Italian, German, French

Armenia

Area: 11,484 sq mi (29,743 sq km)
Population: 3,048,000
Capital: Yerevan, pop. 1,116,000
Currency: dram
Religions: Armenian Apostolic, other Christian
Language: Armenian

Australia

Area: 2,969,906 sq mi (7,692,024 sq km)
Population: 23,106,000
Capital: Canberra, pop. 399,000
Currency: Australian dollar
Religions: Roman Catholic, Anglican
Language: English

Austria

Area: 32,378 sq mi (83,858 sq km)
Population: 8,511,000
Capital: Vienna, pop. 1,720,000
Currency: euro
Religions: Roman Catholic, Protestant, Muslim
Language: German

Azerbaijan

Area: 33,436 sq mi (86,600 sq km)
Population: 9,418,000
Capital: Baku, pop. 2,123,000
Currency: Azerbaijani manat
Religion: Muslim
Language: Azerbaijani (Azeri)

Bahamas

Area: 5,382 sq mi (13,939 sq km)
Population: 350,000
Capital: Nassau, pop. 254,000
Currency: Bahamian dollar
Religions: Baptist, Anglican, Roman Catholic, Pentecostal, Church of God
Languages: English, Creole

Bahrain

Area: 277 sq mi (717 sq km)
Population: 1,131,000
Capital: Manama, pop. 262,000
Currency: Bahraini dinar
Religions: Shiite Muslim, Sunni Muslim, Christian
Languages: Arabic, English, Farsi, Urdu

Bangladesh

Area: 55,598 sq mi (143,998 sq km)
Population: 156,595,000
Capital: Dhaka, pop. 15,391,000
Currency: taka
Religions: Muslim, Hindu
Languages: Bangla (Bengali), English

Barbados

Area: 166 sq mi (430 sq km)
Population: 253,000
Capital: Bridgetown, pop. 122,000
Currency: Barbadian dollar
Religions: Anglican, Pentecostal, Methodist, other Protestant, Roman Catholic
Language: English

Belarus

Area: 80,153 sq mi (207,595 sq km)
Population: 9,463,000
Capital: Minsk, pop. 1,861,000
Currency: Belarusian ruble
Religions: Eastern Orthodox, other (includes Roman Catholic, Protestant, Jewish, Muslim)
Languages: Belarusian, Russian

● Asia   ● Europe   ● North America   ● South America

Belgium

Area: 11,787 sq mi (30,528 sq km)
Population: 11,164,000
Capital: Brussels, pop. 1,949,000
Currency: euro
Religions: Roman Catholic, other (includes Protestant)
Languages: Dutch, French

Belize

Area: 8,867 sq mi (22,965 sq km)
Population: 334,000
Capital: Belmopan, pop. 14,000
Currency: Belizean dollar
Religions: Roman Catholic, Protestant (includes Pentecostal, Seventh-day Adventist, Mennonite, Methodist)
Languages: Spanish, Creole, Mayan dialects, English, Garifuna (Carib), German

Benin

Area: 43,484 sq mi (112,622 sq km)
Population: 9,645,000
Capitals: Porto-Novo, pop. 314,000; Cotonou, pop. 924,000
Currency: Communauté Financière Africaine franc
Religions: Christian, Muslim, Vodoun
Languages: French, Fon, Yoruba, tribal languages

Bhutan

Area: 17,954 sq mi (46,500 sq km)
Population: 733,000
Capital: Thimphu, pop. 99,000
Currencies: ngultrum; Indian rupee
Religions: Lamaistic Buddhist, Indian- and Nepalese-influenced Hindu
Languages: Dzongkha, Tibetan dialects, Nepalese dialects

Bolivia

Area: 424,164 sq mi (1,098,581 sq km)
Population: 11,020,000
Capitals: La Paz, pop. 1,715,000; Sucre, pop. 307,000
Currency: boliviano
Religions: Roman Catholic, Protestant (includes Evangelical Methodist)
Languages: Spanish, Quechua, Aymara

Bosnia and Herzegovina

Area: 19,741 sq mi (51,129 sq km)
Population: 3,834,000
Capital: Sarajevo, pop. 389,000
Currency: konvertibilna marka (convertible mark)
Religions: Muslim, Orthodox, Roman Catholic
Languages: Bosnian, Croatian, Serbian

Botswana

Area: 224,607 sq mi (581,730 sq km)
Population: 1,866,000
Capital: Gaborone, pop. 202,000
Currency: pula
Religions: Christian, Badimo
Languages: Setswana, Kalanga

Brazil

Area: 3,287,612 sq mi (8,514,877 sq km)
Population: 195,527,000
Capital: Brasília, pop. 3,813,000
Currency: real
Religions: Roman Catholic, Protestant
Language: Portuguese

Brunei

Area: 2,226 sq mi (5,765 sq km)
Population: 407,000
Capital: Bandar Seri Begawan, pop. 16,000
Currency: Bruneian dollar
Religions: Muslim, Buddhist, Christian, other (includes indigenous beliefs)
Languages: Malay, English, Chinese

Bulgaria

Area: 42,855 sq mi (110,994 sq km)
Population: 7,260,000
Capital: Sofia, pop. 1,174,000
Currency: lev
Religions: Bulgarian Orthodox, Muslim
Languages: Bulgarian, Turkish, Roma

Burkina Faso

Area: 105,869 sq mi
(274,200 sq km)
Population: 18,015,000
Capital: Ouagadougou,
pop. 2,053,000
Currency: Communauté Financière Africaine franc
Religions: Muslim, indigenous beliefs, Christian
Languages: French, native African languages

Cambodia

Area: 69,898 sq mi (181,035 sq km)
Population: 14,406,000
Capital: Phnom Penh,
pop. 1,550,000
Currency: riel
Religion: Theravada Buddhist
Language: Khmer

Burundi

Area: 10,747 sq mi (27,834 sq km)
Population: 10,892,000
Capital: Bujumbura, pop. 605,000
Currency: Burundi franc
Religions: Roman Catholic, indigenous beliefs,
Muslim, Protestant
Languages: Kirundi, French, Swahili

Cameroon

Area: 183,569 sq mi
(475,442 sq km)
Population: 21,491,000
Capital: Yaoundé, pop. 2,432,000
Currency: Communauté Financière Africaine franc
Religions: indigenous beliefs, Christian, Muslim
Languages: 24 major African language groups,
English, French

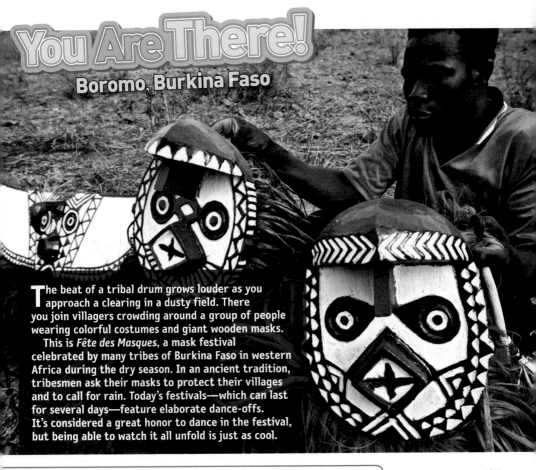

You Are There!
Boromo, Burkina Faso

The beat of a tribal drum grows louder as you approach a clearing in a dusty field. There you join villagers crowding around a group of people wearing colorful costumes and giant wooden masks.

This is *Fête des Masques*, a mask festival celebrated by many tribes of Burkina Faso in western Africa during the dry season. In an ancient tradition, tribesmen ask their masks to protect their villages and to call for rain. Today's festivals—which can last for several days—feature elaborate dance-offs. It's considered a great honor to dance in the festival, but being able to watch it all unfold is just as cool.

Canada

Area: 3,855,101 sq mi (9,984,670 sq km)
Population: 35,250,000
Capital: Ottawa, pop. 1,208,000
Currency: Canadian dollar
Religions: Roman Catholic, Protestant (includes United Church, Anglican), other Christian
Languages: English, French

China

Area: 3,705,405 sq mi (9,596,960 sq km)
Population: 1,357,372,000
Capital: Beijing, pop. 15,594,000
Currency: renminbi (yuan)
Religions: Taoist, Buddhist, Christian
Languages: Standard Chinese or Mandarin, Yue, Wu, Minbei, Minnan, Xiang, Gan, Hakka dialects

Cape Verde

Area: 1,558 sq mi (4,036 sq km)
Population: 515,000
Capital: Praia, pop. 132,000
Currency: Cape Verdean escudo
Religions: Roman Catholic (infused with indigenous beliefs), Protestant (mostly Church of the Nazarene)
Languages: Portuguese, Crioulo

Colombia

Area: 440,831 sq mi (1,141,748 sq km)
Population: 48,028,000
Capital: Bogotá, pop. 8,743,000
Currency: Colombian peso
Religion: Roman Catholic
Language: Spanish

Central African Republic

Area: 240,535 sq mi (622,984 sq km)
Population: 4,676,000
Capital: Bangui, pop. 740,000
Currency: Communauté Financière Africaine franc
Religions: indigenous beliefs, Protestant, Roman Catholic, Muslim
Languages: French, Sangho, tribal languages

ROASTED ANTS are a popular SNACK in Colombia.

Chad

Area: 495,755 sq mi (1,284,000 sq km)
Population: 12,209,000
Capital: N'Djamena, pop. 1,079,000
Currency: Communauté Financière Africaine franc
Religions: Muslim, Catholic, Protestant, animist
Languages: French, Arabic, Sara, more than 120 languages and dialects

Comoros

Area: 863 sq mi (2,235 sq km)
Population: 792,000
Capital: Moroni, pop. 54,000
Currency: Comoran franc
Religion: Sunni Muslim
Languages: Arabic, French, Shikomoro

Chile

Area: 291,930 sq mi (756,096 sq km)
Population: 17,557,000
Capital: Santiago, pop. 6,034,000
Currency: Chilean peso
Religions: Roman Catholic, Evangelical
Language: Spanish

Congo

Area: 132,047 sq mi (342,000 sq km)
Population: 4,355,000
Capital: Brazzaville, pop. 1,611,000
Currency: Communauté Financière Africaine franc
Religions: Christian, animist
Languages: French, Lingala, Monokutuba, local languages

Costa Rica

Area: 19,730 sq mi
(51,100 sq km)
Population: 4,713,000
Capital: San José, pop. 1,515,000
Currency: Costa Rican colón
Religions: Roman Catholic, Evangelical
Languages: Spanish, English

Côte d'Ivoire (Ivory Coast)

Area: 124,503 sq mi
(322,462 sq km)
Population: 21,142,000
Capitals: Abidjan, pop. 4,288,000;
Yamoussoukro, pop. 966,000
Currency: Communauté Financière Africaine franc
Religions: Muslim, indigenous beliefs, Christian
Languages: French, Dioula, other native dialects

Croatia

Area: 21,831 sq mi
(56,542 sq km)
Population: 4,253,000
Capital: Zagreb, pop. 686,000
Currency: kuna
Religions: Roman Catholic, Orthodox
Language: Croatian

Cuba

Area: 42,803 sq mi
(110,860 sq km)
Population: 11,258,000
Capital: Havana, pop. 2,116,000
Currency: Cuban peso
Religions: Roman Catholic, Protestant, Jehovah's
Witnesses, Jewish, Santería
Language: Spanish

Cyprus

Area: 3,572 sq mi (9,251 sq km)
Population: 1,135,000
Capital: Nicosia, pop. 253,000
Currencies: euro; new Turkish
lira in Northern Cyprus
Religions: Greek Orthodox, Muslim, Maronite,
Armenian Apostolic
Languages: Greek, Turkish, English

Czech Republic (Czechia)

Area: 30,450 sq mi (78,866 sq km)
Population: 10,521,000
Capital: Prague, pop. 1,276,000
Currency: koruny
Religion: Roman Catholic
Language: Czech

5 cool things about CZECH REPUBLIC

1. It took nearly 600 years to build St. Vitus Cathedral, the largest church in Prague, the nation's capital.

2. Czech chemist Otto Wichterle invented soft contact lenses.

3. The word "robot" comes from the Czech word *robota*, meaning "work."

4. The sugar cube was invented in the Czech town of Dačice in 1843.

5. Czech astronomers named a newly discovered asteroid after ice hockey star Dominik Hašek, who led the Czech team to gold in the 1998 Olympic Games.

Democratic Republic of the Congo

Area: 905,365 sq mi
(2,344,885 sq km)
Population: 71,128,000
Capital: Kinshasa, pop. 8,798,000
Currency: Congolese franc
Religions: Roman Catholic, Protestant, Kimbanguist, Muslim, syncretic sects, indigenous beliefs
Languages: French, Lingala, Kingwana, Kikongo, Tshiluba

Denmark

Area: 16,640 sq mi (43,098 sq km)
Population: 5,613,000
Capital: Copenhagen, pop. 1,206,000
Currency: Danish krone
Religions: Evangelical Lutheran, other Protestant, Roman Catholic
Languages: Danish, Faroese, Greenlandic, German, English as second language

Djibouti

Area: 8,958 sq mi
(23,200 sq km)
Population: 939,000
Capital: Djibouti, pop. 496,000
Currency: Djiboutian franc
Religions: Muslim, Christian
Languages: French, Arabic, Somali, Afar

Dominican Republic

Area: 18,704 sq mi
(48,442 sq km)
Population: 10,260,000
Capital: Santo Domingo,
pop. 2,191,000
Currency: Dominican peso
Religion: Roman Catholic
Language: Spanish

Dominica

Area: 290 sq mi (751 sq km)
Population: 71,000
Capital: Roseau, pop. 14,000
Currency: East Caribbean
dollar
Religions: Roman Catholic, Seventh-day Adventist,
Pentecostal, Baptist, Methodist, other Christian
Languages: English, French patois

Ecuador

Area: 109,483 sq mi
(283,560 sq km)
Population: 15,789,000
Capital: Quito, pop. 1,622,000
Currency: U.S. dollar
Religion: Roman Catholic
Languages: Spanish, Quechua, other
Amerindian languages

You Are There!

The Galápagos Islands, Ecuador

Slip on a snorkel mask, fins, and a wet suit and dive under the waters surrounding the Galápagos Islands. Soon, you're face-to-face with a marine iguana, the only seagoing lizards on the planet. Watch as these scaly, spiky, dark gray reptiles dive down to feast on algae and seaweed before hopping back on land to warm up on the rocks. You may even see them sneeze out a noseful of salt water, which lands on their head. When the water dries, leaving the salt behind, these lizards get their trademark salty white "wigs."

But that's not all you see. The Galápagos Islands, located 600 miles (1,000 km) from mainland South America, are home to about 9,000 species of animals, including penguins, countless other birds, and the world's largest tortoise. So no matter where you roam, you're bound to spot something wild!

COLOR KEY ● Africa ● Australia, New Zealand, and Oceania

Egypt

Area: 386,874 sq mi
(1,002,000 sq km)
Population: 84,667,000
Capital: Cairo, pop. 11,169,000
Currency: Egyptian pound
Religions: Muslim (mostly Sunni), Coptic Christian
Languages: Arabic, English, French

El Salvador

Area: 8,124 sq mi
(21,041 sq km)
Population: 6,307,000
Capital: San Salvador,
pop. 1,605,000
Currency: U.S. dollar
Religions: Roman Catholic, Protestant
Languages: Spanish, Nahua

Equatorial Guinea

Area: 10,831 sq mi (28,051 sq km)
Population: 761,000
Capital: Malabo, pop. 137,000
Currency: Communauté
Financière Africaine franc
Religions: Christian (predominantly Roman Catholic),
pagan practices
Languages: Spanish, French, Fang, Bubi

Eritrea

Area: 45,406 sq mi
(117,600 sq km)
Population: 5,765,000
Capital: Asmara, pop. 712,000
Currency: nakfa
Religions: Muslim, Coptic Christian, Roman Catholic
Languages: Afar, Arabic, Tigre, Kunama, Tigrinya,
other Cushitic languages

Estonia

Area: 17,462 sq mi (45,227 sq km)
Population: 1,283,000
Capital: Tallinn, pop. 400,000
Currency: euro
Religions: Evangelical Lutheran, Orthodox
Languages: Estonian, Russian

Ethiopia

Area: 426,373 sq mi
(1,104,300 sq km)
Population: 89,209,000
Capital: Addis Ababa,
pop. 2,979,000
Currency: birr
Religions: Christian, Muslim, traditional
Languages: Amharic, Oromigna, Tigrinya, Guaragigna

Fiji

Area: 7,095 sq mi
(18,376 sq km)
Population: 860,000
Capital: Suva, pop. 177,000
Currency: Fijian dollar
Religions: Christian (Methodist, Roman Catholic,
Assembly of God), Hindu (Sanatan), Muslim (Sunni)
Languages: English, Fijian, Hindustani

Finland

Area: 130,558 sq mi
(338,145 sq km)
Population: 5,440,000
Capital: Helsinki, pop. 1,134,000
Currency: euro
Religion: Lutheran Church of Finland
Languages: Finnish, Swedish

France

Area: 210,026 sq mi
(543,965 sq km)
Population: 63,851,000
Capital: Paris, pop. 10,620,000
Currency: euro
Religions: Roman Catholic, Muslim
Language: French

Gabon

Area: 103,347 sq mi (267,667 sq km)
Population: 1,601,000
Capital: Libreville, pop. 686,000
Currency: Communauté Financière
Africaine franc
Religions: Christian, animist
Languages: French, Fang, Myene, Nzebi, Bapounou/
Eschira, Bandjabi

Gambia

Area: 4,361 sq mi (11,295 sq km)
Population: 1,884,000
Capital: Banjul, pop. 506,000
Currency: dalasi
Religions: Muslim, Christian
Languages: English, Mandinka, Wolof, Fula, other indigenous vernaculars

Greece

Area: 50,949 sq mi (131,957 sq km)
Population: 11,081,000
Capital: Athens, pop. 3,414,000
Currency: euro
Religion: Greek Orthodox
Languages: Greek, English, French

Georgia

Area: 26,911 sq mi (69,700 sq km)
Population: 4,541,000
Capital: Tbilisi, pop. 1,121,000
Currency: lari
Religions: Orthodox Christian, Muslim, Armenian-Gregorian
Languages: Georgian, Russian, Armenian, Azeri, Abkhaz

Grenada

Area: 133 sq mi (344 sq km)
Population: 112,000
Capital: St. George's, pop. 41,000
Currency: East Caribbean dollar
Religions: Roman Catholic, Anglican, other Protestant
Languages: English, French patois

ARCHAEOLOGISTS once unearthed a 1.8-million-year-old PREHUMAN SKULL IN GEORGIA.

Guatemala

Area: 42,042 sq mi (108,889 sq km)
Population: 15,428,000
Capital: Guatemala City, pop. 1,168,000
Currency: quetzal
Religions: Roman Catholic, Protestant, indigenous Maya beliefs
Languages: Spanish, 23 official Amerindian languages

Germany

Area: 137,847 sq mi (357,022 sq km)
Population: 80,572,000
Capital: Berlin, pop. 3,462,000
Currency: euro
Religions: Protestant, Roman Catholic, Muslim
Language: German

Guinea

Area: 94,926 sq mi (245,857 sq km)
Population: 11,793,000
Capital: Conakry, pop. 1,786,000
Currency: Guinean franc
Religions: Muslim, Christian, indigenous beliefs
Languages: French, ethnic languages

Ghana

Area: 92,100 sq mi (238,537 sq km)
Population: 26,088,000
Capital: Accra, pop. 2,573,000
Currency: Ghana cedi
Religions: Christian (Pentecostal/Charismatic, Protestant, Roman Catholic, other), Muslim, traditional beliefs
Languages: Asante, Ewe, Fante, Boron (Brong), Dagomba, Dangme, Dagarte (Dagaba), Akyem, Ga, English

Guinea-Bissau

Area: 13,948 sq mi (36,125 sq km)
Population: 1,677,000
Capital: Bissau, pop. 423,000
Currency: Communauté Financière Africaine franc
Religions: indigenous beliefs, Muslim, Christian
Languages: Portuguese, Crioulo, African languages

Guyana

Area: 83,000 sq mi
(214,969 sq km)
Population: 800,000
Capital: Georgetown, pop. 127,000
Currency: Guyanese dollar
Religions: Christian, Hindu, Muslim
Languages: English, Amerindian dialects, Creole, Hindustani, Urdu

Honduras

Area: 43,433 sq mi
(112,492 sq km)
Population: 8,555,000
Capital: Tegucigalpa,
pop. 1,088,000
Currency: lempira
Religions: Roman Catholic, Protestant
Languages: Spanish, Amerindian dialects

Haiti

Area: 10,714 sq mi (27,750 sq km)
Population: 10,421,000
Capital: Port-au-Prince,
pop. 2,207,000
Currency: gourde
Religions: Roman Catholic, Protestant
(Baptist, Pentecostal, other)
Languages: French, Creole

Hungary

Area: 35,919 sq mi (93,030 sq km)
Population: 9,892,000
Capital: Budapest, pop. 1,737,000
Currency: forint
Religions: Roman Catholic, Calvinist, Lutheran
Language: Hungarian

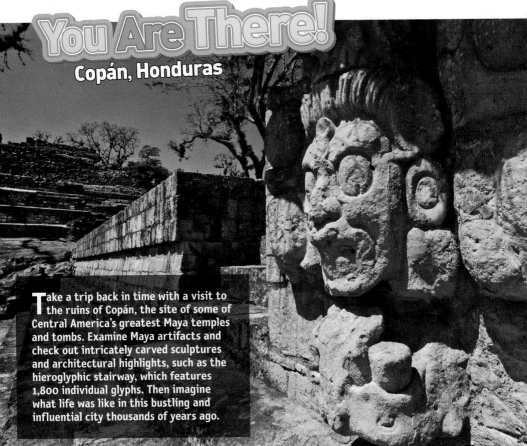

You Are There!
Copán, Honduras

Take a trip back in time with a visit to the ruins of Copán, the site of some of Central America's greatest Maya temples and tombs. Examine Maya artifacts and check out intricately carved sculptures and architectural highlights, such as the hieroglyphic stairway, which features 1,800 individual glyphs. Then imagine what life was like in this bustling and influential city thousands of years ago.

Iceland

Area: 39,769 sq mi
(103,000 sq km)
Population: 323,000
Capital: Reykjavik, pop. 206,000
Currency: Icelandic krona
Religion: Lutheran Church of Iceland
Languages: Icelandic, English, Nordic
languages, German

Indonesia

Area: 742,308 sq mi
(1,922,570 sq km)
Population: 248,527,000
Capital: Jakarta, pop. 9,769,000
Currency: Indonesian rupiah
Religions: Muslim, Protestant, Roman Catholic
Languages: Bahasa Indonesia (modified form of Malay),
English, Dutch, Javanese, local dialects

India

Area: 1,269,221 sq mi (3,287,270 sq km)
Population: 1,276,508,000
Capital: New Delhi, pop. 22,654,000
(part of Delhi metropolitan area)
Currency: Indian rupee
Religions: Hindu, Muslim
Languages: Hindi, 21 other official languages,
Hindustani (popular Hindi/Urdu variant in the north)

Iran

Area: 636,296 sq mi
(1,648,000 sq km)
Population: 76,521,000
Capital: Tehran, pop. 7,304,000
Currency: Iranian rial
Religions: Shiite Muslim, Sunni Muslim
Languages: Persian, Turkic, Kurdish, Luri,
Baluchi, Arabic

You Are There!
Cliffs of Moher, Ireland

Rising 702 feet (214 m) from the churning Atlantic Ocean, the Cliffs of Moher offer some of the most magical views in all of Ireland. Follow the winding path along the top of the cliffs for a gentle hike to cool spots like O'Brien's Tower, one of the highest points around. Climb to the top of the tower to take in the stunning surroundings of Galway Bay and the rocky landscape of the nearby Aran Islands.

Another can't-miss destination? The Hag's Head rock formation, which is said to resemble an old woman staring out to sea.

Iraq

Area: 168,754 sq mi
(437,072 sq km)
Population: 35,095,000
Capital: Baghdad, pop. 6,036,000
Currency: Iraqi dinar
Religions: Shiite Muslim, Sunni Muslim
Languages: Arabic, Kurdish, Assyrian, Armenian

Ireland

Area: 27,133 sq mi
(70,273 sq km)
Population: 4,598,000
Capital: Dublin, pop. 1,121,000
Currency: euro
Religions: Roman Catholic, Church of Ireland
Languages: Irish (Gaelic), English

Israel

Area: 8,550 sq mi (22,145 sq km)
Population: 8,054,000
Capital: Jerusalem, pop. 791,000
Currency: new Israeli sheqel
Religions: Jewish, Muslim
Languages: Hebrew, Arabic, English

Italy

Area: 116,345 sq mi
(301,333 sq km)
Population: 59,831,000
Capital: Rome, pop. 3,298,000
Currency: euro
Religions: Roman Catholic, Protestant, Jewish, Muslim
Languages: Italian, German, French, Slovene

Jamaica

Area: 4,244 sq mi
(10,991 sq km)
Population: 2,712,000
Capital: Kingston, pop. 571,000
Currency: Jamaican dollar
Religions: Protestant (Church of God, Seventh-day Adventist, Pentecostal, Baptist, Anglican, other)
Languages: English, English patois

Japan

Area: 145,902 sq mi (377,887 sq km)
Population: 127,301,000
Capital: Tokyo, pop. 37,217,000
Currency: yen
Religions: Shinto, Buddhist
Language: Japanese

Jordan

Area: 34,495 sq mi
(89,342 sq km)
Population: 7,309,000
Capital: Amman, pop. 1,179,000
Currency: Jordanian dinar
Religions: Sunni Muslim, Christian
Languages: Arabic, English

Kazakhstan

Area: 1,049,155 sq mi
(2,717,300 sq km)
Population: 17,031,000
Capital: Astana, pop. 664,000
Currency: tenge
Religions: Muslim, Russian Orthodox
Languages: Kazakh (Qazaq), Russian

Kenya

Area: 224,081 sq mi (580,367 sq km)
Population: 44,184,000
Capital: Nairobi, pop. 3,363,000
Currency: Kenyan shilling
Religions: Protestant, Roman Catholic, Muslim, indigenous beliefs
Languages: English, Kiswahili, many indigenous languages

Kiribati

Area: 313 sq mi (811 sq km)
Population: 106,000
Capital: Tarawa, pop. 44,000
Currency: Australian dollar
Religions: Roman Catholic, Protestant (Congregational)
Languages: I-Kiribati, English

Kosovo

Area: 4,203 sq mi (10,887 sq km)
Population: 1,824,000
Capital: Prishtina, pop. 600,000
Currency: euro
Religions: Muslim, Serbian Orthodox, Roman Catholic
Languages: Albanian, Serbian, Bosnian, Turkish, Roma

Kuwait

Area: 6,880 sq mi (17,818 sq km)
Population: 3,459,000
Capital: Kuwait City, pop. 2,406,000
Currency: Kuwaiti dinar
Religions: Sunni Muslim, Shiite Muslim
Languages: Arabic, English

Kyrgyzstan

Area: 77,182 sq mi (199,900 sq km)
Population: 5,665,000
Capital: Bishkek, pop. 839,000
Currency: som
Religions: Muslim, Russian Orthodox
Languages: Kyrgyz, Uzbek, Russian

Laos

Area: 91,429 sq mi (236,800 sq km)
Population: 6,736,000
Capital: Vientiane, pop. 810,000
Currency: kip
Religions: Buddhist, animist
Languages: Lao, French, English, various ethnic languages

Latvia

Area: 24,938 sq mi (64,589 sq km)
Population: 2,018,000
Capital: Riga, pop. 701,000
Currency: Latvian lat
Religions: Lutheran, Roman Catholic, Russian Orthodox
Languages: Latvian, Russian, Lithuanian

Lebanon

Area: 4,036 sq mi (10,452 sq km)
Population: 4,822,000
Capital: Beirut, pop. 2,022,000
Currency: Lebanese pound
Religions: Muslim, Christian
Languages: Arabic, French, English, Armenian

Lesotho

Area: 11,720 sq mi (30,355 sq km)
Population: 2,242,000
Capital: Maseru, pop. 239,000
Currencies: loti; South African rand
Religions: Christian, indigenous beliefs
Languages: Sesotho, English, Zulu, Xhosa

Workers discovered a **603-CARAT DIAMOND** in a **LESOTHO** mine.

Liberia

Area: 43,000 sq mi (111,370 sq km)
Population: 4,357,000
Capital: Monrovia, pop. 750,000
Currency: Liberian dollar
Religions: Christian, indigenous beliefs, Muslim
Languages: English, some 20 ethnic languages

Libya

Area: 679,362 sq mi (1,759,540 sq km)
Population: 6,518,000
Capital: Tripoli, pop. 1,127,000
Currency: Libyan dinar
Religion: Sunni Muslim
Languages: Arabic, Italian, English

Liechtenstein

Area: 62 sq mi (160 sq km)
Population: 37,000
Capital: Vaduz, pop. 5,000
Currency: Swiss franc
Religions: Roman Catholic, Protestant
Languages: German, Alemannic dialect

Lithuania

Area: 25,212 sq mi
(65,300 sq km)
Population: 2,956,000
Capital: Vilnius, pop. 546,000
Currency: litas
Religions: Roman Catholic, Russian Orthodox
Languages: Lithuanian, Russian, Polish

Luxembourg

Area: 998 sq mi (2,586 sq km)
Population: 543,000
Capital: Luxembourg,
pop. 94,000
Currency: euro
Religions: Roman Catholic, Protestant,
Jewish, Muslim
Languages: Luxembourgish, German, French

Macedonia

Area: 9,928 sq mi
(25,713 sq km)
Population: 2,066,000
Capital: Skopje, pop. 499,000
Currency: Macedonian denar
Religions: Macedonian Orthodox, Muslim
Languages: Macedonian, Albanian, Turkish

Madagascar

Area: 226,658 sq mi
(587,041 sq km)
Population: 22,550,000
Capital: Antananarivo,
pop. 1,987,000
Currency: Madagascar ariary
Religions: indigenous beliefs, Christian, Muslim
Languages: English, French, Malagasy

Malawi

Area: 45,747 sq mi
(118,484 sq km)
Population: 16,338,000
Capital: Lilongwe, pop. 772,000
Currency: Malawian kwacha
Religions: Christian, Muslim
Languages: Chichewa, Chinyanja, Chiyao, Chitumbuka

Malaysia

Area: 127,355 sq mi (329,847 sq km)
Population: 29,794,000
Capital: Kuala Lumpur,
pop. 1,556,000
Currency: ringgit
Religions: Muslim, Buddhist, Christian, Hindu
Languages: Bahasa Malaysia, English, Chinese, Tamil,
Telugu, Malayalam, Panjabi, Thai, indigenous languages

5 cool things about MALAYSIA

1. The Petronas Towers in Kuala Lumpur, Malaysia, have 32,000 windows.

2. Some Malaysian stick insects are 17 inches (45 cm) long—longer than a toaster!

3. Malaysia is home to about 150 snake species.

4. The giant *Rafflesia arnoldii*—known as the corpse flower for its stinky scent—is the state flower of Sabah, Malaysia.

5. There are over 135 different languages spoken in Malaysia.

Maldives

Area: 115 sq mi (298 sq km)
Population: 360,000
Capital: Male, pop. 132,000
Currency: rufiyaa
Religion: Sunni Muslim
Languages: Maldivian Dhivehi, English

Mali

Area: 478,841 sq mi (1,240,192 sq km)
Population: 15,461,000
Capital: Bamako, pop. 2,037,000
Currency: Communauté Financière Africaine franc
Religions: Muslim, indigenous beliefs
Languages: Bambara, French, numerous African languages

Marshall Islands

Area: 70 sq mi (181 sq km)
Population: 56,000
Capital: Majuro, pop. 31,000
Currency: U.S. dollar
Religions: Protestant, Assembly of God, Roman Catholic
Language: Marshallese

Malta

Area: 122 sq mi (316 sq km)
Population: 448,000
Capital: Valletta, pop. 198,000
Currency: euro
Religion: Roman Catholic
Languages: Maltese, English

Mauritania

Area: 397,955 sq mi (1,030,700 sq km)
Population: 3,712,000
Capital: Nouakchott, pop. 786,000
Currency: ouguiya
Religion: Muslim
Languages: Arabic, Pulaar, Soninke, French, Hassaniya, Wolof

You Are There! Monte Carlo, Monaco

Monaco may be one of the smallest countries in the world, but that doesn't mean it lacks pizazz. Luxury cars, yachts, and hotels are commonplace in this three-mile (4.8-km)-long by half-mile (0.8-km)-wide principality. Adding to the glamour? The Monaco Grand Prix, which welcomes dozens of Formula One cars and their drivers from around the world each year.

COLOR KEY ● Africa ● Australia, New Zealand, and Oceania

Mauritius

Area: 788 sq mi (2,040 sq km)
Population: 1,297,000
Capital: Port Louis, pop. 151,000
Currency: Mauritian rupee
Religions: Hindu, Roman Catholic, Muslim, other Christian
Languages: Creole, Bhojpuri, French

Mexico

Area: 758,449 sq mi (1,964,375 sq km)
Population: 117,574,000
Capital: Mexico City, pop. 20,446,000
Currency: Mexican peso
Religions: Roman Catholic, Protestant
Languages: Spanish, Mayan, other indigenous languages

Micronesia

Area: 271 sq mi (702 sq km)
Population: 107,000
Capital: Palikir, pop. 7,000
Currency: U.S. dollar
Religions: Roman Catholic, Protestant
Languages: English, Trukese, Pohnpeian, Yapese, other indigenous languages

Moldova

Area: 13,050 sq mi (33,800 sq km)
Population: 4,114,000
Capital: Chisinau, pop. 677,000
Currency: Moldovan leu
Religion: Eastern Orthodox
Languages: Moldovan, Russian, Gagauz

Monaco

Area: 0.8 sq mi (2.0 sq km)
Population: 37,000
Capital: Monaco, pop. 35,000
Currency: euro
Religion: Roman Catholic
Languages: French, English, Italian, Monegasque

Mongolia

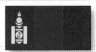

Area: 603,909 sq mi (1,564,116 sq km)
Population: 2,792,000
Capital: Ulaanbaatar, pop. 1,184,000
Currency: togrog/tugrik
Religions: Buddhist Lamaist, Shamanist, Christian
Languages: Khalkha Mongol, Turkic, Russian

Montenegro

Area: 5,333 sq mi (13,812 sq km)
Population: 623,000
Capital: Podgorica, pop. 156,000
Currency: euro
Religions: Orthodox, Muslim, Roman Catholic
Languages: Serbian (Ijekavian dialect), Bosnian, Albanian, Croatian

Morocco

Area: 172,414 sq mi (446,550 sq km)
Population: 32,950,000
Capital: Rabat, pop. 1,843,000
Currency: Moroccan dirham
Religion: Muslim
Languages: Arabic, Berber dialects, French

Mozambique

Area: 308,642 sq mi (799,380 sq km)
Population: 24,336,000
Capital: Maputo, pop. 1,150,000
Currency: metical
Religions: Roman Catholic, Muslim, Zionist Christian
Languages: Emakhuwa, Xichangana, Portuguese, Elomwe, Cisena, Echuwabo, other local languages

Myanmar (Burma)

Area: 261,218 sq mi (676,552 sq km)
Population: 53,259,000
Capitals: Nay Pyi Taw, pop. 1,060,000; Yangon (Rangoon), pop. 4,457,000
Currency: kyat
Religions: Buddhist, Christian, Muslim
Languages: Burmese, minority ethnic languages

Namibia

Area: 318,261 sq mi
(824,292 sq km)
Population: 2,410,000
Capital: Windhoek, pop. 380,000
Currencies: Namibian dollar;
South African rand
Religions: Lutheran, other Christian, indigenous beliefs
Languages: Afrikaans, German, English

Nauru

Area: 8 sq mi (21 sq km)
Population: 11,000
Capital: Yaren, pop. 11,000
Currency: Australian dollar
Religions: Protestant, Roman Catholic
Languages: Nauruan, English

Nepal

Area: 56,827 sq mi
(147,181 sq km)
Population: 26,810,000
Capital: Kathmandu, pop. 1,015,000
Currency: Nepalese rupee
Religions: Hindu, Buddhist, Muslim, Kirant
Languages: Nepali, Maithali, Bhojpuri, Tharu,
Tamang, Newar, Magar

Netherlands

Area: 16,034 sq mi
(41,528 sq km)
Population: 16,798,000
Capital: Amsterdam, pop. 1,056,000
Currency: euro
Religions: Roman Catholic, Dutch Reformed,
Calvinist, Muslim
Languages: Dutch, Frisian

New Zealand

Area: 104,454 sq mi
(270,534 sq km)
Population: 4,450,000
Capital: Wellington, pop. 410,000
Currency: New Zealand dollar
Religions: Anglican, Roman Catholic, Presbyterian,
other Christian
Languages: English, Maori

Nicaragua

Area: 50,193 sq mi
(130,000 sq km)
Population: 6,043,000
Capital: Managua, pop. 970,000
Currency: gold cordoba
Religions: Roman Catholic, Evangelical
Language: Spanish

Niger

Area: 489,191 sq mi (1,267,000 sq km)
Population: 16,916,000
Capital: Niamey, pop. 1,297,000
Currency: Communauté
Financière Africaine franc
Religions: Muslim, other (includes indigenous
beliefs and Christian)
Languages: French, Hausa, Djerma

Nigeria

Area: 356,669 sq mi
(923,768 sq km)
Population: 173,615,000
Capital: Abuja, pop. 2,153,000
Currency: naira
Religions: Muslim, Christian, indigenous beliefs
Languages: English, Hausa, Yoruba, Igbo (Ibo), Fulani

The National ANIMAL of Nigeria is the EAGLE.

North Korea

Area: 46,540 sq mi
(120,538 sq km)
Population: 24,720,000
Capital: Pyongyang,
pop. 2,843,000
Currency: North Korean won
Religions: Buddhist, Confucianist, some Christian
and syncretic Chondogyo
Language: Korean

Norway

Area: 125,004 sq mi
(323,758 sq km)
Population: 5,084,000
Capital: Oslo, pop. 915,000
Currency: Norwegian krone
Religion: Church of Norway (Lutheran)
Languages: Bokmal Norwegian, Nynorsk Norwegian, Sami

Pakistan

Area: 307,374 sq mi
(796,095 sq km)
Population: 190,709,000
Capital: Islamabad, pop. 919,000
Currency: Pakistani rupee
Religions: Sunni Muslim, Shiite Muslim
Languages: Punjabi, Sindhi, Siraiki, Pashto, Urdu, Baluchi, Hindko, English

Oman

Area: 119,500 sq mi
(309,500 sq km)
Population: 3,983,000
Capital: Muscat, pop. 743,000
Currency: Omani rial
Religions: Ibadhi Muslim, Sunni Muslim, Shiite Muslim, Hindu
Languages: Arabic, English, Baluchi, Urdu, Indian dialects

Palau

Area: 189 sq mi (489 sq km)
Population: 21,000
Capital: Melekeok, pop. 1,000
Currency: U.S. dollar
Religions: Roman Catholic, Protestant, Modekngei, Seventh-day Adventist
Languages: Palauan, Filipino, English, Chinese

You Are There!

Franz Josef Glacier, New Zealand

As your helicopter lifts into the cloudless sky, the landscape below rapidly changes from a lush green to an icy blue. You are flying high above New Zealand's Westland Tai Poutini National Park, home to the Franz Josef Glacier. Ranging from a height of 8,858 feet (2,700 m) above sea level down to just 787 feet (240 m), Franz Josef is one of the world's steepest glaciers. But it's also one of the most accessible, welcoming up to 2,700 visitors a day.

The best way to take in all of the glacier's glory? The chopper, of course, which gives you a brilliant bird's-eye view before landing. Then hike past funky formations, curving tunnels, and towering peaks—all formed by the majestic blue glacial ice.

Panama

Area: 29,157 sq mi (75,517 sq km)
Population: 3,850,000
Capital: Panama City, pop. 1,426,000
Currencies: balboa; U.S. dollar
Religions: Roman Catholic, Protestant
Languages: Spanish, English

Peru

Area: 496,224 sq mi (1,285,216 sq km)
Population: 30,475,000
Capital: Lima, pop. 9,130,000
Currency: nuevo sol
Religion: Roman Catholic
Languages: Spanish, Quechua, Aymara, minor Amazonian languages

Papua New Guinea

Area: 178,703 sq mi (462,840 sq km)
Population: 7,179,000
Capital: Port Moresby, pop. 343,000
Currency: kina
Religions: indigenous beliefs, Roman Catholic, Lutheran, other Protestant
Languages: Melanesian Pidgin, 820 indigenous languages

Philippines

Area: 115,831 sq mi (300,000 sq km)
Population: 96,209,000
Capital: Manila, pop. 11,862,000
Currency: Philippine peso
Religions: Roman Catholic, Muslim, other Christian
Languages: Filipino (based on Tagalog), English

Paraguay

Area: 157,048 sq mi (406,752 sq km)
Population: 6,798,000
Capital: Asunción, pop. 2,139,000
Currency: guarani
Religions: Roman Catholic, Protestant
Languages: Spanish, Guarani

Poland

Area: 120,728 sq mi (312,685 sq km)
Population: 38,517,000
Capital: Warsaw, pop. 1,723,000
Currency: zloty
Religion: Roman Catholic
Language: Polish

5 cool things about PARAGUAY

1. Paraguay's flag features different designs on the front and back.

2. Located in the center of South America, Paraguay is sometimes called *Corazon de America* ("Heart of America").

3. Lace-making is a popular Paraguayan craft.

4. A musician in Paraguay makes instruments out of recycled trash from the country's largest landfill.

5. Paraguay completed the first railroad system in South America in 1889.

Portugal

Area: 35,655 sq mi (92,345 sq km)
Population: 10,460,000
Capital: Lisbon, pop. 2,843,000
Currency: euro
Religion: Roman Catholic
Languages: Portuguese, Mirandese

Qatar

Area: 4,448 sq mi (11,521 sq km)
Population: 2,169,000
Capital: Doha, pop. 567,000
Currency: Qatari rial
Religions: Muslim, Christian
Languages: Arabic; English commonly a second language

COLOR KEY ● Africa ● Australia, New Zealand, and Oceania

Romania

Area: 92,043 sq mi
(238,391 sq km)
Population: 21,269,000
Capital: Bucharest, pop. 1,937,000
Currency: new leu
Religions: Eastern Orthodox, Protestant,
Roman Catholic
Languages: Romanian, Hungarian

Russia

Area: 6,592,850 sq mi
(17,075,400 sq km)
Population: 143,493,000
Capital: Moscow, pop. 11,621,000
Currency: ruble
Religions: Russian Orthodox, Muslim
Languages: Russian, many minority languages
*Note: Russia is in both Europe and Asia, but its capital is in Europe,
so it is classified here as a European country.*

Rwanda

Area: 10,169 sq mi
(26,338 sq km)
Population: 11,116,000
Capital: Kigali, pop. 1,004,000
Currency: Rwandan franc
Religions: Roman Catholic, Protestant,
Adventist, Muslim
Languages: Kinyarwanda, French, English, Kiswahili

Samoa

Area: 1,093 sq mi (2,831 sq km)
Population: 190,000
Capital: Apia, pop. 37,000
Currency: tala
Religions: Congregationalist, Roman Catholic,
Methodist, Church of Jesus Christ of Latter-day
Saints, Assembly of God, Seventh-day Adventist
Languages: Samoan (Polynesian), English

San Marino

Area: 24 sq mi (61 sq km)
Population: 33,000
Capital: San Marino, pop. 4,000
Currency: euro
Religion: Roman Catholic
Language: Italian

Sao Tome and Principe

Area: 386 sq mi (1,001 sq km)
Population: 188,000
Capital: São Tomé,
pop. 64,000
Currency: dobra
Religions: Roman Catholic, Evangelical
Language: Portuguese

Saudi Arabia

Area: 756,985 sq mi
(1,960,582 sq km)
Population: 30,054,000
Capital: Riyadh, pop. 5,451,000
Currency: Saudi riyal
Religion: Muslim
Language: Arabic

Senegal

Area: 75,955 sq mi
(196,722 sq km)
Population: 13,497,000
Capital: Dakar, pop. 3,035,000
Currency: Communauté
Financière Africaine franc
Religions: Muslim, Christian (mostly Roman Catholic)
Languages: French, Wolof, Pulaar, Jola, Mandinka

Serbia

Area: 29,913 sq mi (77,474 sq km)
Population: 7,136,000
Capital: Belgrade, pop. 1,135,000
Currency: Serbian dinar
Religions: Serbian Orthodox, Roman Catholic, Muslim
Languages: Serbian, Hungarian

Seychelles

Area: 176 sq mi (455 sq km)
Population: 93,000
Capital: Victoria, pop. 27,000
Currency: Seychelles rupee
Religions: Roman Catholic, Anglican, other Christian
Languages: Creole, English

Sierra Leone

Area: 27,699 sq mi (71,740 sq km)
Population: 6,242,000
Capital: Freetown, pop. 941,000
Currency: leone
Religions: Muslim, indigenous beliefs, Christian
Languages: English, Mende, Temne, Krio

Slovakia

Area: 18,932 sq mi (49,035 sq km)
Population: 5,414,000
Capital: Bratislava, pop. 434,000
Currency: euro
Religions: Roman Catholic, Protestant, Greek Catholic
Languages: Slovak, Hungarian

Singapore

Area: 255 sq mi (660 sq km)
Population: 5,444,000
Capital: Singapore, pop. 5,188,000
Currency: Singapore dollar
Religions: Buddhist, Muslim, Taoist, Roman Catholic, Hindu, other Christian
Languages: Mandarin, English, Malay, Hokkien, Cantonese, Teochew, Tamil

Slovenia

Area: 7,827 sq mi (20,273 sq km)
Population: 2,060,000
Capital: Ljubljana, pop. 273,000
Currency: euro
Religions: Roman Catholic, Muslim, Orthodox
Languages: Slovene, Croatian, Serbian

You Are There!

Singapore Flyer, Singapore

Imagine strapping yourself into a Ferris wheel and being lifted so high in the sky, you can see nearly 30 miles (45 km) away. Well, in Singapore, you don't have to imagine: You can do just that in real life! Just take a spin on the Singapore Flyer—one of the world's highest observation wheels, which, at 541 feet (165 m), stands about 50 stories high. A standout on Singapore's iconic skyline along the Singapore River, the Flyer offers an unrivaled 360° view of famous sites and even neighboring countries.

COLOR KEY ● Africa ● Australia, New Zealand, and Oceania

Solomon Islands

Area: 10,954 sq mi (28,370 sq km)
Population: 581,000
Capital: Honiara, pop. 68,000
Currency: Solomon Islands dollar
Religions: Church of Melanesia, Roman Catholic, South Seas Evangelical, other Christian
Languages: Melanesian pidgin, 120 indigenous languages

Somalia

Area: 246,201 sq mi (637,657 sq km)
Population: 10,383,000
Capital: Mogadishu, pop. 1,554,000
Currency: Somali shilling
Religion: Sunni Muslim
Languages: Somali, Arabic, Italian, English

South Africa

Area: 470,693 sq mi (1,219,090 sq km)
Population: 52,982,000
Capitals: Pretoria (Tshwane), pop. 1,501,000; Bloemfontein, pop. 468,000; Cape Town, pop. 3,562,000
Currency: rand
Religions: Zion Christian, Pentecostal, Catholic, Methodist, Dutch Reformed, Anglican, other Christian
Languages: IsiZulu, IsiXhosa, Afrikaans, Sepedi, English

South Korea

Area: 38,321 sq mi (99,250 sq km)
Population: 50,220,000
Capital: Seoul, pop. 9,736,000
Currency: South Korean won
Religions: Christian, Buddhist
Languages: Korean, English

South Sudan

Area: 248,777 sq mi (644,329 sq km)
Population: 9,782,000
Capital: Juba, pop. 269,000
Currency: South Sudan pound
Religions: animist, Christian
Languages: English, Arabic, regional languages (Dinke, Nuer, Bari, Zande, Shilluk)

Spain

Area: 195,363 sq mi (505,988 sq km)
Population: 46,647,000
Capital: Madrid, pop. 6,574,000
Currency: euro
Religion: Roman Catholic
Languages: Castilian Spanish, Catalan, Galician, Basque

Sri Lanka

Area: 25,299 sq mi (65,525 sq km)
Population: 20,501,000
Capitals: Colombo, pop. 693,000; Sri Jayewardenepura Kotte, pop. 126,000
Currency: Sri Lankan rupee
Religions: Buddhist, Muslim, Hindu, Christian
Languages: Sinhala, Tamil

St. Kitts and Nevis

Area: 104 sq mi (269 sq km)
Population: 55,000
Capital: Basseterre, pop. 12,000
Currency: East Caribbean dollar
Religions: Anglican, other Protestant, Roman Catholic
Language: English

St. Lucia

Area: 238 sq mi (616 sq km)
Population: 170,000
Capital: Castries, pop. 21,000
Currency: East Caribbean dollar
Religions: Roman Catholic, Seventh-day Adventist, Pentecostal
Languages: English, French patois

St. Vincent and the Grenadines

Area: 150 sq mi (389 sq km)
Population: 108,000
Capital: Kingstown, pop. 31,000
Currency: East Caribbean dollar
Religions: Anglican, Methodist, Roman Catholic
Languages: English, French patois

Sudan

Area: 718,722 sq mi
(1,861,484 sq km)
Population: 34,186,000
Capital: Khartoum, pop. 4,632,000
Currency: Sudanese pound
Religions: Sunni Muslim, indigenous beliefs, Christian
Languages: Arabic, Nubian, Ta Bedawie, many diverse
dialects of Nilotic, Nilo-Hamitic, Sudanic languages

Suriname

Area: 63,037 sq mi (163,265 sq km)
Population: 558,000
Capital: Paramaribo, pop. 278,000
Currency: Suriname dollar
Religions: Hindu, Protestant (predominantly
Moravian), Roman Catholic, Muslim, indigenous beliefs
Languages: Dutch, English, Sranang Tongo,
Hindustani, Javanese

Swaziland

Area: 6,704 sq mi (17,363 sq km)
Population: 1,238,000
Capitals: Mbabane, pop. 66,000;
Lobamba, pop. 4,557
Currency: lilangeni
Religions: Zionist, Roman Catholic, Muslim
Languages: English, siSwati

Sweden

Area: 173,732 sq mi
(449,964 sq km)
Population: 9,592,000
Capital: Stockholm, pop. 1,385,000
Currency: Swedish krona
Religion: Lutheran
Languages: Swedish, Sami, Finnish

Switzerland

Area: 15,940 sq mi
(41,284 sq km)
Population: 8,078,000
Capital: Bern, pop. 353,000
Currency: Swiss franc
Religions: Roman Catholic, Protestant, Muslim
Languages: German, French, Italian, Romansh

Syria

Area: 71,498 sq mi (185,180 sq km)
Population: 21,898,000
Capital: Damascus, pop. 2,650,000
Currency: Syrian pound
Religions: Sunni, other Muslim (includes Alawite,
Druze), Christian
Languages: Arabic, Kurdish, Armenian, Aramaic,
Circassian

Tajikistan

Area: 55,251 sq mi
(143,100 sq km)
Population: 8,085,000
Capital: Dushanbe,
pop. 739,000
Currency: somoni
Religions: Sunni Muslim, Shiite Muslim
Languages: Tajik, Russian

Tanzania

Area: 364,900 sq mi (945,087 sq km)
Population: 49,122,000
Capitals: Dar es Salaam, pop.
2,930,000; Dodoma, pop. 226,000
Currency: Tanzanian shilling
Religions: Muslim, indigenous beliefs, Christian
Languages: Kiswahili, Kiunguja, English, Arabic,
local languages

Thailand

Area: 198,115 sq mi
(513,115 sq km)
Population: 66,185,000
Capital: Bangkok, pop. 8,426,000
Currency: baht
Religions: Buddhist, Muslim
Languages: Thai, English, ethnic dialects

Timor-Leste (East Timor)

Area: 5,640 sq mi
(14,609 sq km)
Population: 1,108,000
Capital: Dili, pop. 180,000
Currency: U.S. dollar
Religion: Roman Catholic
Languages: Tetum, Portuguese, Indonesian, English,
indigenous languages

Togo

Area: 21,925 sq mi (56,785 sq km)
Population: 6,168,000
Capital: Lomé, pop. 1,524,000
Currency: Communauté Financière Africaine franc
Religions: indigenous beliefs, Christian, Muslim
Languages: French, Ewe, Mina, Kabye, Dagomba

Trinidad and Tobago

Area: 1,980 sq mi (5,128 sq km)
Population: 1,341,000
Capital: Port of Spain, pop. 66,000
Currency: Trinidad and Tobago dollar
Religions: Roman Catholic, Hindu, Anglican, Baptist
Languages: English, Caribbean Hindustani, French, Spanish, Chinese

Tonga

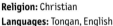

Area: 289 sq mi (748 sq km)
Population: 103,000
Capital: Nuku'alofa, pop. 25,000
Currency: pa'anga
Religion: Christian
Languages: Tongan, English

Tunisia

Area: 63,170 sq mi (163,610 sq km)
Population: 10,882,000
Capital: Tunis, pop. 790,000
Currency: Tunisian dinar
Religion: Muslim
Languages: Arabic, French

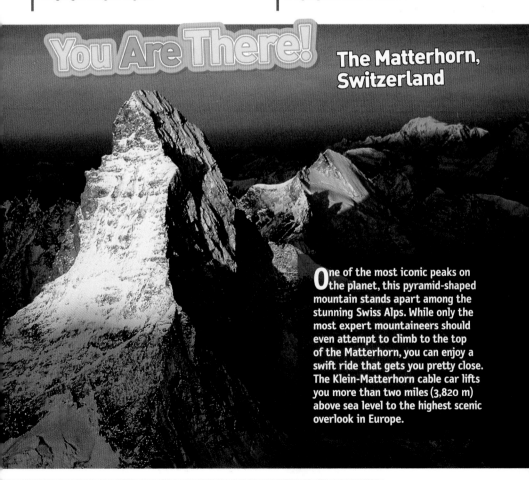

You Are There!

The Matterhorn, Switzerland

One of the most iconic peaks on the planet, this pyramid-shaped mountain stands apart among the stunning Swiss Alps. While only the most expert mountaineers should even attempt to climb to the top of the Matterhorn, you can enjoy a swift ride that gets you pretty close. The Klein-Matterhorn cable car lifts you more than two miles (3,820 m) above sea level to the highest scenic overlook in Europe.

Turkey

Area: 300,948 sq mi
(779,452 sq km)
Population: 76,083,000
Capital: Ankara, pop. 4,194,000
Currency: new Turkish lira
Religion: Muslim (mostly Sunni)
Languages: Turkish, Kurdish, Dimli (Zaza), Azeri, Kabardian, Gagauz

Turkmenistan

Area: 188,456 sq mi
(488,100 sq km)
Population: 5,240,000
Capital: Ashgabat, pop. 683,000
Currency: Turkmen manat
Religions: Muslim, Eastern Orthodox
Languages: Turkmen, Russian, Uzbek

1. There are more white marble buildings in the capital city of Ashgabat than in any other city in the world.

2. The massive Karakum Desert covers about 70 percent of Turkmenistan.

3. Turkmenistan is home to the world's largest indoor Ferris wheel.

4. Dinosaur footprints have been discovered in eastern Turkmenistan.

5. A crater in the Karakum Desert has been on fire for over 40 years.

Tuvalu

Area: 10 sq mi (26 sq km)
Population: 11,000
Capital: Funafuti, pop. 5,000
Currencies: Australian dollar; Tuvaluan dollar
Religion: Church of Tuvalu (Congregationalist)
Languages: Tuvaluan, English, Samoan, Kiribati

Uganda

Area: 93,104 sq mi
(241,139 sq km)
Population: 36,890,000
Capital: Kampala, pop. 1,659,000
Currency: Ugandan shilling
Religions: Protestant, Roman Catholic, Muslim
Languages: English, Ganda, other local languages, Kiswahili, Arabic

Ukraine

Area: 233,090 sq mi
(603,700 sq km)
Population: 45,513,000
Capital: Kiev, pop. 2,829,000
Currency: hryvnia
Religions: Ukrainian Orthodox, Orthodox, Ukrainian Greek Catholic
Languages: Ukrainian, Russian

United Arab Emirates

Area: 30,000 sq mi
(77,700 sq km)
Population: 9,346,000
Capital: Abu Dhabi, pop. 942,000
Currency: Emirati dirham
Religion: Muslim
Languages: Arabic, Persian, English, Hindi, Urdu

United Kingdom

Area: 93,788 sq mi
(242,910 sq km)
Population: 64,092,000
Capital: London, pop. 9,005,000
Currency: British pound
Religions: Anglican, Roman Catholic, Presbyterian, Methodist
Languages: English, Welsh, Scottish form of Gaelic

United States

Area: 3,794,083 sq mi
(9,826,630 sq km)
Population: 316,158,000
Capital: Washington, D.C., pop. 617,996
Currency: U.S. dollar
Religions: Protestant, Roman Catholic
Languages: English, Spanish

Uruguay

Area: 68,037 sq mi
(176,215 sq km)
Population: 3,392,000
Capital: Montevideo, pop. 1,672,000
Currency: Uruguayan peso
Religion: Roman Catholic
Language: Spanish

Vietnam

Area: 127,844 sq mi
(331,114 sq km)
Population: 89,721,000
Capital: Hanoi, pop. 2,955,000
Currency: dong
Religions: Buddhist, Roman Catholic
Languages: Vietnamese, English, French, Chinese, Khmer

Uzbekistan

Area: 172,742 sq mi
(447,400 sq km)
Population: 30,215,000
Capital: Tashkent,
pop. 2,227,000
Currency: Uzbekistani sum
Religions: Muslim (mostly Sunni), Eastern Orthodox
Languages: Uzbek, Russian, Tajik

Yemen

Area: 207,286 sq mi
(536,869 sq km)
Population: 25,235,000
Capital: Sanaa, pop. 2,419,000
Currency: Yemeni rial
Religions: Muslim, including Shaf'i (Sunni) and Zaydi (Shiite)
Language: Arabic

Vanuatu

Area: 4,707 sq mi (12,190 sq km)
Population: 265,000
Capital: Port Vila, pop. 47,000
Currency: vatu
Religions: Presbyterian, Anglican, Roman Catholic, other Christian, indigenous beliefs
Languages: more than 100 local languages, pidgin (known as Bislama or Bichelama)

Zambia

Area: 290,586 sq mi
(752,614 sq km)
Population: 14,187,000
Capital: Lusaka, pop. 1,802,000
Currency: Zambian kwacha
Religions: Christian, Muslim, Hindu
Languages: English, Bemba, Kaonda, Lozi, Lunda, Luvale, Nyanja, Tonga, about 70 other indigenous languages

Vatican City

Area: 0.2 sq mi (0.4 sq km)
Population: 798
Capital: Vatican City, pop. 798
Currency: euro
Religion: Roman Catholic
Languages: Italian, Latin, French

Zimbabwe

Area: 150,872 sq mi
(390,757 sq km)
Population: 13,038,000
Capital: Harare, pop. 1,542,000
Currency: Zimbabwean dollar
Religions: Syncretic (part Christian, part indigenous beliefs), Christian, indigenous beliefs
Languages: English, Shona, Sindebele, tribal dialects

Venezuela

Area: 352,144 sq mi
(912,050 sq km)
Population: 29,679,000
Capital: Caracas, pop. 3,242,000
Currency: bolivar
Religion: Roman Catholic
Languages: Spanish, numerous indigenous dialects

THE SPRAY from Victoria Falls—a waterfall in ZIMBABWE—can be seen from more than 12 MILES (20 KM) away.

● Asia   ● Europe   ◐ North America   ● South America

POLITICAL CANADA

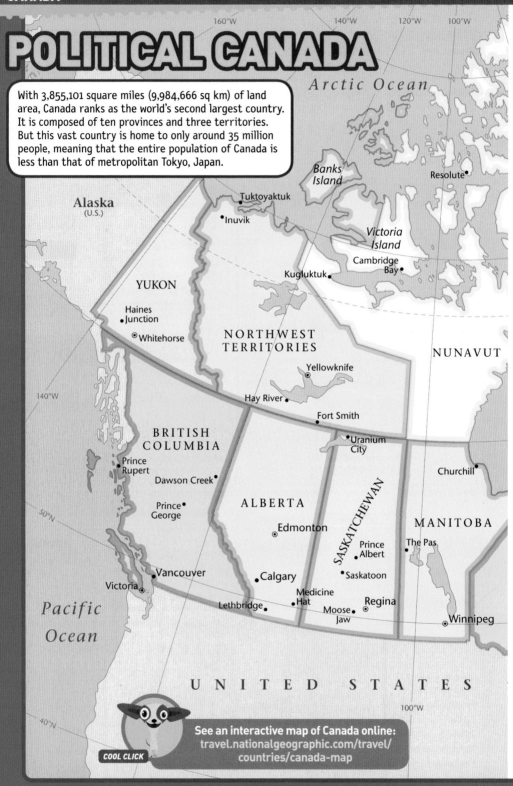

With 3,855,101 square miles (9,984,666 sq km) of land area, Canada ranks as the world's second largest country. It is composed of ten provinces and three territories. But this vast country is home to only around 35 million people, meaning that the entire population of Canada is less than that of metropolitan Tokyo, Japan.

Arctic Ocean

Banks Island

Resolute

Alaska (U.S.)

Tuktoyaktuk

Inuvik

Victoria Island

Cambridge Bay

Kugluktuk

YUKON

Haines Junction

Whitehorse

NORTHWEST TERRITORIES

NUNAVUT

Yellowknife

Hay River

Fort Smith

BRITISH COLUMBIA

Uranium City

Churchill

Prince Rupert

Dawson Creek

Prince George

ALBERTA

SASKATCHEWAN

MANITOBA

Edmonton

Prince Albert

The Pas

Vancouver

Calgary

Saskatoon

Victoria

Medicine Hat

Regina

Lethbridge

Moose Jaw

Winnipeg

Pacific Ocean

UNITED STATES

100°W

See an interactive map of Canada online:
travel.nationalgeographic.com/travel/
countries/canada-map

COOL CLICK

ICELAND

Ellesmere
Island

Greenland
(Denmark)

80°N
40°W
20°W

ARCTIC CIRCLE

70°N

60°N

Baffin Island

Igloolik

Map Key

⊗ National capital

⊙ Provincial or
territorial capital

• Other city

40°W

Cape Dorset

Iqaluit ⊙

0   400 Miles
0   400 Kilometers

Azimuthal Equidistant Projection

Ivujivik

Kuujjuaq

NEWFOUNDLAND AND LABRADOR

*Atlantic
Ocean*

*Hudson
Bay*

Schefferville
Happy Valley-
Goose Bay

L'Anse aux
Meadows

50°N

Fort
Severn

St.
John's

Chisasibi

QUEBEC

Sept-Îles

PRINCE EDWARD
ISLAND

Fort
Albany

ONTARIO

Saguenay

Charlottetown

Thunder
Bay

Timmins

Québec ⊙

NEW
BRUNSWICK

Fredericton ⊙

Greater
Sudbury

Montréal

Halifax ⊙

NOVA
SCOTIA

Sault
Ste. Marie

Ottawa ⊗

Kingston

40°N

Toronto ⊙
Hamilton
London
Niagara
Falls
Windsor

80°W

60°W

317

PHYSICAL CANADA

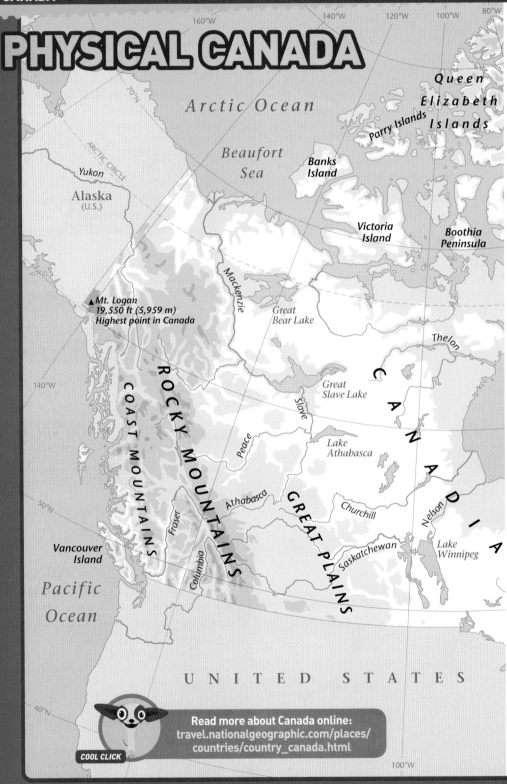

160°W 140°W 120°W 100°W 80°W

Arctic Ocean

Queen Elizabeth Islands

Parry Islands

70°N

ARCTIC CIRCLE

Yukon

Alaska
(U.S.)

Beaufort
Sea

Banks
Island

Victoria
Island

Boothia
Peninsula

▲ Mt. Logan
19,550 ft (5,959 m)
Highest point in Canada

Mackenzie

Great
Bear Lake

Thelon

140°W

ROCKY MOUNTAINS

COAST MOUNTAINS

Slave

Great
Slave Lake

C A N A D I A

Peace

Lake
Athabasca

50°N

Fraser

Athabasca

GREAT PLAINS

Churchill

Nelson

Vancouver
Island

Columbia

Saskatchewan

Lake
Winnipeg

Pacific
Ocean

U N I T E D   S T A T E S

40°N

COOL CLICK

Read more about Canada online:
travel.nationalgeographic.com/places/
countries/country_canada.html

100°W

Located in northern North America, Canada shares land borders with the United States and is across the Arctic Ocean from Russia.

From the deepest lake in Canada, Great Slave Lake in the Northwest Territories (2,014 ft/614 m), to the country's highest waterfall, Della Falls on Vancouver Island (1,445 ft/440 m), Canada has a unique relationship with water. It has more than half of the world's lakes within its borders. Canada is surrounded by the Atlantic, Pacific, and Arctic Oceans and has the longest coastline of any country (151,023 mi/243,048 km). All together, Canada is a country rich in natural resources and beauty.

Map Key (Elevation)

▲ Highest point

6,600 ft	2,000 m
3,300 ft	1,000 m
1,650 ft	500 m
650 ft	200 m
0 ft	0 m

0   400 Miles
0   400 Kilometers

Azimuthal Equidistant Projection

Greenland
(Denmark)

ICELAND

Ellesmere Island

Baffin Bay

Baffin Island

Davis Strait

Melville Peninsula

Hudson Strait

Ungava Peninsula

Caniapiscau

Labrador

Labrador Sea

Hudson Bay

La Grande Riviére

SHIELD

Laurentide Scarp

Island of Newfoundland

Albany

Gaspé Peninsula

St. Lawrence

Gulf of St. Lawrence

Ottawa

Bay of Fundy

Nova Scotia

Lake Superior

L. Michigan

L. Huron

L. Ontario

L. Erie

Atlantic Ocean

CANADA'S PROVINCES AND TERRITORIES

Canada, the world's second largest country by area, is made up of ten provinces and three territories. Its capital is Ottawa, Ontario. Provinces can exercise constitutional powers on their own, while territories have only the legal powers delegated to them by the federal government. City population counts provided in this section represent metropolitan areas, with the exception of Iqaluit, Nunavut, for which the city's population is listed.

Capital   # Ottawa

Ottawa

Province: Ontario
City land area: 1,073 sq mi (2,779 sq km)
Metro land area: 2,053 sq mi (5,319 sq km)
Population: 1,273,300

There's a sanctuary for **STRAY CATS**, with little wooden houses and food, **behind Canada's Parliament Buildings** in Ottawa.

Province   # Alberta

Area: 255,541 sq mi (661,848 sq km)
Population: 4,025,100
Capital: Edmonton, pop. 1,230,100
Largest city: Calgary, pop. 1,309,200

YOU CAN SCUBA DIVE in a mountain lake at an altitude of **4,750 feet** (1,450 m) in Banff National Park.

Province

British Columbia

Area: 364,764 sq mi (944,735 sq km)
Population: 4,582,000
Capital: Victoria, pop. 363,100
Largest city: Vancouver, pop. 2,463,700

The town of **Nanaimo** is considered the
BATHTUB RACING
Capital of the World.

Province

Manitoba

Area: 250,116 sq mi (647,797 sq km)
Population: 1,265,000
Capital: Winnipeg, pop. 778,400
Largest city: Winnipeg, pop. 778,400

Each fall, migrating **POLAR BEARS**
wander through the town
of Churchill.

Province — New Brunswick

Area: 28,150 sq mi (72,908 sq km)
Population: 756,100
Capital: Fredericton, pop. 94,398
Largest city: Saint John, pop. 128,900

right whale

In summer, **THE BAY OF FUNDY*** is home to **eight species of whales**— including humpbacks and right whales.

Province — Newfoundland & Labrador

Area: 156,453 sq mi (405,212 sq km)
Population: 526,700
Capital: St. John's, pop. 200,600
Largest city: St. John's, pop. 200,600

Icebergs **THE SIZE OF SMALL CRUISE SHIPS** float down **"Iceberg Alley"** off the coast of Newfoundland.

*The Bay of Fundy is located between New Brunswick and Nova Scotia.

Territory

Northwest Territories

Area: 519,734 sq mi (1,346,106 sq km)
Population: 43,500
Capital: Yellowknife, pop. 19,819
Largest city: Yellowknife, pop. 19,819

Yellowknife is the **COLDEST CITY IN CANADA**, with an average winter temperature of **-20.02°F** (-28.9°C).

Province

Nova Scotia

Area: 21,345 sq mi (55,284 sq km)
Population: 940,800
Capital: Halifax, pop. 413,700
Largest city: Halifax, pop. 413,700

The Nova Scotia **Duck Tolling Retriever** is the **OFFICIAL PROVINCIAL DOG of Nova Scotia.**

Territory — Nunavut

Area: 808,185 sq mi (2,093,190 sq km)
Population: 35,600
Capital: Iqaluit, pop. 7,081
Largest city: Iqaluit, pop. 7,081

The town of Alert, on the tip of Ellesmere Island, is the **northernmost** permanently inhabited place **in the world.**

Province — Ontario

Area: 415,598 sq mi (1,076,395 sq km)
Population: 13,538,000
Capital: Toronto, pop. 5,941,500
Largest city: Toronto, pop. 5,941,500

A street in **TORONTO**—Yonge St. to Highway 11—is **1,178 miles** (1,896 km) **long**—longer than the distance from **London, England, to Madrid, Spain.**

Province

Prince Edward Island

Area: 2,185 sq mi (5,660 sq km)
Population: 145,200
Capital: Charlottetown, pop. 67,836
Largest city: Charlottetown, pop. 67,836

Prince Edward Island is nicknamed "**SPUD ISLAND**" for all the **potatoes** that grow there.

Province

Quebec

Area: 595,391 sq mi (1,542,056 sq km)
Population: 8,155,300
Capital: Quebec City, pop. 769,600
Largest city: Montreal, pop. 3,957,700

Northern Quebec is home to some of the **OLDEST ROCKS** ever found on Earth's surface.

Province

Saskatchewan

Area: 251,366 sq mi (651,036 sq km)
Population: 1,108,300
Capital: Regina, pop. 226,300
Largest city: Saskatoon, pop. 284,000

Regina is home to the
ONLY TRAINING ACADEMY for the
Royal Canadian Mounted Police.

Territory

Yukon

Area: 186,272 sq mi (482,443 sq km)
Population: 36,700
Capital: Whitehorse, pop. 27,222
Largest city: Whitehorse, pop. 27,222

The capital city of **Whitehorse** is
said to have the **FRESHEST AIR**
of any city **in the world.**

THE GREAT OUTDOORS

Canada's national parks collectively cover almost 86,667 square miles (224,466 sq km) and are home to some of the planet's most scenic and geographically diverse spots. Check out some of the country's most popular parks.

BANFF

JASPER

Banff National Park

Where: Alberta
What to see: More than 1,000 glaciers, sparkling lakes, and the largest cave system in Canada
Cool fact: Banff's ancient mountains range from 45 to 120 million years old.

Jasper National Park

Where: Alberta
What to see: Soaring mountains, deep valleys, hot springs, glaciers, and plenty of wildlife like grizzly bears, moose, and elk
Cool fact: Jasper's Columbia Icefield—a huge mass of ice—is as thick as the Eiffel Tower is tall.

AUYUITTUQ

Auyuittuq National Park

Where: Nunavut
What to see: A vast, uninhabited tundra; glacier-carved fjords; and majestic mountain peaks
Cool fact: Auyuittuq, which means the "land that never melts" in a native language, is home to Mount Thor, the world's tallest and steepest cliff.

Point Pelee National Park

Where: Ontario
What to see: A diverse collection of plants and flowers, plus more than 350 species of migrating birds
Cool fact: During August and September, thousands of monarch butterflies land on Point Pelee as they migrate south.

POINT PELEE

GROS MORNE

Gros Morne National Park

Where: Newfoundland and Labrador
What to see: Jagged mountains, glacier-carved lakes, towering waterfalls, sandy beaches, and sea caves
Cool fact: In the Tablelands area in Gros Morne, you can walk on part of the Earth's mantle that has been pushed above ground.

1

China's mountainous bamboo forests can rise sharply—but pandas can easily climb as much as **13,000 FEET** (3,962 m) up the slopes.

2

BEFORE THE 1400s IN EUROPE, PORTUGAL'S SOUTHERN COAST WAS THOUGHT TO BE THE EDGE OF THE KNOWN WORLD.

3

About **12,000 years ago**, the **Sahara** was covered with millions of trees.

15 COOL THINGS ABOUT

4

More people live in TAMPA, FLORIDA, U.S.A., than in all of ICELAND.

5

CANADA'S THOR PEAK IS THOUGHT TO HAVE THE WORLD'S LONGEST UNINTERRUPTED CLIFF FACE.

6

In Jordan's ancient city of Petra, buildings were carved directly into cliff walls.

7

BEIJING
BERLIN
BAKU
BERN

MORE CAPITAL CITIES START WITH THE LETTER *B* THAN WITH ANY OTHER LETTER.

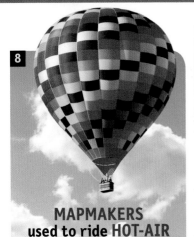

8

MAPMAKERS used to ride HOT-AIR **BALLOONS** to view and map land.

9
WHEN FORESTS FLOOD ALONG THE AMAZON RIVER, RIVER DOLPHINS SOMETIMES HAVE TO SWIM AROUND TREES.

11
THE SURFACE OF THE PACIFIC OCEAN COULD COVER ALL OF EARTH'S CONTINENTS COMBINED.

10
A MOTORCYCLE SWEPT TO SEA BY A 2011 TSUNAMI DRIFTED ALL THE WAY FROM JAPAN TO CANADA.

THE WORLD

12
INDONESIA'S REMOTE FOJA MOUNTAINS ARE HOME TO BIZARRE SPECIES SUCH AS THE PINOCCHIO-NOSED FROG.

13
HURRICANES NORTH OF THE EQUATOR SPIN IN THE OPPOSITE DIRECTION FROM ONES SOUTH OF THE EQUATOR.

15
The scorching deserts of North Africa don't hurt the sand cat—the animal's paw pads are covered in fur to protect its feet from heat.

14
THE CHOCOLATE HILLS IN THE PHILIPPINES ARE SHAPED LIKE **GIANT HERSHEY'S KISSES.**

KISSES™

Coolest Coasters

Check out the tallest, fastest, loopiest rides on the planet.

hurl -o- meter ★★★★★

THE LOOPIEST: COLOSSUS

WHERE Thorpe Park in Surrey, England

RIDE Riders on Colossus blast through ten upside-down loops, including two dizzying corkscrew turns and a loop shaped like a snake's head. One last loop awaits just when you think the ride is over.

COOL SCIENCE As riders enter a loop, the acceleration produces a force that pushes them away from the center of the circle. The force presses riders into their seats—even while upside down.

hurl -o- meter ★★★★★

THE FASTEST: FORMULA ROSSA

WHERE Ferrari World in Abu Dhabi, United Arab Emirates

RIDE This coaster jumps from 0 to 149 miles an hour (0 to 240 kph) in less than five seconds. Because of its launch system, which is similar to those used in jet planes, riders must wear goggles to protect their eyes from sand and bugs.

COOL SCIENCE Formula Rossa's launch system is powered by hydraulics, which uses the pressure of fluids to build power. This power can be stored up and released with so much force that the ride hits incredible speeds.

hurl -o- meter ★★★★★

THE TALLEST: KINGDA KA

WHERE Six Flags Great Adventure in Jackson, New Jersey, U.S.A.

RIDE Ka launches riders up a record-breaking 456-foot (139-m)-tall tower—higher than a 40-story building.

COOL SCIENCE When the ride reaches the top of the tower, it has built up potential energy for later. Once it begins to roll back down, potential energy becomes kinetic energy—the energy of motion, which helps the ride move without additional motors.

EXTREME WEIRDNESS

From AROUND the WORLD

WHAT'S HIS HAIR LOOK LIKE UNDER THE HAT?

ROTTEN APPLE

ORANGE YOU GLAD YOU KNOW ABOUT THIS APPLE?

WHAT Apple-shaped race car

WHERE Kiev, Ukraine

DETAILS This is one sour apple. The scowling fruit-shaped cart was part of a race against about 50 other wacky-looking vehicles. More than 30,000 people came to watch the event. The apple wasn't the fastest thing on wheels, but it did provide some juicy competition.

BEARD VS. BEARD

WHAT European Beard and Mustache Championships

WHERE Leogang, Austria

DETAILS Talk about a manly competition. More than 150 well-groomed gentlemen participated in the contest, which included 17 categories—and a lot of hair spray. Contestants spruced up their facial art with curling irons, blow-dryers, and sculpting wax. Clippers were not welcome.

SHARK GETS FRIENDLY

WHAT Polar Bear Swim

WHERE Vancouver, Canada

DETAILS One fake shark brings new meaning to the phrase "biting cold." Celebrating the new year, participants in this annual event wade into the chilly 44°F (6.7°C) waters of the English Bay wearing kooky costumes—or just their bathing suits. The plunge also raises money for charity. No coldhearted people here.

HE'S NOT FOOLING ANYONE.

HAUNTED HOTELS

Ghosts could be fellow guests in these creepy quarters.

Trips to historical sites can really make the past come to life. But at some popular spots, "living history" takes on a new meaning. Some people believe that these landmarks are home to ghosts, spirits, and downright spooky activity. Decide for yourself if these places are just creepy ... or actually haunted.

GREEN GHOST

WHAT: Tulloch Castle Hotel
WHERE: Dingwall, Scotland, U.K.
THE STORY: The daughter of a former owner of this 12th-century castle is said to wander the halls whispering "Why?" over and over. The ghost is nicknamed the Green Lady since she wears a long, elegant green dress.

CREEPY CASTLE

WHAT: Hampton Court Palace
WHERE: London, England, U.K.
THE STORY: King Henry VIII's palace is said to be haunted by one of his executed wives, whose screams have reportedly been heard echoing throughout one of the galleries. Numerous visitors have fainted in one particular spot within the palace, and security cameras once recorded the fire doors bursting open and a mysterious unidentified figure closing them. Ooh, creepy!

GHOST HORSES

WHAT: Hotel Castello della Castelluccia
WHERE: Rome, Italy
THE STORY: Built between the 10th and 13th centuries by an Italian noble family, this hotel rests on the site of an ancient Roman villa. Three ghosts are thought to haunt the hotel, including the Roman emperor Nero, who restlessly wanders the gardens seeking somewhere to sleep. Guests have also reported hearing the hooves of ghostly horses who supposedly circle the castle at night.

SPOOKY SIGNALS

WHAT: St. Augustine Lighthouse and Museum
WHERE: St. Augustine, Florida, U.S.A.
THE STORY: When a cart carrying people and supplies tumbled into the ocean near this lighthouse, some victims disappeared forever—unless you believe the spooky tales. There have been reports of mysterious giggling in the lighthouse, ghostly faces peering out of windows, and a strange man in a blue lighthouse keeper's uniform.

Wild Vacations

Tree House Hotel!

The Chinese invented toilet paper in the 1300s—but back then it was only for emperors.

Table tennis is one of China's most popular sports. Some players start training for the Olympics at 10 years old.

HAINAN, CHINA

WHAT YOU'LL DO Sleep in tree houses overlooking the South China Sea; walk from tree to tree on a suspension bridge; admire some of the island's 600 butterfly species.

ACT LIKE A LOCAL Pick your snack. Hainan's tamarind trees produce tasty sweet-and-sour fruit to peel and eat.

SAY HELLO (in Mandarin)
ni hao (nee haow)

SOUTH AFRICA

WHAT YOU'LL DO Go on safari to see **zebras**, lions, and elephants; get face-to-face with a great white shark. (Don't worry—you'll be in a cage.)

ACT LIKE A LOCAL Cheer on a local soccer team—just make sure to call it football, not soccer.

SAY HELLO (in Zulu) *sawubona* (sow-BOH-nah)

ITALY

WHAT YOU'LL DO Float down **Venice**'s canals in a gondola; pretend you're watching ancient gladiators battle at the Colosseum in Rome.

ACT LIKE A LOCAL Grab some gelato—like ice cream, only creamier—while taking a late afternoon stroll.

SAY HELLO (in Italian) *ciao* (CHOW)

HAWAII

WHAT YOU'LL DO Snorkel with **sea turtles** and tropical fish; hike on an active volcano at Hawaii Volcanoes National Park.

ACT LIKE A LOCAL Catch some waves on a surfboard, just as Hawaiians have done for hundreds of years.

SAY HELLO (in Hawaiian) *aloha* (ah-LOH-hah)

STUMP YOUR PARENTS

GEOGRAPHY ROCKS QUIZ

Are your parents rock stars when it comes to geography? Quiz them on info based in this chapter to find out!

ANSWERS BELOW

1 There are _____ countries in Asia.
- **a.** 79
- **b.** 46
- **c.** 27
- **d.** 2,048

2 Where in Europe do macaques live?
- **a.** Bavarian Forest
- **b.** Swiss Alps
- **c.** Rock of Gibraltar
- **d.** South of France

3 Where is the world's largest indoor Ferris wheel?
- **a.** Tunisia
- **b.** Texas
- **c.** Thailand
- **d.** Turkmenistan

4 The ghost of which famous person is said to haunt Italy's Hotel Castello della Castelluccia?
- **a.** Nero
- **b.** Julius Caesar
- **c.** Michelangelo
- **d.** Gepetto

5 **True or false?** South America is the third largest continent.

Not **STUMPED** yet? Check out the *National Geographic Kids Quiz Whiz* collection for more crazy **GEOGRAPHY** questions!

ANSWERS:
1. b; 2. c; 3. d; 4. a; 5. False. It's the fourth largest. Asia, Africa, and North America are larger.

HOMEWORK HELP

Finding Your Way Around

Every map has a story to tell, but first you have to know how to read one. Maps represent information by using a language of symbols. Knowing how to read these symbols provides access to a wide range of information. Look at the scale and compass rose or arrow to understand distance and direction (see box below).

To find out what each symbol on a map means, you must use the key. It's your secret decoder—identifying information by each symbol on the map.

Latitude

Longitude

90°N (North Pole)

LATITUDE AND LONGITUDE

Latitude and longitude lines (above) help us determine locations on Earth. Every place on Earth has a special address called absolute location. Imaginary lines called lines of latitude run west to east, parallel to the Equator. These lines measure distance in degrees north or south from the Equator (0° latitude) to the North Pole (90°N) or to the South Pole (90°S). One degree of latitude is approximately 70 miles (113 km).

Lines of longitude run north to south, meeting at the Poles. These lines measure distance in degrees east or west from 0° longitude (prime meridian) to 180° longitude. The prime meridian runs through Greenwich, England.

SCALE AND DIRECTION

The scale on a map can be shown as a fraction, as words, or as a line or bar. It relates distance on the map to distance in the real world. Sometimes the scale identifies the type of map projection. Maps may include an arrow or compass rose to indicate north on the map.

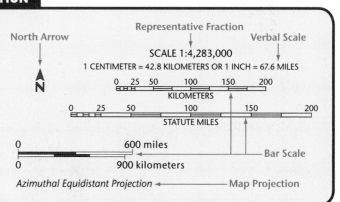

North Arrow

Representative Fraction

Verbal Scale

SCALE 1:4,283,000

1 CENTIMETER = 42.8 KILOMETERS OR 1 INCH = 67.6 MILES

0 25 50 100 150 200
KILOMETERS

0 25 50 100 150 200
STATUTE MILES

0 600 miles

0 900 kilometers

Bar Scale

Azimuthal Equidistant Projection ← Map Projection

GAME ANSWERS

What in the World?, page 162
Top row: **sweaters, rainbow, sprinkles.**
Middle row: **colored pencils, umbrella, toothbrushes.**
Bottom row: **licorice, towels, feathers.**
Bonus: **a pot of gold.**

Animal Jam, page 164
1. **panda**; 2. **monkey**; 3. **bunny**; 4. **koala**; 5. **avatar**; 6. **tiger**; 7. **fox.**

In Plane Sight, page 167

A-maze-ing Paris, pages 156–157

Up, Up, and Away, page 170

Color Café, page 158

Signs of the Times, page 160
Sign #1 and #3 are fake.

Windy Jumble, page 161
Eleanor, **A**; Sam, **J**; Nicole, **E**; Steve, **H**; Carlos, **F**; Zak, **B**; Ava, **C**; Jill, **I**; Isabel, **G**; Daniel, **D**.

What in the World?, page 171
Top row: **frog, bat, sloth.**
Middle row: **jaguar, viper, piranha.**
Bottom row: **grasshopper, tapir, toucan.**
Bonus: **a howler monkey business.**

Your World 2015 (8–17)

All articles by Sarah Wassner Flynn

Amazing Animals (18–81)

pp. 20–21 "What Is Taxonomy?" & "Vertebrates"/"Invertebrates" by Susan K. Donnelly; pp. 22–23 "Gorilla Goes Ape for Rabbit" & "Pup Babysits Piglets" by Kitson Jazynka, "Baboon Befriends Bush Baby" by Andrea Silen; p. 25 "Ape Brushes Teeth" by John Micklos, Jr.; "Cat Has Two Faces" by Elisabeth Deffner; pp. 26–27 "Do Animals Love Each Other?" by Aline Alexander Newman; pp. 30–31 "Ocean Superstars" by Ruth A. Musgrave; pp. 32–33 "Meet the Penguins" by Ruth A. Musgrave; p. 34 "5 Cool Things About Koalas" by Crispin Boyer; p. 35 "Snowy Owls" by Karen De Seve; pp. 36–37 "Freaky Frogs!" by Ruth A. Musgrave; p. 38 "Meerkat City" by Graeme Stemp-Morlock; p. 39 "Wild Dogs of Africa" by Crispin Boyer; pp. 40–41 "Super Snakes" by Chana Stiefel; p. 42 "5 Cool Things About Harp Seals" by Sharon Thompson; p. 43 "Monkey Trouble" by Robyn Keene-Young; pp. 44–45 "Dolphin" & "Elephant" by Scott Elder, "Koala" by Kitson Jazynka; p. 46 "Rock-a-Bye Monkey" by Ruth A. Musgrave; p. 47 "Secrets of the Spirit Bear" by Karen De Seve; pp. 48–49 "Big Cats" by Elizabeth Carney; p. 50 "Cheetahs: Built for Speed" by Fiona Sunquist; pp. 51–55 "Snow Leopard Secrets," "Tigers in the Snow" & "Family Pride" by Karen De Seve; pp. 56–57 "Bizarre Insects" by Sarah Wassner Flynn; pp. 58–59 "5 Silly Pet Tricks" by Kitson Jazynka; pp. 60–61 "Lifestyles of the Rich and Furry" by Bridget A. English; p. 62 "Real Animal Heroes!" by Aline Alexander Newman; pp. 64–65 "Paw Enforcement" by Scott Elder; pp. 66–71 "15 Cutest Animals of 2015" by Sarah Wassner Flynn; p. 72 "What Killed the Dinosaurs?" nationalgeographic.com; pp. 72–74 "Prehistoric Time Line" & "Dino Classification" by Susan K. Donnelly; pp. 75–77 "Newly Discovered Dinos" & "Dynamite Dino Awards" by Sarah Wassner Flynn; pp. 78–79 "Dino Myths Busted!" by Suzanne McIntire

Going Green (82–99)

pp. 86–87 "Habitat Destruction" by Crispin Boyer; pp. 88–89 "Global Warming" & "Greenland's Giant Canyon" by Sarah Wassner Flynn; pp. 90–91 "Pollution," "Declining Biodiversity," & "Habitats Threatened" by David George Gordon; p. 93 "Electric Tricycle" by Crispin Boyer, "Musical Shower" by Cathy Lu; pp. 94–95 "8 Fun Ways to Get Outside" by Sarah Wassner Flynn; pp. 96–97 "World Energy & Minerals" by Mark Bockenhauer

Awesome Adventure (100–117)

pp. 102–105 "Dare to Explore" by C.M. Tomlin; p. 106 "Montana Adventure" by Catherine D. Hughes; p. 107 "Mystery in the Skies" by Sarah Wassner Flynn; pp. 108–109 "Secrets of the Blue Holes" by Kristin Baird Rattini; p. 112 "Orangutan to the Rescue" by Sarah Wassner Flynn; p. 113 "How to Survive a Killer Bee Attack!" & "How to Survive a Bee Sting!" by Rachel Buchholz; pp. 114–115 "Extreme Action Sports" by Sarah Wassner Flynn

Super Science (118–153)

pp. 120–121 "...Big Bang" by David A. Aguilar; p. 120 "Powerful Particle" by Sarah Wassner Flynn; p. 124 "Dwarf Planets" by Sarah Wassner Flynn; p. 125 "Super Sun!" by Sarah Wassner Flynn; p. 127–129 "Destination Space" & "5 Freaky Places in Space" by Stephanie Warren; p. 131 "The Three Domains of Life" by Susan K. Donnelly; pp. 132–134 "Your Amazing Eyes," "Your Amazing Heart," & "Your Amazing Brain" by Douglas E. Richards; pp. 136–137 "That's Gross!" by Crispin Boyer; p. 138 "All About You: Birth Order" by Amanda Pressner; p. 141 "Rock Stars" by Steve Tomecek; pp. 142–143 "15 Cool Things About Rocks and Minerals" by Sean McCollum; pp. 144–145 "Kaboom!" by Sarah Webb; pp. 146–147 "Cool Inventions" by Crispin Boyer; p. 148 "Get Ready for Robots" by Douglas E. Richards; p. 149 "GPS" by Sarah Wassner Flynn; pp. 150–151 "Animal Killers Busted!" by Kristin Baird Rattini

Culture Connection (174–199)

p. 178 "What's Your Chinese Horoscope?" by Geoff Williams; p. 180 "Halloween Pet Parade" by Andrea Silen; pp. 184–185 "Handimals" by B.F. Summers and Kelley Miller; pp. 186–187 "Food That Fools You" by Andrea Silen; pp. 188–189 "Chew on This" by Kay Boatner; pp. 192–193 "Money Around the World!" by Kristin Baird Rattini; pp. 194–195 "Mythology" by Susan K. Donnelly; pp. 196–197 "World Religions" by Mark Bockenhauer

Wonders of Nature (200–221)

p. 202 "Weather and Climate" by Mark Bockenhauer; p. 203 "Weather Comparisons" by Kathy Furgang; p. 206 "Hurricane!" by Renee Skelton; p. 207 "Wildfire!" & "Flood!" by Sarah Wassner Flynn; p. 208 "How to Survive Lightning" by Rachel Buchholz; p. 209 "Tsunami Heroes" by Scott Elder; pp. 210–211 "The Water Cycle" by Kathy Furgang; p. 214 "Coral Reefs" by Crispin Boyer; p. 216 "How Does Your Garden Grow?" by Susan K. Donnelly; p. 217 "Food for Your Garden!" by Jill Yaworski; pp. 218–219 "Biomes" by Susan K. Donnelly

History Happens (222–253)

pp. 224–225 "Packing for the Afterlife" & pp. 230–231 "Knight Life" by Crispin Boyer; p. 232 "Mystery of the Buried Treasure" by Molly Lyons; p. 233 "The Amazing Houdini" by Michael N. Smith and Debora L. Smith; pp. 234–235 "Secrets of the Titanic" by Kristin Baird Rattini; pp. 236–237 "War!" by Susan K. Donnelly/Sarah Wassner Flynn; p. 237 "Remembering Anne Frank" by Sarah Wassner Flynn; pp. 238–241 by Susan K. Donnelly; pp. 242–247 by Susan K. Donnelly/Sarah Wassner Flynn; pp. 248–249 "Aboriginal Canada" by Susan K. Donnelly/Sarah Wassner Flynn; pp. 250–251 "Women Fighting for Equality" by Sarah Wassner Flynn

Geography Rocks (254–337)

pp. 256–261 by Mark Bockenhauer; pp. 262–289 by Sarah Wassner Flynn, Mark Bockenhauer, and Susan K. Donnelly; pp. 290–315 "You Are There!" by Sarah Wassner Flynn; pp. 320–326 "Canada's Provinces and Territories" by Sarah Wassner Flynn; p. 327 "The Great Outdoors" by Sarah Wassner Flynn; pp. 328–329 "15 Cool Things About the World" by Zachary Petit; p. 330 "Coolest Coasters" by Sean McCollum; p. 331 "Extreme Weirdness" by Kay Boatner and Molly Marcot; pp. 332–333 "Haunted Vacations" by Zachary Petit and Sarah Wassner Flynn

All "Homework Help" by Vicki Ariyasu

ABBREVIATIONS:

CO: Corbis
GI: Getty Images
IS: iStockphoto
IS.com: iStockphoto.com
MP: Minden Pictures
NGC: National Geographic Creative
NGS: National Geographic Stock
NGS.com: National Geographic Stock.com
NPL: Nature Picture Library
PR: Photo Researchers, Inc.
SPS: SuperStock
SS: Shutterstock

All Maps
By NGS unless otherwise noted.

All Illustrations & Charts
By Stuart Armstrong unless otherwise noted.

Zipper Artwork
By Nathan Jurevicius

Front Cover/Spine
Tiger, Tom & Pat Leeson/Kimball Stock;
Colosseum, Samot/SS; butterfly, James Laurie/SS;
kayaker, technotr/IS; meerkats, tratong/SS; snake,
fivespots/SS

Back Cover
Snake, fivespots/SS; globe, SS; hang glider, Alex-
andra Lande/SS; frog, Dirk Ercken/SS; Hong Kong,
Sean Pavone/SS; gecko, irin-k/SS; dirt bikes, Nildo
Scoop/SS; zebras, Curioso/SS

Inside Front Cover
Giraffe, Roy Toft/NGS; (*T. rex*) CO

Front Matter (2–7)
2–3 (background), Kim Taylor/NPL; 5 (top), SS;
5 (top, center left), Dave Stamboulis/Alamy;
5 (bottom, center left), Paul Nicklen/NGC; 5 (bottom, left), Michael Hubbard/Captsure; 6 (top,
left), PatitucciPhoto; 6 (top, center left), Courtesy
PAL-V/Spark design and innovation; 6 (top, center
left), Jeremy Woodhouse/Photodisc/GI; 6 (bottom, center left), Paul Souders/DanitaDelimont.
com; 6 (bottom, left), © Dennis Cox/ChinaStock;
7 (top, left), age fotostock/SPS; 7 (left, center),
Travel Pix Collection/JAI/CO; 7 (bottom, left), age
fotostock/SPS

Your World 2015 (8–17)
8–9, Dave Stamboulis/Alamy; 10 (left, center),
Mark Gurney for Smithsonian via GI; 10 (right,
center), AP Photo/Wildlife Conservation Society,
Ashish John; 10 (top, left), Conservation Interna-
tional/photo by Mark Erdmann; 10 (bottom,
right), Jodi J. L. Rowley/Australian Museum;
11 (top), akg-images/Alamy; 11 (center), Bettmann/
CO; 11 (right, center), The Granger Collection,
NYC—All rights reserved; 11 (bottom, right),
National Maritime Museum, London/The Image
Works; 12 (top, right), Courtesy ElephantVoices;
12 (left, center), Courtesy ElephantVoices;
12 (bottom, left), Courtesy ElephantVoices;
12 (right, center), Courtesy ElephantVoices;
13 (top), NASA/JPL-Caltech; 13 (top, right), Walter
Myers/Science Source; 13 (bottom, left), Rex
Features via AP Images; 14 (top), Ronald Grant/
LUCASFILM/Mary Evans; 14 (left, center), Photos
12/Alamy; 14 (bottom, center right), DREAMWORKS
SKG © 2008 DreamWorks Animation, L.L.C. All
Rights Reserved Ronald Grant Archive/Mary
Evans; 14 (bottom, left), Columbia Pictures/
Courtesy Everett Collection, Inc.; 15 (top, right),
University of Leicester/Rex Features World
(Rex Features via AP Images); 15 (left, center),
GL Archive/Alamy; 15 (right, center), AP Photo/
University of Leicester, file; 15 (bottom, right),
Jane Burton/NPL; 16 (top, left), Marc Dietrich/
SS; 16 (top, center left), mt1278/SS; 16 (bottom,
center left), Constantine Pankin/SS; 16 (bottom,
left), Andrei Shumskiy/SS; 16 (top, right), Mathee
Suwannarak/SS; 16 (top, center right), zhu
difeng/SS; 16 (bottom, center right), Andia/Alamy;
16 (bottom, right), Walker Art Library/Alamy; 17
(bottom, right), Toru Hanai/Reuters/CO; 17 (top),
Courtesy Sandstorm Events; 17 (bottom, left),
Tony Quinn/Icon SMI/CO

Amazing Animals (18–81)
18–19, Paul Nicklen/NGC; 20 (left, center), Eric
Isselée/SS; 20 (top, right), Planetpix/Alamy;
20 (bottom, right), Joel Sartore/NGC; 21 (top,
left), FloridaStock/SS; 21 (right, center), Karen
Massier/IS.com; 21 (top, right), cbpix/SS; 21 (left,
center), mashe/SS; 21 (bottom), Eric Isselée/SS;
22 (background), AP Images; 22 (inset), Toni Dil-
lon; 23 (top, left), AP Images; 23 (top, center left),
AP Images; 23 (bottom, right), Thomas Mukoya/
Reuters; 23 (bottom, center), Thomas Mukoya/
Reuters; 24 (background), Paul Souders/CO;
25 (top), Juergen Freund/Caters News Agency;
25 (bottom), Courtesy VenusMommy; 26 (top),
Andy Rouse/NPL; 26 (bottom), Kathy Jo Ferguson;
27 (top, left), Anup Shah/NPL; 27 (right, center),
Corbis Premium RF/Alamy; 27 (bottom, left), Cour-
tesy of Philadelphia Zoo; 28 (1), guentermanaus/
SS; 28 (2), Christian Mussat/SS; 28 (3), Goncha-
ruk/SS; 28 (4), Nickolay Stanev/SS; 28 (5), Flip
Nicklen/MP; 28 (6), Brandon Bordages/SS; 28 (7),
urosr/SS; 29 (9), Skip O'Donnell/IS; 29 (10), Willyam
Bradbury/SS; 29 (11), Jenny Solomon/SS; 29 (12),
Hiroshi Sato/SS; 29 (13), Tubuceo/SS; 30 (bottom),
Norbert Wu/MP; 30 (bottom), Claudio Contreras/
NPL/MP; 31 (top), Doug Perrine/NPL; 31 (center),
SA Team/Foto Natura/MP; 31 (bottom, left),
Claudio Contreras/NPL; 31 (bottom, right), Doug
Perrine/NPL; 32 (top, left), Solvin Zankl/NPL/MP;
32 (left, center), Tui De Roy/MP; 32 (right), Peter
Barritt/SPS; 32 (bottom), Martha Holmes/NPL/
MP; 33 (top), Tui De Roy/MP; 33 (top, center left),
Mitsuaki Iwago/MP; 33 (center), Tui De Roy/
MP; 33 (bottom, center left), Suzi Eszterhas/MP;
33 (bottom, left), imagebroker/Alamy; 33 (bottom,
right), Tony Heald/NPL; 34 (top), Jouan & Rius/
NPL; 34 (bottom), J-L. Klein & M-L. Hubert/Pho-
toLibrary/GI; 35 (top, right), Andy Rouse/NPL; 35
(right, center), Michio Hoshino/MP; 35 (bottom,
left), Bruce Corbett/Alamy; 36 (top), Stephen
Dalton/NPL; 36 (bottom, right), Andrew Murray/
NPL; 36 (bottom, left), Pete Oxford/NPL; 37 (top,
right), Stephen Dalton/NPL; 37 (right, center),
Thomas Marent/MP; 37 (right, center), Mark
Moffet/MP; 37 (bottom, center left), National
News/Zuma Press; 37 (bottom, right), Michael &
Patricia Fogden/MP; 38 (top, left), Paul Souders/
GI; 38 (top, left), EcoPrint/SS; 38 (bottom, left),
age fotostock/SPS; 38 (bottom, right), Beverly
Joubert/NGS; 39 (top), Andy Rouse/Stone/GI; 39
(bottom), Albert Froneman; 40 (top, left), Michael
D. Kern; 40 (bottom, center right), Brian Kenney;
40 (bottom, left), Heidi & Hans-Juergen Koch/MP;
41 (top, right), Andrew Bannister/Gallo Images/
CO; 41 (top, center left), Michael Kern and the
Gardens of Eden; 41 (bottom, left), Michael Kern
and the Gardens of Eden; 41 (bottom, right),
Michael Kern and the Gardens of Eden; 42 (top),
Lisa & Mike Husar/Team Husar; 42 (bottom), Keren
Su/GI; 43 (top, right), Adrian Bailey; 43 (left,
center), Adrian Bailey; 43 (bottom, center right),
Adrian Bailey; 43 (bottom, center left), Adrian Bailey;
44 (top), Dr. Amber Gillett; 44 (bottom), Nichola
Chapman/Born Free Foundation; 45 (top, right),
Andy Rouse/NPL; 45 (right, center), Norman
Carr Safaris; 45 (bottom, right), Jeff Foster;
46 (top, background), Djuna Ivereigh; 46 (center),
Djuna Ivereigh; 46 (bottom), Djuna Ivereigh;
47 (top), Mark Carwardine/ARDEA; 47 (inset),
Steven J. Kazlowski/Alamy; 47 (bottom, left),
Steven J. Kazlowski/Alamy; 48, Staffan Widstrand/
NPL; 49 (top, left), worldswildwonders/SS;
49 (top, center left), Kesu/SS; 49 (top, center
right), WitR/SS; 49 (top, right), Eric Isselée/SS;
49 (left, center), DLILLC/CO; 49 (right, center),
Eric Isselée/SS; 49 (bottom, left), Eric Isselée/SS;
49 (bottom, right), Eric Isselée/SS; 50 (top), Andy
Rouse/NHPA/Photoshot; 50 (center), Stephen
Belcher/MP; 50 (bottom, left), Martin Harvey/
PhotoLibrary/GI; 50 (bottom, right), Suzi Eszter-
has/MP; 51 (top), Steve Winter/NGS; 51 (center),
Purple Pilchards/Alamy; 51 (bottom), NHPA/SPS;
52 (top), Image Source/CO; 52 (bottom), Juniors/
SPS; 53 (top, right), Tom & Pat Leeson/ARDEA;
53 (bottom, right), Lisa & Mike Husar/Team Husar;
54 (top), Chris Harvey/ARDEA; 54 (bottom), NHPA/
SPS; 55 (top), Anup Shah/NPL; 55 (center), Mit-
suaki Iwago/MP; 56 (top, center left), Beverly Joubert/
NGC; 56 (top, center right), Ingo Arndt/NPL; 56
(top, center right), Dr. James L. Castner/Visuals
Unlimited, Inc.; 56 (bottom, center), Alex Hyde/
NPL; 56 (bottom, left), NHPA/SPS; 56 (bottom,
right), Chris Mattison/FLPA/MP; 56 (top, right), Cosmin
Manci/SS; 57 (top, left), Photolibrary.com; 57 (top,
right), PREMAPHOTOS/NPL; 57 (right, center),
Kazuo Unno/Nature Production/MP; 57 (left,
center), Christopher Smith/Alamy; 58 (top), Kelley
Miller/NGS Staff; 58 (bottom), Kelley Miller/NGS
Staff; 59 (top, left), Kesu/SS; 59 (top, center
right), Stacey M. Warnke; 59 (top,
right), Dan Larson; 59 (bottom, right), Mark
Steiger; 60 (top), Kate Pinney; 60 (bottom), La
Petite Maison; 60—61, PhotoDisc/Punchstock;
61 (top), artpaw.com; 61 (center), David Blattel;
61 (bottom, left), Robert Ochoa; 61 (bottom, right),
Robert Ochoa; 62 (top), Courtesy of Carly Riley;
62 (center), Courtesy of Michelle and Rod Ramsey;
62 (bottom), Biosphoto/SPS; 63 (top, left), Rebecca
Richardson/GI; 63 (top, right), Darwin Wiggett-
oopoomoo; 63 (bottom, right), Bartussek/ARCO/
NPL; 63 (bottom, left), Philip J. Brittan/GI;
64 (top), Richard T. Nowitz; 64 (inset), Richard T.
Nowitz; 64 (top, left), Richard T. Nowitz; 65 (top),
Richard T. Nowitz; 65 (center), Richard T. Nowitz;
66 (top), Paul Nicklen/NGC; 66 (bottom), China
Daily/Reuters/CO; 67 (top), Paul Maguire/Dream-
stime.com; 67 (bottom, left), Yva Momatiuk & John
Eastcott/MP; 67 (bottom, right), Adam Jones/
Visuals Unlimited/CO; 68 (top, left), Stephanie
Swartz; 68 (bottom, left), Michio Hoshino/MP;
68 (right), Courtney Dasher; 69 (top), iDigital
Art/SS; 69 (bottom), Cusp/SPS; 70 (top, left), Tony
Heald/NPL; 70 (bottom, left), Eric Baccega/NPL;
70 (top, right), Cyril Ruoso/MP; 70 (bottom, right),
Michael Kern and the Gardens of Eden/All Rights
Reserved; 71, Konrad Wothe/MP; 72 (top), Chris
Butler/Science Photo Library/PR; 72 (center),
Publiphoto/PR; 72 (bottom), Pixeldust Studios/
NGC; 73 (B), Laurie O'Keefe/PR; 73 (C), Chris But-
ler/PR; 73 (D), Publiphoto/PR; 73 (A), Publiphoto/
PR; 73 (E), image Courtesy of Project Exploration;
74 (top), Paul B. Moore/SS; 74 (bottom), Andrea
Meyer/SS; 75 (1), AP Photo/Natural History
Museum of Utah, Andrey Atuchin; 75 (3), Nobu-
michi Tamura; 75 (2), Masato Hattori; 75 (4), Julius
Csotonyi; 76 (top), Franco Tempesta; 76 (center),
Franco Tempesta; 76 (bottom), Photo by Roderick
Mickens, © American Museum of Natural
History; 77 (bottom, left), Julius Csotonyi; 77 (top,
left), Franco Tempesta; 77 (top, right), Franco
Tempesta; 77 (bottom, right), Franco Tempesta; 78, Dean
Macadam; 79 (top), Dean Macadam; 79 (bottom,
right), Dean Macadam; 80 (bottom, left), Chris
Harvey/ARDEA; 80 (top, right), Stephen Dalton/
NPL; 80 (top, center left), Tom & Pat Leeson/
ARDEA; 80 (bottom, left), Brian Kenney;
81 (top, right), CampCrazy Photography/SS

Going Green (82–99)
82–83, Michael Hubbard/Captsure; 84 (6), Peter
Forsberg/Alamy; 84 (1), topseller/SS; 84 (2),
Sandra Caldwell/SS; 84 (3), Dinga/SS; 84 (4), Plati

Photography/SS; 84 (5), Zadiraka Evgenii/SS; 84 (7), italianestro/SS; 85 (9), jannoon028/SS; 85 (8), Eric Isselée/SS; 85 (10), SS; 85 (11), Liv friis-larsen/SS; 85 (12), Veniamin Kraskov/SS; 85 (13), Ivaschenko Roman/SS; 85 (14), Nuno Andre/SS; 85 (15), Picsfive/SS; 86 (top, right), David J. Southall; 86 (top, center left), Rod Williams/MP; 86 (right, center), Ernie Janes/NHPA/Photoshot; 87 (top), Pete Oxford/MP; 87 (bottom), Pete Oxford/MP; 88 (bottom), Erlend Kvalsvik/IS.com; 88 (top), Paul Souders/CO; 89 (bottom, left), AP Photo/Extreme Ice Survey, James Balog; 89 (center), James Balog/NGC; 90 (left), Stéphane Bidouze/SS; 90 (background), Mujka Design Inc./IS.com; 91 (top), 33karen33/IS.com; 91, Nick Garbutt/NPL; 92 (bottom, left), GrigoryL/SS; 92 (bottom, right), Alexey Stiop/Alamy; 93 (top, right), Emcycle/Rex/Rex USA; 93 (top, left), Emcycle/Rex/Rex USA; 93 (bottom, right), Courtesy of Tango Group Limited; 94 (bottom, left), Ambient Images Inc./SPS; 94 (top), SPS; 94 (bottom, right), Rebecca Hale, NGS; 95 (top, right), Larry Landolfi/Science Source; 95 (left, center), Dex Image/Alamy; 95 (bottom, center right), Courtesy Uncharted Play; 95 (bottom, left), FLPA/Gary K Smith/MP; 95 (top left, background), plainpicture; 95 (bottom, right), Alan Tansey; 95 (top left, left inset), Begsteiger/McPhoto/Capital Pictures; 95 (top left, center left inset), Vivian Fung/SS; 95 (top left, center right inset), Don Klumpp/Photographer's Choice/GI; 95 (top left, right inset), Sarah Leen; 95 (top left, right inset), Gary S Chapman/Photographer's Choice/GI; 96 (bottom, right), Jason Lee/Reuters/CO; 97 (left, center), Walter Rawlings/CO; 97 (center), Richard Nowitz/NGC; 97 (top), Marc Moritsch/NGC; 97, WENN/Newscom; 98 (top), Pete Oxford/MP; 98 (right, center), IS; 98 (bottom, left), Rod Williams/MP; 99, Albo003/SS

Awesome Adventure (100–117)

100–101, PatitucciPhoto; 102 (top, right), Mark Thiessen, NGS; 102 (top, center), koya979/SS; 102 (background), Monty Graham; 102 (bottom, left), Mint Images - Paul Edmondson/GI; 103 (top, center), koya979/SS; 103 (background), photo Courtesy of Brady Barr; 103 (top, right), Simon Boyce; 104 (top, right), imago sportfotodienst/Newscom; 104 (background), Ralf Dujmovits; 104 (top, center), koya979/SS; 105 (top, right), Edmund J. Coppa/Splash News/Newscom; 105 (background), Jon Ross Photography; 105 (bottom, left), Robert Mayer/MCT/Newscom; 105 (top, center), koya979/SS; 105 (top, center), koya979/SS; 106 (top), Daniel R. Westergren; 106 (top, center right), Daniel R. Westergren; 106 (bottom, center right), Daniel R. Westergren; 106 (bottom), Daniel R. Westergren; 107 (top), Famous Aircraft and Their Pilots: Lockheed Ten Electra—Amelia Earhart by Hardy, Wilf (Wilfred) (20th century)/Private Collection; Look and Learn/The Bridgeman Art Library; 107 (bottom), 2009 AP Images; 108–109, Wes C. Skiles/NGC; 108 (bottom, right), Wes C. Skiles/NGC; 108 (bottom, left), Wes C. Skiles/NGC; 109 (bottom, right), Andrew Hounslea/GI; 110 (1), Potapov Alexander/SS; 110 (2), Ocean/CO; 110 (4), Longjourneys/SS; 110 (5), nednapa/SS; 110 (6), Mariana Bazo/Reuters/CO; 110 (7), Stephen Rees/SS; 110 (3), Victor Maff/IS; 111 (9), Eric Nguyen/CO; 111 (10), Nixx Photography/SS; 111 (11), Maria Dryfhout/SS; 111 (12), Biosphoto/SPS; 111 (13), LJM Photo/Design Pics/CO; 111 (8), Petoo/SS; 112 (top, left), Fairfax Media New Zealand/Lawrence Smith; 112 (right), Shin Yoshino/MP; 113 (top), Tony Campbell/SS; 113 (bottom), PMACD|PHOTOGRAPHY/SS; 114 (top), Berbar Halim/SIPA/Newscom; 114 (bottom, left), James Cheadle; 114 (bottom, right), Thomas Lohnes/AFP/GI/Newscom; 115 (top, right), imago sportfotodienst/Newscom; 115 (top, left), Jason Kenworthy/A-Frame Media; 115 (bottom), Barry Bland/Alamy; 116 (top), 2009 AP Images; 116 (bottom),

PMACD|PHOTOGRAPHY/SS; 116, Wes C. Skiles/NGC; 116 (top), Berbar Halim/SIPA/Newscom; 117, Grady Reese/IS.com

Super Science (118–153)

118–119 (foreground), Courtesy PAL-V/Spark design and innovation; 118–119 (background), Jeremy Woodhouse/Photodisc/GI; 120–121 (background), Take 27 Ltd/PR; 121 (A), David Aguilar; 121 (B), David Aguilar; 121 (C), David Aguilar; 121 (D), David Aguilar; 121 (E), David Aguilar; 122–123, David Aguilar; 124, David Aguilar; 125 (top), NASA/Science Faction/SPS; 125 (bottom), NASA; 126, Tony & Daphne Hallas/PR; 126 (background), Gabe Palmer/CO; 126 (top, right), Walter Myers/Stocktrek Images/CO; 126 (bottom, right), NASA; 127 (bottom), Mondolithic Studio; 127 (background), Mondolithic Studio; 128 (2), NASA/Galileo; 128 (1), NASA/JPL-Caltech/T. Pyle; 128–129 (5), NASA/JPL-Caltech/STScI/CXC/SAO; 129 (3), David Aguilar; 129 (4), NASA/Dana Berry; 130, David Aguilar; 131 (E), Marie C. Fields/SS; 131 (D), Fedor A. Sidorov/SS; 131 (F), sgame/SS; 131 (A), Sebastian Kaulitzki/SS; 131 (B), Steve Gschmeissner/PR; 131 (C), Volker Steger/Christian Bardele/PR; 131 (G), Benjamin Jessop/IS.com; 132 (top), Dennis Cooper/CO; 132 (bottom), Linda Nye; 133, Mondolithic Studio; 134, Robert J. Demarest; 134 (top, center), Guido Daniele/Sipa; 134 (top, right), Christian Schmalhofer/Dreamstime.com; 134 (bottom, left), Guido Daniele/Sipa; 134 (bottom, right), R. Gino Santa Maria/Dreamstime.com; 135 (top, center), Guido Daniele/Sipa; 135 (top, right), Donald M. Jones/MP; 135 (bottom, left), Mark Thiessen, NGS; 135 (bottom, right), Guido Daniele/Sipa; 135 (bottom), Stockjiggo/Dreamstime.com; 135 (center), BC_DS Photo Illustration/Alamy; 136 (1), Science Photo Library/Alamy; 136 (top), Irochka/Dreamstime.com; 136–137 (2), Scimat Scimat/GI; 137 (3), Sebastian Kaulitzki/SS; 137 (4), PR/GI; 137 (right, center), Liubov Grigoryeva/Dreamstime.com; 137 (bottom, center right), Shirley Hu/Dreamstime.com; 137 (bottom, right), Sebastian Kaulitzki/Dreamstime.com; 138, IT Stock Free/Jupiter Images; 139 (top), sdominick/IS; 139 (bottom), Javier Brosch/SS; 141 (top), Ralph Lee Hopkins/NGS; 141 (top, center left), Visuals Unlimited/GI; 141 (top, center right), Visuals Unlimited/GI; 141 (bottom, center left), Doug Martin/PR; 141 (bottom, center right), DEA/C. Dani/GI; 141 (bottom, center left), Michael Baranski/SS; 142 (1), Chip Clark/NMNH/Smithsonian Institution; 142 (2), Joel Arem/PR/Science Source; 142 (3), Joel Arem/PR/Science Source; 142 (4), age fotostock/SPS; 142 (5), Food and Drink/SPS; 142 (6), Chip Clark/NMNH/Smithsonian Institution; 142 (7), Colin Monteath/Hedgehog House/MP; 143 (8), Chip Clark/NMNH/Smithsonian Institution; 143 (9), Bob Krist/CO; 143 (10), Mark A. Schneider/PR/Science Source; 143 (11), CO/SPS; 143 (12), Kenneth Garrett/NGC; 143 (13), Sinclair Stammers/PR/Science Source; 143 (14), NASA; 144 (1), Dykon Explosive Demolition Corp.; 144 (2), Dykon Explosive Demolition Corp.; 144 (3), Dykon Explosive Demolition Corp.; 145 (1), Zou Haibin/Xinhua Press/CO; 145 (2), Zou Haibin/Xinhua Press/CO; 145 (3), Zou Haibin/Xinhua Press/CO; 146 (top), Courtesy USU Ascending Aggies Team Members; 146 (center), Courtesy USU Ascending Aggies Team Members; 146 (bottom), TBWA/RAAD; 147 (top, center), Anna Utekhina/Dreamstime.com; 147 (top, right), Adam Bettcher; 147 (bottom), James Lee Needham; 148 (top), Aldebaran Robotics; 148 (bottom), Aldebaran Robotics; 149 (top), SS; 149 (bottom, left), Dieter Spannknebel/Stockbyte/GI; 149 (top, center right), plainpicture/Kniel Synnatzschke; 149 (top, center right), SS; 149 (right, center), SS; 149 (bottom, center right), SS; 150 (bottom), Mark Raycroft/MP; 150 (top), Stockbyte/GI; 150 (right, center), David McGlynn/Taxi/GI; 151 (top, left), Siede Preis/GI; 151 (top, right), Theo Allofs/MP; 151 (center), Stockbyte/GI; 151 (bottom, right), Otmar Thormann/Nordic

Photos/GI; 151 (left, center), Alaska Stock/Alamy; 151 (bottom, left), PureStock/GI; 152 (bottom, center right), Shirley Hu/Dreamstime.com; 152 (top, right), Chip Clark/NMNH/Smithsonian Institution; 152 (bottom), Mondolithic Studio; 152 (right, center), Colin Monteath/Hedgehog House/MP; 153 (bottom), Chris Gorgio/IS.com; 153, AVAVA/SS

Fun and Games (154–173)

154–155, Paul Souders/DanitaDelimont.com; 156–157, CTON; 158, James Yamasaki; 159, Dan Sipple; 160 (1), Andrew Woodley/Alamy; 160 (2), John Warden/Alaska Stock Images/Pacific Stock; 160 (3), SS; 160 (4), SS; 160 (5), CO; 160 (6), Dreamstime.com; 160, CO; 161, James Yamasaki; 162 (A), Dreamstime.com; 162 (B), Dreamstime.com; 162 (C), Dreamstime.com; 162 (D), Dreamstime.com; 162 (E), Dreamstime.com; 162 (F), Dreamstime.com; 162 (G), Dreamstime.com; 162 (H), Dreamstime.com; 162 (I), Dreamstime.com; 163 (top, right), Jason Gallier/Alamy; 163 (left, center), fStop/Alamy; 163 (right, center), Jeffrey Hamilton/GI; 163 (bottom, right), Tim Davis/CO; 164, Smart Bomb Interactive; 165 (top, left), Gary Fields; 165 (top, right), Gary Fields; 165 (right, center), Gary Fields; 165 (bottom, left), Gary Fields; 165 (bottom, right), Gary Fields; 166, Dan Sipple; 167, James Yamasaki; 168–169, Strika Entertainment; 170, CTON; 171 (A), Dreamstime.com; 171 (B), Dreamstime.com; 171 (C), Dreamstime.com; 171 (D), Dreamstime.com; 171 (E), Dreamstime.com; 171 (F), Dreamstime.com; 171 (G), Dreamstime.com; 171 (H), Dreamstime.com; 171 (I), Dreamstime.com; 172 (top), Lynn M. Stone/NPL; 172 (left, center), Elvele Images Ltd/Alamy; 172 (center), Konrad Wothe/NPL; 172 (right, center), Bradley Mason/GI; 172 (bottom, right), S & D & K Maslowski/MP; 173, Dan Sipple

Culture Connection (174–199)

174–175, © Dennis Cox/ChinaStock; 176 (5), Tubol Evgeniya/SS; 176–177 (header), Madlen/SS; 176 (1), fotohunter/SS; 176 (6), pattarastock/SS; 176 (9), Charles B. Ming Onn/SS; 177 (11), Dinodia/age fotostock; 177 (13), Plutonius 3d/SS; 177 (16), Dinodia/age fotostock; 177 (18), Zee/Alamy; 177 (19), wacpan/SS; 177 (15), Shaffer/Smith/SPS; 178, Scott Matthews; 180 (top, left), Timothy A. Clary/AFP/GI; 180 (top, right), Pixtal/SPS; 180 (bottom, left), Vickie Burt/Photographers Direct; 181 (top, right), Rebecca Hale, NGS; 181 (left, center), Rebecca Hale, NGS; 181 (bottom, left), Rebecca Hale, NGS; 181 (bottom, right), Rebecca Hale, NGS; 182 (1), anarhist/SS; 182 (2), Hway Kiong Lim/SS; 182 (3), SS; 182 (5), arkady/SS; 182 (6), Alex Staroseltsev/SS; 182 (7), Damien Palus/IS; 183 (9), Keith Hanson/IS; 183 (11), Andersphoto/SS; 183 (13), Maxphotographer/SS; 183 (14), Brooks Craft/CO; 183 (15), SS; 184 (top, left), Mark Thiessen, NGS; 184 (center), Mark Thiessen, NGS; 185 (top, left), Mark Thiessen, NGS; 185 (top, center left), Mark Thiessen, NGS; 186–187, Photography/Renee Comet, Food Styling/Lisa Cherkasky; 188 (center), Rebecca Hale, NGS; 189, Rebecca Hale, NGS; 190, Ocean/CO; 191 (top), Courtesy Disney Publishing Worldwide; 192 (A), INTERFOTO/Alamy; 192 (B), Paul Harrison/Alamy; 192 (C), Radomir Tarasov/Dreamstime.com; 192 (D), Glyn Thomas/Alamy; 192 (E), Erwan Galesne/Numista; 192 (F), Michael Mitin/Dreamstime.com; 192 (G), Used with the permission of the Bank of Canada; 192 (H), Daniel Krylov/Dreamstime.com; 192, JTB Photo Communications, Inc./Alamy; 193 (A), The Perth Mint; 193 (B), AFP/GI; 193 (C), Courtesy Tazmic Enterprises; 193 (D), Ron Nickel/Design Pics/CO; 193 (E), Won Park; 193 (F), Susan Law Cain/Dreamstime.com; 193 (G), Sam Sloan/Alamy; 193 (H), Mohamed Osama/Dreamstime.com; 193 (I), Kelley Miller, NGS Staff; 194 (top, left), John Hazard; 194 (top, right), Jose Ignacio Soto/SS; 194 (bottom), Photosani/SS; 195 (left), Corey Ford/Dreamstime.com; 195 (right), IS.com; 196 (top), Randy Olson; 196 (bottom, left), Martin Gray/NGC; 196 (bottom, right), Sam Panthaky/AFP/GI; 197 (bottom, left), Reza/NGC; 197 (bottom, right), Richard Nowitz/NGC; 197 (top), Winfield Parks/NGC; 198 (top, right), Sam Panthaky/AFP/GI; 198 (bottom, center), John Hazard; 198 (bottom, right), Scott Matthews; 199 (top), Neftali/SS; 199 (center), Ajay Bhaskar/IS.com; 199 (bottom), Sunil Menon/IS.com

Wonders of Nature (200–221)

200–201, age fotostock/SPS/SS; 202, Steve Mann/SS; 203 (top, left), AISPIX/SS; 203 (top, right), tiorna/SS; 203 (left, center), Warren Faidley/Oxford Scientific/PhotoLibrary/GI; 203 (right, center), Sergei Bachlakov/SS; 203 (bottom, right), Jessie Jean/Iconica/GI; 204 (1), NASA; 204 (2), rvlsoft/SS; 204 (3), Craig Tuttle/CO; 204 (4), Jim Reed/Science Source; 204 (5), Menna/SS; 204 (6), Leo & Mandy Dickinson/NPL; 204 (7), Willi Rolfes/Foto Natura/MP; 205 (top), Rob Marmion/SS; 205 (8), Adam Jones/Science Source; 205 (9), John A. Ey III/Science Source; 205 (10), David Kjaer/NPL; 205 (11), Ocean/CO; 205 (12), European Space Agency/AOES Medialab/Science Source; 205 (13), Carl D. Walsh/Aurora Photos; 205 (14), Arend/Smith/Alaska Stock Images/NGC; 205 (15), ISA/Science Source; 206, NOAA; 207 (top, right), AP Photo/U.S. Forest Service; 207 (bottom, left), Helmut Fohringer/epa/CO; 207 (left, center), Reuters/Wolfgang Rattay/CO; 208 (B), Arcady/SS; 208 (background), Shane Kirk/NGC; 208 (A), koya979/SS; 208 (C), Natutik/SS; 208 (D), Picksell/SS; 208 (E), Giuseppe_R/SS; 208 (F), StockLite/SS; 209 (top), AP Images/The Yomiuri Shimbun; 209 (top, center), AP Images/Kyodo; 209 (bottom, left), AP Images/Dogwood; 209 (bottom, right), STR/AFP/GI; 210–211, Bamboosil/age fotostock; 212–213, Jason Edwards/NGC; 212 (bottom, left), Brandon Cole; 212 (bottom, right), Reinhard Dirscherl/Visuals Unlimited, Inc.; 213 (bottom, left), Dray van Beeck/SS; 213, Brandon Cole; 214 (bottom), GI; 214–215 (background), John A. Anderson/IS.com; 214 (top), Paul Souders/CO; 215 (top), Vilainecrevette/SS; 215 (center), Reinhard Dirscherl/FLPA/MP; 215 (bottom), Stephen Frink/CO; 216 (top), FotograFFF/SS; 216 (bottom), Craig Tuttle/CO; 218 (top), AVTG/IS.com; 218 (bottom), Brad Wynnyk/SS; 219 (A), Rich Carey/SS; 219 (B), Richard Walters/IS.com; 219 (C), Karen Graham/IS.com; 219 (D), Michio Hoshino/MP/NGC

History Happens (222–253)

222–223, Travel Pix Collection/JAI/CO; 224 (top), Victor R. Boswell Jr./NGC; 224 (center), DeAgostini/GI; 224 (bottom), Sandro Vannini/CO; 225 (top, left), Leemage/Universal Images Group/GI; 225 (top, right), Werner Forman/Art Resource, NY; 225 (bottom, left), Mark Moffett/NGS/MP; 225 (bottom, right), Photolibrary.com/GI; 225 (right, center), Kenneth Garrett/NGC; 226 (top, left), Mika Stock/DanitaDelimont.com; 226 (top, right), Jon Arnold Images/DanitaDelimont.com; 226 (bottom), Fengling/SS; 227 (top), David Sutherland; 227 (bottom, left), Kenneth Garrett/NGC; 227 (bottom, right), Yoshio Tomii/SPS; 228 (1), Luca Tettoni/Robert Harding Picture Library; 228 (2), design56/SS; 228 (3), Design Pics Inc/NGC; 228 (4), Sandro Vannini; 228 (5), Luigi Vaccarella/Grand Tour/CO; 228 (6), Emilio Ereza/Alamy; 228 (7), Ed Darack/Science Faction/CO; 229 (top, right), Seamas Culligan/Zuma/CO; 229 (bottom), Roger Ressmeyer/CO; 229 (8), Universal History Archive/GI; 229 (9), The Granger Collection, NYC—All rights reserved; 229 (10), The Granger Collection, NYC—All rights reserved; 229 (11), Kenneth Garrett/NGC; 229 (12), Kristel Richard/NPL; 229 (13), Sites & Photos/Alamy; 229 (14), Nearby/Alamy; 229 (15), Volosina/SS; 230–231 (background), age fotostock/SPS; 231 (bottom, right), North Wind Picture Archives/Alamy; 232, Tibor Bognar/CO; 232, Art by Daniel Dociu/Source: Kevin Leahy, Portable Antiquities Scheme; 232 (bottom, right),

Robert Clark; 232 (bottom, left), Robert Clark; 232 (top), Robert Clark; 233 (left), Bettmann/CO; 233 (top, center), McManus-Young Collection/Library of Congress Prints & Photographs Division; 233 (bottom, right), Bettmann/CO; 234, Disney Enterprises, Inc./Walden Media, LLC; 234–235, Corey Ford; 235, Mark Thiessen, NGS; 235 (top, right), Ocean/CO; 236–237, AP Images/Adam Butler; 237 (top, right), World History Archive/TopFoto/The Image Works; 238 (top), Travel Inc/GI; 239 (top), Three Lions/GI; 240 (bottom), Suzanne Plunkett/Reuters/CO; 241 (top, left), AP Images/Adrian Wyld/The Canadian Press; 241 (top, right), Chris Wattie/Reuters/CO; 241 (bottom, right), Howard Sandler/SS; 242 (A), CP Photo/Irma Coucill/Canadian Press Images; 242 (B), CP Photo/Irma Coucill/Canadian Press Images; 242 (C), CP Photo/Irma Coucill/Canadian Press Images; 242 (D), Ken Paul/All Canada Photos/CO; 242 (E), CP Photo/Irma Coucill/Canadian Press Images; 242 (F), CP Photo/Irma Coucill/Canadian Press Images; 242 (G), CP Photo/Irma Coucill/Canadian Press Images; 243 (A), CP Photo/Irma Coucill/Canadian Press Images; 243 (B), CP Photo/Irma Coucill/Canadian Press Images; 243 (C), CP Photo/Irma Coucill/Canadian Press Images; 243 (D), CP Photo/Irma Coucill/Canadian Press Images; 243 (E), Lipowski Milan/SS; 243 (F), CP Photo/Irma Coucill/Canadian Press Images; 243 (G), CP Photo/Irma Coucill/Canadian Press Images; 243 (H), CP Photo/Irma Coucill/Canadian Press Images; 243 (I), Mega Pixel/SS; 243 (J), CP Photo/Irma Coucill/Canadian Press Images; 244 (A), CP Photo/Irma Coucill/Canadian Press Images; 244 (B), Hong Vo/SS; 244 (C), CP Photo/Irma Coucill/Canadian Press Images; 244 (D), CP Photo/Irma Coucill/Canadian Press Images; 244 (E), CP Photo/Irma Coucill/Canadian Press Images; 244 (F), CP Photo/Irma Coucill/Canadian Press Images; 244 (G), CP Photo/Irma Coucill/Canadian Press Images; 244 (H), C Squared Studios/Photodisc/GI; 244 (I), CP Photo/Irma Coucill/Canadian Press Images; 244 (J), CP Photo/Irma Coucill/Canadian Press Images; 245 (bottom), Arkadia/SS; 246 (top, right), AP Images/Paul Hawthorne, File; 246 (top, center left), rook76/SS; 246 (top, center right), National Archives of Canada/Canadian Press Images; 246 (bottom, center left), Public Domain; 246 (bottom, right), Saeed Khan/AFP/GI; 247 (top), Trinacria Photo/SS; 247 (right, center), falk/SS; 247 (bottom), Robert Wagenhoffer/CO; 248 (background), John E. Marriott/All Canadian Photos/GI; 248 (inset), Rolf Hickler/All Canada Photos/GI; 249 (top, left), Wayne R. Bilenduke/Stone/GI; 249 (bottom, right), Norbert Rosing/NGC; 250 (top), Glenbow Archives NA-2204-5; 251 (top, left), Richard Lautens/Toronto Star/ZUMA Press/Newscom; 251 (top, right), Bill Becker/Canadian Press Images; 251 (bottom, right), Adrien Veczan/Canadian Press Images; 252, Art by Daniel Dociu/Source: Kevin Leahy, Portable Antiquities Scheme; 252 (left, center), Jon Arnold Images/DanitaDelimont.com; 252 (top, right), Ocean/CO; 253 (top, right), Michael Frost/Disney Publishing Worldwide

Geography Rocks (254–337)

254–255, age fotostock/SPS; 257 (center, center), Maria Stenzel/NGC; 257 (bottom, center), Bill Hatcher/NGC; 257 (top), Carsten Peter/NGC; 257 (right, center), Gordon Wiltsie/NGC; 257 (bottom, left), James P. Blair/NGC; 257 (center, left), Thomas J. Abercrombie/NGC; 257 (bottom, right), Bill Curtsinger/NGC; 262, Neil Aldridge/NPL; 263 (bottom, right), THEGIFT777/IS.com; 263 (top, left), Pete Oxford/NPL/MP; 263 (bottom, center right), Kevin Schafer/The Image Bank/GI; 263 (left, center), AWL Images/GI; 263 (top, right), jsbdueck/SS; 263 (top, center right), Joao Nunes de Almeida/SS; 266, Paul Nicklen/NGC; 267 (top, left), Jack Stein Grove/DanitaDelimont.com; 267 (left, center), Norbert Wu/MP; 267 (top, right), Aurora Creative/GI; 267 (top, center right), McPHOTO MDF/age fotostock;

267 (bottom, center right), Courtesy Liam Quinn; 267 (bottom, right), Jan Vermeer/Foto Natura/MP; 268–269, Jonah Light; 268 (top, left), blickwinkel/Alamy; 269 (bottom), Courtesy of LEGOLAND; 269 (top), Courtesy of LEGOLAND Florida; 270, David Santiago Garcia/Aurora Photos/Robert Harding Picture Library; 271 (bottom, left), porkrithap/SS; 271 (bottom, center right), Nancy Brown/Photographer's Choice/GI; 271 (top, left), Jon Arnold Images/DanitaDelimont.com; 271 (top, right), Rod Williams/NPL; 271 (top, center right), Charles Marden Fitch/SPS; 271 (bottom, right), JudyKennamer/IS; 274, Ingrid Visser/Hedgehog House/MP; 275 (top, left), Cusp/SPS; 275 (bottom, center right), Jeff Hunter/The Image Bank/GI; 275 (left, center), nimu1956/IS; 275 (top, right), DEAN LEWINS/epa/CO; 275 (top, center right), Travellinglight/Dreamstime.com; 275 (bottom, right), Martin Withers/FLPA/MP; 278, Rudy Sulgan/CO; 279 (top, center right), Annette Hopf/IS; 279 (bottom, center right), Diego Lezama Orezzoli/CO; 279 (top, left), Steven Vidler/Eurasia Press/CO; 279 (top, right), fStop/SPS; 279 (left, center), David Osborn/Alamy; 279 (bottom, right), holg/IS; 279 (bottom, center right), AFP/GI; 282, Fred J. Lord/Jaynes Gallery/DanitaDelimont.com; 282 (top, center right), Julius Csotonyi; 283 (top, left), W. Bertsch/Robertstock; 283 (bottom, right), David Rose/SS; 283 (left, center), Javier Trueba/MSF/Science Source; 283 (top, right), Tatiana Popova/SS; 283 (bottom, center right), Ken Canning/IS; 286, Claus Meyer/MP; 287 (bottom, center right), Jason Edwards/NGS; 287 (bottom, right), Bernardo Galmarini/Alamy; 287 (top, left), Photononstop/SPS; 287 (left, center), David Tipling/Alamy; 287 (top, right), CO; 287 (bottom, center right), AFP/GI; 287 (bottom, center right), Dr. Morley Read/Science Source; 293, Cubo Images/SPS; 296, Wolfgang Kaehler/SPS; 299 (bottom), Dennis Cox/WorldViews; 300, Lukasz Pajor/SS; 304 (bottom), anshar/SS; 307, B.S.P.I./CO; 310 (bottom), YAY Media AS/Alamy; 313 (bottom), Aurora Creative/GI; 320 (top), REDSTARSTUDIO/SS; 320 (bottom), Nelu Goia/SS; 321 (top), Gunter Marx Photography/CO; 321 (bottom), Action Press/Zuma Press/Newscom; 322 (top), Brian Skerry/NGC; 322 (bottom), Melissa King/SS; 323 (top), Design Pics Inc./Alamy; 323 (bottom), Tierfotoagentur/Alamy; 324 (top), Jerry Kobalenko/age fotostock; 324 (bottom), David Giral/Alamy; 325 (top), Mike Grandmaison/All Canada Photos/SPS; 325 (bottom), Science/AAAS; 326 (top), J. Baylor Roberts/NGC; 326 (bottom), Miles Ertman/Masterfile; 327 (top), Matt Champlin/National Geographic My Shot; 327 (top, center right), BGSmith/SS; 327 (right, center), Biosphoto/SPS; 327 (bottom, center right), Tom Vezo/DanitaDelimont.com; 327 (bottom, right), Barrett & MacKay/All Canada Photos/CO; 328 (2), James Steidl/Dreamstime.com; 328 (1), Pete Oxford/MP; 328 (3), Wrangel/Dreamstime.com; 328 (4), Universal Images Group (Lake County Discovery Museum)/Alamy; 328 (5), Michael Nichols/NGC; 328 (6), Giuliachristin/Dreamstime.com;328 (7), John Takai/Dreamstime.com; 329 (8), Vladimir Ovchinnikov/Dreamstime.com; 329 (9), Kevin Schafer/MP; 329 (11), Chen Po Chuan/Dreamstime.com; 329 (12), Tim Laman/NGC; 329 (13), Courtesy of NOAA; 329 (14), Steven Mark Needham/Envision/CO; 329 (15), Photononstop/Alamy; 330 (top, left), Thorpe Park; 330 (top, right), Chris Batson/Alamy; 330 (bottom, left), Joel A. Rogers; 331 (top, left), Herwig Prammer/Reuters; 331 (bottom), Andy Clark/Reuters; 331 (top, right), Sergey Dolzhenko/epa/CO; 332 (top, right), Roy Hunt; 332 (bottom, center), David Sanger Photography/Alamy; 332–333, Fogline Studio/GI; 333 (center), Courtesy Castello della Castelluccia; 333 (top, right), Sandro Vannini/CO; 334 (background), David Greenberg; 334 (inset), David Greenberg; 335 (top), Andy Rouse/NPL; 335 (center), Reinhard Dirscherl/GI; 335 (bottom), David B. Fleetham/SeaPics.com; 336 (left, center), David Osborn/Alamy; 336 (center), Courtesy Castello della Castelluccia

ILLUSTRATION CREDITS AND INDEX

346

Published by the National Geographic Society

Gary E. Knell,
President and Chief Executive Officer

John M. Fahey,
Chairman of the Board

Declan Moore
*Executive Vice President;
President, Publishing and Travel*

Melina Gerosa Bellows
*Publisher and Chief Creative Officer,
Books, Kids, and Family*

Prepared by the Book Division

Hector Sierra, *Senior Vice President and General Manager*
Nancy Laties Feresten, *Senior Vice President,
Kids Publishing and Media*
Jennifer Emmett, *Vice President, Editorial Director,
Kids Books*
Eva Absher-Schantz, *Design Director,
Kids Publishing and Media*
Jay Sumner, *Director of Photography, Kids Publishing*
R. Gary Colbert, *Production Director*
Jennifer A. Thornton, *Director of Managing Editorial*

Staff for This Book

Robin Terry, Shelby Alinsky, *Project Managers*
Mary Varilla Jones, *Project Editor*
James Hiscott, Jr., *Art Director*
Ruth Ann Thompson, *Designer*
Hillary Leo, *Associate Photo Editor*
Kris Hanneman, *Illustrations Editor*
Sarah Wassner Flynn, *Contributing Writer*
Michelle Harris, *Researcher*
Sara Zeglin, *Digital Content Producer*
Ariane Szu-Tu, *Editorial Assistant*
Carl Mehler, *Director of Maps*
Michael McNey, David B. Miller, and Martin S. Walz
Map Research and Production
Stuart Armstrong, *Graphics Illustrator*
Callie Broaddus, *Design Production Assistant*
Grace Hill, *Associate Managing Editor*
Joan Gossett, *Production Editor*
Lewis R. Bassford, *Production Manager*
Susan Borke, *Legal and Business Affairs*

Production Services

Phillip L. Schlosser, *Senior Vice President*
Chris Brown, *Vice President, NG Book Manufacturing*
George Bounelis, *Vice President, Senior
Production Manager*
Nicole Elliott, *Director of Production*
Rachel Faulise, *Manager*
Robert L. Barr, *Manager*

In Partnership With
NATIONAL GEOGRAPHIC KIDS Magazine
Julie Vosburgh Agnone, *Vice President, Editorial Operations*
Rachel Buchholz, *Editor and Vice President*

Catherine D. Hughes, *Senior Editor, Science*
Photo: Kelley Miller, *Senior Editor;* Lisa Jewell, *Editor*
Art: Eileen O'Tousa-Crowson, *Art Director;*
Julide Obuz Dengel, *Designer;*
Stephanie Rudig, *Digital Design Assistant*
Editorial: Andrea Silen, *Associate Editor;* Nick Spagnoli,
Copy Editor; Kay Boatner, *Assistant Editor*
Administration: Bianca Bowman, *Editorial Assistant;*
Tammi Colleary, *Financial Analyst*
Production: David V. Showers, *Director*
Online: Anne A. McCormack, *Director*

For more information, please visit nationalgeographic.com, call 1-800-NGS LINE (647-5463), or write to the following address:

National Geographic Society, 1145 17th Street N.W.,
Washington, D.C. 20036-4688 U.S.A.

Visit us online at nationalgeographic.com/books

For librarians and teachers: ngchildrensbooks.org

More for kids from National Geographic:
kids.nationalgeographic.com

For information about special discounts for bulk purchases, please contact National Geographic Books Special Sales: ngspecsales@ngs.org

For rights or permissions inquiries, please contact National Geographic Books Subsidiary Rights:
ngbookrights@ngs.org

Paperback edition ISBN: 978-1-4263-1463-6

Printed in the United States of America

14/QGT-CML/1